THE LIBRARY
ST. MARY'S COLLEGE OF MARYLAND
ST. MARY'S CITY, MARYLAND 20686

75954

A DANCE IN A GARDEN
From a manuscript of the *Roman de la Rose*.
Flemish illumination of the end of the fifteenth century.
By permission of the Trustees of the British Museum

THE BOOK OF CRAFTSMEN

The Story of Man's Handiwork through the Ages

BY

MARJORY BRUCE

WITH NUMEROUS ILLUSTRATIONS

> He hath given men skill, that He might be honoured in His marvellous works. . . . They will maintain the state of the world, and their desire is in the work of their craft. *Ecclesiasticus* xxxviii

NEW YORK
DODD, MEAD & COMPANY
PUBLISHERS

Republished by Gale Research Company, Book Tower, Detroit, 1974

Library of Congress Cataloging in Publication Data

Bruce, Marjory.
　　The book of craftsmen.

　　Reprint of the 1937 ed.
　　1. Art industries and trade--History. 2. Industrial arts--History. I. Title.
NK600.B7　　1974　　　　600　　　　70-185352
ISBN 0-8103-3960-9

FOREWORD

On fine days, especially when they are holidays as well, most boys and girls like to be out of doors *doing* something: playing games, riding, swimming, walking, climbing trees, picking blackberries, sailing boats, or some other equally strenuous occupation. But on wet days, and on winter evenings, they usually like to *make* things. *What* they make depends on the taste of each child. One will put together model aeroplanes, or make bridges and dams with the aid of Meccano; another will whittle out a boat; another will pat coloured clay into many shapes. A girl may want to knit or sew; either a boy or a girl may want to draw and paint pictures. But always the instinct to create, to fashion, to put together, is at work.

Now, children who like making things also like to know how things are made; and it will usually be found that it interests them to hear how things were made in the past, and what sort of men they were who first began to make them. This is largely unexplored ground, both for teachers and children, since the subject is a vast and complicated one, full of human colour and character. In learning about the potters and weavers, woodcarvers and masons, metal-workers and cobblers of Egypt and Babylonia, Greece and Rome, and medieval Europe, the child absorbs incidentally a great deal of vivid and varied knowledge of daily life in those far-off lands and distant times, a knowledge not only of art and archæology in their most engaging and least academic aspect, but of conditions of labour and methods of craftsmanship. How little, in some ways, those methods have altered, and how greatly those conditions have improved, emerges in every chapter.

The aim of this book is to give a clear picture of the development of the principal crafts evolved by mankind through the ages,

The Book of Craftsmen

and at the same time a series of lifelike sketches of the craftsmen of other days. It is hoped that it may encourage that active interest in handicrafts which most children are quite ready to feel, and which an increasing number of parents and teachers now desire to foster.

As the Right Hon. Oliver Stanley, President of the Board of Education, recently observed, children over the age of eleven are developing all sorts of active and curious desires; they are, as the Hadow Report put it, " waking to various new interests suggested by the world about them," and handicraft in wood and metal, and craft-work generally, are a splendid way of interesting the growing boy.

That boy and his sister are all the more likely to take pleasure in the work of their own hands if they know something about the craftsmen of other days.

M. B.

CONTENTS

CHAPTER		PAGE
I.	THE POTTER AND THE WORKER IN CLAY	11
II.	THE WORKER IN METALS	36
III.	THE WORKER IN WOOD	66
IV.	THE WEAVER	92
V.	THE SCULPTOR AND THE BUILDER	121
VI.	THE TAILOR AND THE HATTER	153
VII.	THE PAINTER	181
VIII.	THE BAKER AND THE COOK	201
IX.	THE WORKER IN LEATHER	221
X.	THE FURNITURE-MAKER	247
XI.	THE MAKER OF WEAPONS	265
	INDEX	281

FULL-PAGE ILLUSTRATIONS

	PAGE
A Dance in a Garden	*Frontispiece*
Terra-cotta Figurine from Tanagra	22
Figure of an Early Sumerian Royal Personage or Priestly Official	22
Figure of a Lady of the T'ang Dynasty	22
The Goddess Kwannon	23
The British Museum Lohan	23
Japanese Porcelain	23
Majolica Plate depicting a Majolica-painter at Work	26
Figure in Enamelled Terra-cotta by Luca della Robbia	26
Two Figures made by the Bow Potters	27
Three Derby Figures, about 1775	27
Tureen made at Sèvres in 1759	30
Polish Gentleman and Lady: Group made at Meissen	30
Figures made at Derby after the Style of Chelsea	34
Bristol China Figures	34
Saxon Jewels found at Prittlewell	46
The Shrine of St Patrick's Bell	50
From Ghiberti's Second Bapistery Door	51
Salt-cellar made for Francis I by Benvenuto Cellini	51
Wooden Statue of Egyptian Overseer	68
Wooden Figure of Egyptian Girl playing the Harp	69
Angel carved in Wood	69
Tyrolean Crucifix carved in Wood	76
An Example of Polynesian Wood-carving	77

The Book of Craftsmen

	PAGE
A Chinese Lantern in Carved Wood	77
Carving at Petworth by Grinling Gibbons	90
The Great Door of the Close, Canterbury Cathedral	91
Lace Cravat carved out of Limewood by Grinling Gibbons	91
Chinese Brocade of the Eighteenth Century	106
The Tower of Babel Reconstructed	124
Lifelike Figures of Man and Horse from the Frieze of the Parthenon	125
Roman Marble Relief of the Third Century	125
Horseshoe Arches in the Alcazar at Seville	150
Tomb of Charles the Bold at Bruges	151
The Merchant Taylors' Hall	168
An Elizabethan Elegant	169
The Tailor	174
Queen Elizabeth	175
The Cave-dweller as an Artist	182
Painted Wall in the Throne-room at Knossos	183
Wall-painting on a Tomb at Thebes	184
Moonlight and Mist	186
Banners of the Knights of the Garter in St George's Chapel at Windsor	187
Corner Cupboard from David Garrick's Bedroom	198
The Chef of the Hotel Chatham, Paris	218

CHAPTER I
THE POTTER AND THE WORKER IN CLAY

Long, long ago, in the very dawn of human history, queer-looking men who lived in dark caves took to kneading lumps of clay between their hands and fashioning from them rough vessels in which to hold water. Such a man would make a dint or a hollow with his fist in a dab of moist earth which he would then leave to dry in the sun: but to his annoyance these bowls often melted back into mud again when they had contained water for any length of time. Then, perhaps by mere chance, one man dried an earthen vessel in the red ashes of his hearth, and thus produced *fired* pottery, much harder and better than anything he had had before.

As the long, dim centuries passed, his descendants found many uses for pottery. They made little lamps, with bison-tallow for oil and a tuft of moss for a wick; they made beakers and urns and jars; they made beads to hang round their wives' necks—and probably round their own—and toys for their children to play with. Later, when a rude sort of loom had been invented, they made weights of clay for it: and they made spindle-whorls of the same useful substance.

The pottery of these long-vanished people tells us a great deal about them, and historians are able, with the help of the fragments which remain, to trace the wanderings of the primitive tribes who moved about the continent of Europe seeking pasture for their flocks and herds. The earliest tribes were hunters, and were 'stay-at-homes' in comparison with those that followed them; then came the herdsmen, who were more civilized, and whose pottery was more varied and more beautiful than that of the hunting folk.

The Book of Craftsmen

One reason why the pottery of the second Stone Age is so shapeless is that man had not as yet discovered the potter's wheel. The exact date of that discovery is not known, but it was very far back in human history, and, like several other discoveries, including sails, glass, and the mariner's compass, was probably accidental. Primitive man learned how to make a sort of basket-work with supple twigs, and we know from the markings on some of his pots that he often used a shallow wicker basket as a support for the lump of clay which he was moulding with his hands. Then one potter, more resourceful than his brethren, found that by beginning to shape his pot on the flat side of a boulder he could make the support revolve and so apply pressure evenly and steadily to every part. Thus was created the potter's wheel, a familiar sight in the East to this day, and, much elaborated, a necessary item in the equipment of every great factory where china and earthenware are made.

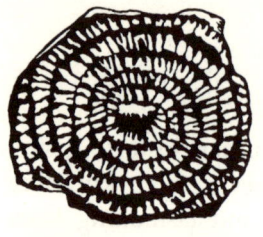

BASE OF AN ANCIENT EARTHENWARE VESSEL
Found at Moussian, near Gouva. It shows the structure of the mat on which it was built up. Similar impressions are often found in Egypt.
The Childhood of Art, Spearing

ANCIENT EGYPTIAN POTTERS AT WORK
1. Shaping on the wheel. 2. Tending the kiln. 3. Stacking the pots. 4. Carrying the pots away.

It has been suggested that in prehistoric times most of the pottery was fashioned by women. If this be true, the potter's wheel may have been invented by some intelligent housewife whose house was a cave! In any case it is highly probable that at first each family made for itself the vessels that it needed; but by degrees

The Potter

new uses were found for such things, and long before the end of the Bronze Age the craft of the potter had become what would now be called a 'skilled occupation.' The growth of religious ideas and of religious ceremonies gave the potter fresh work to do. He—or she—had to make special cups to hold 'libations' or drink-offerings for the gods, and incense-burners from which sweet odours ascended for their delight. When, about fifteen hundred years before Christ, cremation became the usual method of disposing of the dead over the greater part of Europe, large urns, known as cinerary urns, were necessary to hold the ashes. Many such urns have been unearthed in Great Britain, dug up, discovered by pure chance, or uncovered by the plough.

We have seen how man learned first to harden pots by means of fire and then how to mould them on a wheel. Their colour would depend upon the colour of the clay from which they were formed, and might be brown, grey, red or buff: the process of firing sometimes darkened the clay and made it almost black. Bands of dots, or zigzags, or wavy stripes, scratched with a thumb-nail or a thorn, were the earliest attempts at decoration. But in districts where the earth was of various tints the potter took to applying streaks or dabs of one hue on another, buff on grey, black on red, red on brown, and so *coloured* pottery came into existence. When one colour is applied upon another in this way the ware is said to be decorated 'in slip' or 'with slip,' and is sometimes called 'slipware.' Long before King Khufu built the Great Pyramid the dwellers in the Nile Valley were producing beautiful pottery of a

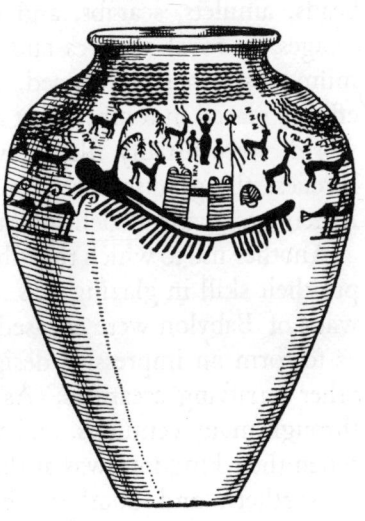

PREHISTORIC EGYPTIAN JAR
It bears one of the earliest known representations of a mother and children.

The Book of Craftsmen

thousand different shapes, decorated with all sorts of quaint figures. The design might include birds, fishes, men, or hippopotami, but the drawing is so crude that it is often difficult to tell exactly what was in the potter's mind. Upon one very ancient Egyptian jar found at Abydos there is, among various odd-looking beasts and birds, what is probably the earliest representation in art of a mother with two small children. She is holding her hands above her head, and the taller of the two seems to be clutching at her gown.

These same artistic and inventive people are believed to have been the first to beautify their pottery with brilliantly tinted glaze. Into the composition of this glaze various oxides enter, chiefly those of copper and manganese. The result is absolutely dazzling. The Egyptians applied glaze to many objects, large and small, to beads, amulets, scarabs, and seals, to jars, vases, statuettes, and images, to royal sceptres and to the fine beaded mesh in which mummies were often draped. The queer little *ushabtiu*, miniature effigies placed in tombs to act as servants to the dead in the underworld, were usually filmed with vivid blue glaze. Among the loveliest things discovered in the sepulchre of King Tut-ankh-Amen was a vase of delicate purple pottery.

Another use to which the inhabitants of Egypt and Mesopotamia put their skill in glazing was the production of *tiles*. The famous walls of Babylon were encased in glittering tiles fitted together so as to form an impressive design of lions, winged monsters, and other terrifying creatures. As we shall see, this fashion endured through many centuries, and was adopted by the rulers of Persia when their kingdom was at the height of its splendour.

Northern and Southern Babylonia were called Akkad and Sumer, and in those lands workers in clay had much to do, for wood and stone were hard to come by, and clay was made to take their place. The Sumerians kept accounts, wrote records, and inscribed contracts on cylinders of clay, using the wedge-shaped (cuneiform) script: they fashioned figures of their friends, their kinsfolk and their gods in the same useful and abundant material:

The Potter

they built terraced towers and huge temples and proud palaces with brick walls and gates of bronze.

The Egyptians were a seafaring people, which is as much as to say that they were a trading people. Among the distant kingdoms with which they traded in the days of the greatest Pharaohs was the kingdom of Crete. And the Cretans were skilful potters, whose handiwork testifies to their skill after more than four thousand years. Their kingdom was a centre of civilization in the Ægean, and examples of their characteristic pottery have been unearthed in great numbers from the ruins of their capital city of Knossos. Favourite designs were shells, seaweeds, octopods, and lotus-lilies. Votive offerings in the form of little idols and models were laid upon the altars of the snake-goddess who was the chief divinity of the race. Some of these models, made in glazed and coloured clay, represented ladies' dresses with long flounced skirts and tight waists, not unlike the dresses worn by Victorian ladies in England.

Although the Cretans were neighbours of the Greeks, they were Greek neither in blood, nor in speech, nor in religion. It was not until after their splendour had passed away that Greece rose to the height of her artistic and intellectual power. In the sixth, fifth, and fourth centuries before Christ the Greeks produced wonderful vases, jars, mixing-bowls, wine-cups and libation-dishes, covered with a fine, silky glaze, and decorated with figures of gods and heroes, men and women, children and animals. In the earlier type of Greek vase the design is black upon red, in the later red upon black. Yet another type has figures in black and red on a white background. At the Panathenaic Games, held every four years in honour of the mythical founder of the city of Athens, the prize took the form of a large and beautiful vase. The Greek potters delighted in depicting the legendary events in the lives of the heroes of the race, and you find the myths of the gods and the tale of Troy repeated again and again, sometimes in quaint and stiff forms, sometimes with exquisite purity of line. By way of variety they also chose familiar and homely scenes, such as a boy

The Book of Craftsmen

playing with a pet quail in a cage, or dragging a toy cart, or having a lesson on the double pipe; or a girl at her mirror, or at her loom, or two girls bouncing on a see-saw. These clay workers of ancient Greece made many things besides jars and bowls. They made lamps; they made dolls and toys. They also made tombstones, curious, dumpy little monuments with figures of the dead person

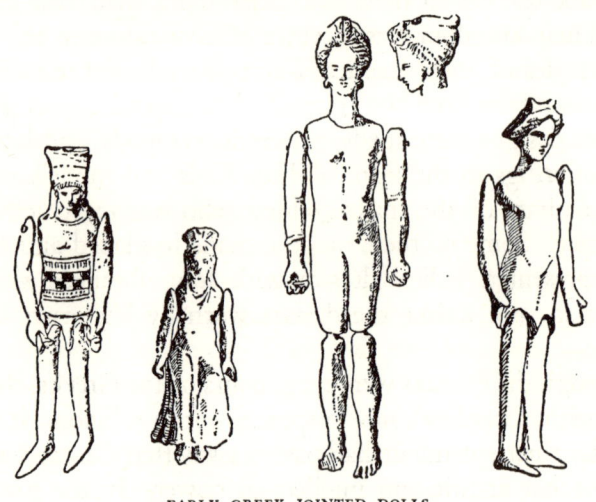

EARLY GREEK JOINTED DOLLS
From Athens, Myrina, and Rhodes.

moulded in what is called ' low relief '—that is to say, not completely detached from the background. And they made tiny models to be put in the tomb itself. For example,

> in a girl's tomb near Athens was found a whole collection of small clay objects, a seated doll with movable arms, a pair of boots, a vase for lustral water (to be used in religious purifications), and a model of an *onos*, the semi-cylindrical shield placed on the knee by women when carding wool.[1]

Among the loveliest productions of the Greek potters were little statuettes such as those of which large quantities have been discovered at Tanagra, on the coast of Bœotia. The ancient Greeks

[1] D. M. Stuart, *The Girl through the Ages*, p. 48 (Harrap).

The Potter

who lived in other parts of the Grecian archipelago professed to regard the Bœotians as a very unintelligent set of people, and the word 'Bœotian' came to mean 'stupid' or 'dull': but the potters of Tanagra must have had keenly artistic brains as well as skilful fingers, for these images are things of pure beauty. Most of them represent women or young girls wearing long draperies and standing or sitting in poses of natural, unaffected grace. When two are modelled together they are very often playing the game of knucklebones, or bending their heads towards each other as if exchanging confidences. Some of them wear the most fascinating broad-brimmed hats! Other Tanagra designs include cupids, satyrs, pet animals, and small children.

West of the Tiber and the Apennines, along the valley of the Arno, lay the land of Etruria, where in the sixth and fifth centuries before Christ there flourished two groups or confederations of powerful cities. Rome itself was at one time included in the Etruscan dominions and governed by Etruscan kings. We all remember Lars Porsena of Clusium, the Etruscan chieftain whose warlike attempt to restore the Etruscan dynasty of Tarquin was so gloriously defeated by the "dauntless three" who held back his army until the City Fathers of Rome had hewn down the Sulpician Bridge. This ancient, interesting, and rather mysterious race, whose literary records have all perished, made extensive use of pottery in their daily lives, and imported large quantities from Greece, as well as encouraging Greek potters to settle in their domains. Such enormous numbers of vases have been unearthed from Etruscan tombs that for a long time people believed that the craftsmen of Etruria had been especially skilful in the making of pottery. They *did* make a certain amount, mostly black in colour with ornamental mouldings in low relief, but the terra-cotta ware attributed to them is now known to have been Greek in origin.

The term *terra-cotta* means literally 'cooked earth,' and is applied to a mixture of sand and clay hardened by fire. The Etruscans used this material for many purposes, and when a wealthy Etruscan died his relatives prepared a magnificent terra-

The Book of Craftsmen

cotta tomb for him, surmounted by a life-sized effigy of himself painted a reddish tawny colour. His wife's effigy would be of a much paler tint, and it has been suggested that the ladies of Etruria spent so great a part of their time indoors that their complexions were actually several shades lighter than those of their husbands. The Romans were not an artistic people, but they encouraged the fine arts, especially those which increased the comfort of everyday life. Under Roman rule the potters of the various provinces of the Empire, especially Gaul and the Rhineland, attained a high degree of skill. The worker in terra-cotta, as distinct from the maker of bowls and vases, was kept busy producing the flues and hot-air pipes needed for the hypocaust system of heating houses. Wherever you find traces of prolonged Roman occupation you will find hypocausts: and the chances are that you will also find specimens of a particular kind of light red pottery which is known by three different names, each of which tells you something about it.

From the fact that it was first fashioned in the Greek island of Samos this pottery is sometimes called 'Samian ware': from the fact that it was afterwards made in the Roman city of Aretium (the modern Arezzo) it is sometimes called 'Aretine ware': and from the fact that it was almost always decorated with figures or designs in low relief, it was sometimes called *terra sigillata*, *sigilla* being the Latin for images impressed in this manner, as if by a seal. Most of these beautiful red bowls and cups bear the name of the potter who made them. They were imported from Gaul and Germany into Roman Britain by the shipload. One of the ships thus laden foundered off the coast of Kent, and her cargo, after lying for many centuries in the salt ooze of the sea, may now be seen in the British Museum. Favourite designs on Samian ware were combats of gladiators, or hunting subjects, with dogs pursuing deer.

Native British potters endeavoured with some success to imitate these vessels, so vivid in colour, so graceful in form. In the matter of colour they could not compete with their rivals on the Continent,

The Potter

as the raw material was different in Britain, and the clay necessary to produce that lovely red was lacking. At Castor, in Northamptonshire, a rather fine type of dark-coloured ware was made, with ornamentations applied in the form of fluid clay moulded before firing. Black pottery decorated with white slip was common, and in the New Forest district buff vessels were made with patterns in shades of brown. The potters of Castor imitated the characteristic gladiatorial and sporting designs of the Gaulish and Germanic craftsmen, and some of their helmeted fighters and fleeting hounds are very lifelike and energetic.

Meanwhile, in quite another part of the world, far beyond the reach of Roman influences, the potters' art was being brought to wonderful perfection. This was in the Empire of China, which, as we all know, has given its name to the finest sort of pottery in use at the present day. By the third century before Christ the Chinese, always very skilful potters, had learned to mould many objects in green-glazed earthenware. Like the ancient Egyptians and the Etruscans they placed in tombs models of various belongings likely to be useful to the dead person in the world of shades. A powerful prince would have his horses, his servants, his house, his wine-jars and lamps and incense-burners, all fashioned carefully in clay and filmed with moss-green or honey-yellow glaze. The custom of tea-drinking led to the introduction of teapots and teacups: Chinese love of flowers encouraged Chinese potters to design vases specially to hold branches of wistaria or roses, or slender tufts of bamboo.

One great advantage which these potters enjoyed over their unknown fellow-craftsmen in other lands was the presence in China of large deposits of those special kinds of fine clay from which translucent and delicate vessels of many lovely colours can be made. At one time, owing to the high temperature needed to melt the glaze, blue and white were the only colours seen in Chinese porcelain.[1] Some of the most valuable pieces of ancient

---

[1] The English word ' porcelain ' comes from the Italian *porcellana*, a cowrie shell. The highly polished surface of the shell suggested comparison with the highly glazed pottery from the Far East.

The Book of Craftsmen

china in modern collections are of this blue-and-white, and from time to time this particular type becomes a fashionable craze. This was the case in England in the eighteenth century and again late in the nineteenth: and that is why an English dandy of King George II's reign who gave up collecting china and took to planning a garden observed to a friend that now he was interested in *green* trees instead of in *blue* ones!

One of the most famous designs of blue-and-white Chinese pottery is the Willow Pattern. To the right you see a two-storeyed house, the home of a rich mandarin; in the foreground is a pavilion, in the background an orange-tree, and to the right of the pavilion a peach-tree. At one end of a graceful bridge is the celebrated willow-tree, at the other is a humble cottage, with a solitary fir-tree behind it. In the distance is a small island with a sort of summer-house. On the bridge are three figures, the mandarin's young daughter, her lover, and the mandarin himself. Below, in a boat, are the fleeing couple; overhead hover two turtle-doves. According to the legend, Li-Chi, the girl, fell in love with a youth called Chang, who had been her father's secretary. They crept away together and, after hiding for a time in the gardener's cottage, escaped in a boat, trying to reach the island home of Chang. The furious mandarin pursued and overtook them, and would have beaten them both to death had not the pitying gods changed them into doves. These events were said to have happened " at the season when the willow begins to shed its leaves."

As early as the sixth century of the Christian era there were flourishing potteries in China, especially in the district of Ching-te-Chen where the surrounding hills were rich in the two sorts of earth, china-stone (*kaolin*) and china-clay, necessary to the manufacture of delicate porcelain. The first of these, being infusible, forms what the Chinese called the 'bones' of the ware: the 'flesh' was provided by the china-clay, which melts at a high temperature and becomes a glittering, semi-transparent substance resembling glass. It was by skilfully combining these two clays that the craftsmen of Ching-te-Chen—and elsewhere in the far-stretched Chinese

The Potter

Empire—were able to make such marvellous vessels, large and small. As we shall see later, it was not until the eighteenth century that the chance discovery of deposits of *kaolin* in Saxony enabled the potters of Europe to introduce anything resembling—much less equalling—the china of the Far East.

When once the Chinese mastered the art of applying various colours to their porcelain their range of design became enormous. Learned students of ceramics—or the art of pottery—can tell at a glance where and when the finest of the famous pieces in modern collections were made. Flowers are a favourite subject: the shaggy, loose-petalled Chinese rose, wistaria, bamboo, willow, plum-blossom, and many others. Human figures often appear, warriors in armour riding forth to battle on dumpy grey steeds, mandarins fishing, or playing chess, or walking in prim gardens where fir-trees droop over red lacquer bridges; dragons, the emblem of Imperial China, abound—terrifying dragons with long, sharp toe-nails and wildly protruding eyes. Animals, birds and fishes, some of them very lifelike, some of them decidedly quaint, are not infrequently seen. The hare and the tortoise are both familiar figures, but they are not the emblems of speed and of perseverance as they are in Æsop's fable; the tortoise signifies long life, and the hare is a holy hare who lives in the moon. The carp means literary success!

Being a methodically minded people, the Chinese were very fond of arranging their designs in groups of regular numbers. For example, seven sages in a bamboo-grove, eight horses of the Emperor Mu Wang, or four liberal accomplishments—writing, painting, music, and chess.

One of the devices which occurs most frequently in ancient pottery of all lands and periods is the 'swastika.' In Chinese it signifies the word *wan*—ten thousand—and expresses a wish for long life.

Some of the inscriptions on Chinese pottery, stating the place of origin, suggest that the Chinese craftsmen gave very fanciful and pretty names to their workshops. These they describe

The Book of Craftsmen

sometimes as a hall, sometimes as a studio, sometimes as a retreat. Two blue-and-white saucers dating from the seventeenth century are marked as having been " made in the hall of rare jade," and a coloured dish with a design of lotus-lilies was " made in the studio of peace and tranquillity." Short sentences wishing good luck to the possessor of the ware are very usual. The Chinese held learning and long life in equally high esteem; so we find inscriptions such as these:

> May you have scholarship as lofty as the hills and the Great Bear!
> May you enjoy eternal prosperity and enduring Spring!
> Knowledge, virtue, and long life be yours!

Apart from the many-coloured porcelains designed for use or for ornament, Chinese potters produced beautifully modelled images of the gods and goddesses of their land. Kwannon, the goddess of mercy, is represented in greyish-white, highly glazed ware, with a blandly simpering countenance, an elaborate headdress, and wonderful tapering fingers and toes. The god of luck has a fat 'tummy' and a smiling face; the judges of the Nether Regions have glaring eyes and grinning mouths. These figures ranged in size from dainty things only a few inches in height to impressive forms larger than life. The largest usually portrayed sages, philosophers, or holy men.

> Some years ago a hoard of such figures was discovered in a lonely cave among the mountains of Ichnofu, and one of them is now among the treasures of the British Museum. This shows a Lohan, one of the sixteen apostles of Buddha, seated in meditation, modelled in hard white clay glazed with orange, buff, and green. Even the hair is green! The expression of the face is surprisingly lifelike, and so is the hint of physical strength and spiritual tranquillity in the position of the hands.[1]

The Persians were at every period in their history very skilful potters. Darius, one of their most famous kings, cased his palace at Susa in magnificent coloured tiles, and the blue glaze, violet,

[1] E. W. Walters, *The Book of Art*, p. 32 (Harrap).

TERRA-COTTA FIGURINE FROM TANAGRA
Fourth century B.C.

FIGURE OF AN EARLY SUMERIAN ROYAL PERSONAGE OR PRIESTLY OFFICIAL
British Museum

FIGURE OF A LADY OF THE T'ANG DYNASTY (618–907 A.D.)

THE GODDESS KWANNON
Victoria and Albert Museum

THE BRITISH MUSEUM LOHAN

JAPANESE PORCELAIN
About 1700.
Dresden, Porzellansammlung

The Potter

turquoise, and sky blue, which Persian craftsmen applied to their earthenware jars and bowls has never been surpassed for brilliance and beauty.

After the rise and spread of the Mohammedan religion in the seventh century of the Christian era there came into being a new form of art called Islamic art. (The word 'Islam,' usually applied to Mohammedanism in general, means, literally, surrender.) As Mohammed, like Moses before him, forbade the representation of any living creature, human or otherwise, Islamic designers had to fall back upon geometrical patterns, foliage, imaginary monsters, and texts—in Arabic letters—from the Koran, their holy book. These patterns appear on the tiles which glitter in the mosques of Constantinople and Cairo, Jerusalem and Cordova, Ispahan and Agra; they appear upon the jars in which True Believers kept water, since they might not keep wine, upon the cups whence they drank sherbet, and the dishes whence they ate Turkish delight, or almonds and dates, or *pilau* made of rice and spice and chicken. In Moorish Spain there were many clever physicians, both Mohammedans and Jews, and these needed vessels of various shapes and sizes wherein to hold their drugs. Hence arose a demand which the potters were not slow to meet. The result is that in modern museums one finds exceedingly beautiful pots and vials inscribed in Arabic characters

EARTHENWARE TILE FROM SPAIN
Early nineteenth century.

and glazed in purple, yellow, white, and blue; they are described on case-labels as 'Hispano-Moresque'—'Spanish-Moorish.' And long after the last of the Moors had been expelled from Spain the Spaniards ornamented their houses with shining tiles of the Moorish type. The removal of Islamic customs allowed them to introduce human figures and animals, sometimes with very quaint effects.

The Book of Craftsmen

The European potters of the Middle Ages were nothing like as skilful as their forerunners of Egyptian and Greek times. Though they lived more than three thousand years after the men who wrought Tut-ankh-Amen's purple and peacock-hued jars, and nearly two thousand after those who fashioned the red-and-black vases given as prizes in the Panathenaic festivals, their handiwork set side by side with Egyptian and Greek—and even with Roman—pottery looks curiously crude and uncouth. The medieval potter worked, as his predecessors of far-off lands had worked, with the aid of the kiln and the wheel: yet almost all the skill laboriously acquired by them had been lost by him. Through the pottery of *his* fashioning one seems to see the original, unwrought and unbaked clay. His glazes are thin and patchy, reddish brown, buff yellow, or mossy green: sometimes the film of colour drips down the brims and sides of his pots as if it were soup or jam that had boiled over and then dried hard.

GLAZED PITCHER WITH HUMAN FACE
Fourteenth century.

SLIP-WARE JUG
Fifteenth century.

One reason for the roughness of medieval European pottery may perhaps have been the rough and homely uses to which it was most frequently put. The secret of the Chinese porcelain was as yet unguessed-at, unknown, and the day was still far ahead in the dim future when wealthy Englishmen and Frenchmen and Italians, Germans and Austrians and Spaniards, should eat off plates and drink from cups of delicate and lovely china. In medieval times the platters upon lordly tables were often platters of wood, and the flagons, tankards, and drinking-cups were almost always of silver,

The Potter

silver-gilt, or gold. Not until the fifteenth century did the potters of Italy perfect a brilliantly glazed and tinted ware known as *majolica*. We shall have more to say about majolica before long.

    The potter of Plantagenet England plied his craft chiefly for the benefit of the humbler folk. He made the great high-shouldered pitchers in which villagers carried water from their well and Londoners from their conduit; he made the sturdy mugs from which his fellow-craftsmen quaffed their frothing ale, and the pots and pans and pipkins that their wives used in cooking, storing, and serving their solid, if simple, fare. He made cake-moulds in the form of saints' heads and money-boxes like towers and pigeon-cotes. For pilgrims he made gourd-shaped flasks, for clerks little green inkpots. For chilly people he made small, basket-shaped braziers to hold charcoal embers and to be held between the palms. Occasionally his handiwork *did* find its way into the company of the great, as when he made drinking-troughs for the pet-birds of the long-fingered ladies, or pitchers from which the pages poured water over the sticky hands of the knights after a banquet. This type of pitcher was called an *aquamanile*, and was often modelled to represent a knight on horseback.[1]

    During the Tudor period a type of stoneware jug with a bearded face moulded upon it was popular in England, especially in taverns and inns. The largest held about eight pints, the smallest only one. Most of these jugs were imported from Holland and Flanders. They were sometimes called *Bellarmines*, after Cardinal Robert Bellarmine, a zealous and hard-favoured Churchman much disliked among the Protestants of the Continent. In 1626 Charles I granted the sole right to make " stone pottes, stone juggs and stone bottells " for a period of fourteen years to two Londoners, Thomas Rous and Abraham Cullyn. The King's object was not only to break a foreign monopoly

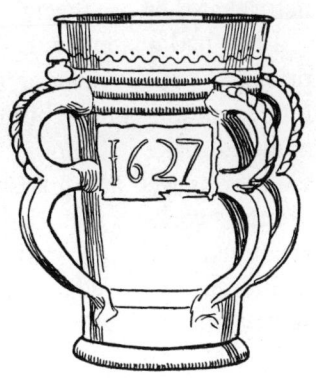

STUART SLIP-WARE MUG, 1627

[1] D. M. Stuart, *Men and Women of Plantagenet England*, p. 94 (Harrap).

The Book of Craftsmen

and encourage a new industry; he was also influenced by the fact that through the enterprise of these men "many poore people may be sett on worke and put to labour and good employment."

In the beautiful city of Florence the fine arts flourished exceedingly during the fifteenth century, and artists had no difficulty in finding wealthy patrons to reward and inspire them. A certain Florentine goldsmith called Luca della Robbia, born in the year 1400, turned his attention from gold to clay, and invented a method of applying a very hard, very durable, and very brilliant glaze to models or reliefs in terra-cotta. He began by making wall-ornaments with designs of foliage, fruit, masks, birds, or heraldic coats-of-arms: then he modelled human figures, often in white against a background of deep, clear blue. When he introduced other tints they were dim and pale, not attempting to imitate the stronger colours of real life. He excelled at reproducing the chubby softness of a baby's limbs, and his groups of the Madonna and Child, or the Adoration of the Three Kings, are as lifelike and natural as they are lovely.

STUART SALT-CELLAR

Luca had a nephew called Andrea della Robbia, who was his principal pupil, and four great-nephews, all of whom worked as modellers and potters, but none of whom equalled the first of their name to make it famous. Luca himself was a remarkable man, a sculptor as well as a goldsmith and a potter. Among the most delightful works of the della Robbia family are the medallions of swaddled babies decorating the walls of the Foundling Hospital in Florence: and what could be more charming than the solemn, podgy little fellow playing a big blue bagpipe in the Victoria and Albert Museum?

Meanwhile another—and in some ways a very beautiful—type of earthenware had been introduced and developed in Italy. The Spanish potters of the fifteenth century had not lost or forgotten the processes by which, as we have seen, the Moorish craftsmen

MAJOLICA PLATE DEPICTING A MAJOLICA-PAINTER AT WORK

Victoria and Albert Museum

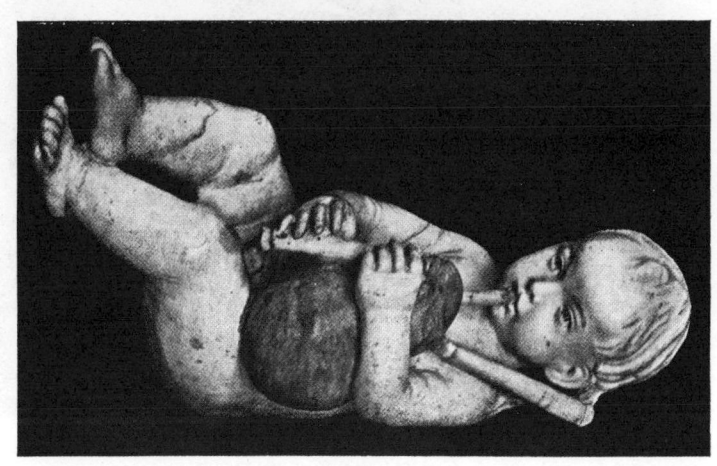

FIGURE IN ENAMELLED TERRA-COTTA BY LUCA DELLA ROBBIA

TWO FIGURES MADE BY THE BOW POTTERS
About 1750.
Victoria and Albert Museum

THREE DERBY FIGURES, ABOUT 1775
John Wilkes, James Quin as Falstaff, and Field-Marshal Conway.
Victoria and Albert Museum

The Potter

used to make gorgeous and glittering jugs and jars. A great deal of this Spanish ware was shipped to the island of Majorca, a dependency of the kingdom of Aragon, and thence to Italy, and the Italians gave it the name of 'Majolica,' a name which stuck to it even after the place of manufacture shifted from Spanish to Italian territory. Faenza, an ancient city in the province of Ravenna, on the old Roman Road known as the Via Æmilia, became the centre of the majolica industry, and as years passed the designs enamelled upon this ware showed more and more clearly the influence of the great painters then living and working in Italy. Scenes from classical mythology and from Biblical history were very popular, especially upon dishes made to commemorate betrothals or weddings. Upon a brilliant white background figures and patterns were applied in various colours, blue and yellow being the most common. Heroes of legend and fable appear with blue faces and limbs and yellow hair. So famous did the potteries at Faenza become that the word *faïence* soon meant brightly glazed earthenware in general, and is still used in that sense by experts upon the subject.

DELFT POSSET POT

Other Italian cities produced rich and glowing majolica ware, and the craft was practised in France as early as the fourteenth century. That luxurious and art-loving monarch François I proved a generous patron to the French potters, whose works during his reign showed much ingenuity and skill. German potters did not lag very far behind, and in Holland during the sixteenth and seventeenth centuries glazed earthenware was put to a variety of purposes. It was used for candlesticks, inkpots, knife-handles, pipe-bowls, stoves, hearth-tiles, and wall-ornaments. Delft, the greatest of the Dutch pottery-towns, traded extensively with Japan and the East Indies during the seventeenth century,

The Book of Craftsmen

and Oriental influence is strong in the patterns chosen by the Delft potters.

Japanese porcelain, though not equal to the Chinese which it closely resembled, was often exceedingly beautiful. The Japanese liked brighter colours, and more complicated, crowded designs. Their cups and vases were often ornamented with masses of either grotesque or dainty little figures; like the Chinese, they delighted in fierce, curly dragons, shaggy chrysanthemums, delicate plum-blossom, and flying storks and cranes. Under Chinese influence Japanese designs were sometimes very simple and graceful, without too much detail.

Now let us take a very long stride, from the volcanic islands of the Japanese archipelago to the quite village of Fulham on the north bank of the river Thames, opposite Putney. It *was* a village, and a quiet village, too, in the middle of the seventeenth century when John Dwight established a pottery there near the old church whose massive grey tower still stands. John Dwight was a bookish man, an M.A. of Oxford, and had been secretary in turn to three Bishops of Chester. Abandoning his secretarial duties, he obtained a royal patent in 1671 authorizing him to produce " transparent earthenware."

Being an inventive and enterprising fellow, he produced a great variety of wares, and succeeded in breaking the foreign monopoly in earthenware which had annoyed English potters in the days of good Queen Bess. He made not only jugs, bottles, tobacco-pipes, bowls, and jars; he modelled wonderfully lifelike figures in full relief—that is to say, completely separated from any background—and in bas-relief—that is, only partly separated from the panel or slab against which we see them. He fashioned two figures of his baby daughter Lydia. There is one little statuette of her draped in a loosely flowing mantle and looking upward: and another, lying as if asleep, with a lace-edged cap on her head and a posy of flowers in her small chubby hands. The inscription on the back of this second model explains the posy and the fast-shut eyes. It is: *Lydia Dwight, died March* 3, 1673.

The Potter

Charles II, like all the Stuarts, was keenly interested in inventions and discoveries. Dwight found in him an intelligent patron, and many of the productions of the Fulham kilns bear the letters C.R. (*Carolus Rex*), either as a token that they were manufactured expressly for his Majesty or to remind the world that Mr Dwight worked under royal patronage.

Perhaps the most magnificent piece of Fulham ware which has survived is the life-sized bust of Charles II's cousin, Prince Rupert, now in the British Museum. It is modelled in grey glazed pottery, the collar and badge of the Order of the Garter being faintly touched with gold, and it gives us a vivid glimpse of the gallant cavalier Captain in his later years, when his battles on land and sea had been left far behind, and he was solacing his leisure with scientific experiments.

The closely curled periwigs worn by Prince Rupert and his royal kinsmen, those periwigs so characteristic of the Restoration period, were re-curled by means of small cylinders of heated pipe-clay. The name of this clay indicates the use to which it was first put. When tobacco was first introduced from Virginia it was smoked in rather short-stemmed clay pipes: at a later date came the very long-stemmed, graceful pipe known as the 'Churchwarden.' Pipes of briar-wood or of meerschaum are comparatively recent in date.

In the first patent granted to John Dwight his invention is said to concern "transparent earthenware, commonly known by the name of porcelain or china," but the very finest and most delicate of his productions fell far short of the genuine Chinese porcelain in the quality of transparency. This was also true of the wares which came from a rival pottery set up by a Dutchman called Van Hamme at Lambeth. This Lambeth ware, closely resembling real Delft, remained popular in England till the eighteenth century, when Staffordshire took the place of London as the centre of the industry.

A set of six Lambeth plates in the British Museum bears the following quaint inscriptions:

The Book of Craftsmen

(1) What is a merry man?
(2) Let him do what he can
(3) To entertain his guests
(4) With wine and merry jests;
(5) But if his wife do frown
(6) All merriment goes down.

Two men played a very important part in the development of European porcelain: they were Augustus the Strong, Elector of Saxony (afterwards King of Poland), and an apothecary called Böttger, whom he kept in his employment to make secret experiments in alchemy. In the opening years of the eighteenth century Augustus, a man of many hobbies, began to collect specimens of the beautiful chinaware which the Dutch traders were then shipping in large quantities from China and Japan. He was seized with an enthusiastic desire to discover the secret of the Far Eastern potters, and to this end he set Böttger to work. By mere chance, a rather comical chance, the discovery was made. One day Herr Böttger sent his wig to be freshly powdered. When it came back from the hairdresser's he put it on, and found that it was unusually heavy. Concluding, quite rightly, that some new sort of powder had been applied to it, he snatched it off his head, shook some of the stuff out of it, and began to examine and analyse. To his excitement and surprise, he discovered that the white, dusty substance was *kaolin*, the clay upon which the Chinese potters depended to give transparency to their china. Inquiries revealed that the powder had been obtained from a large deposit of this clay near the village of Aue.

DRINKING-VESSEL OF BÖTTGER'S PORCELAIN
The monogram is that of Augustus the Strong.

Two years later visitors to the Leipzig Fair were able to admire some examples of fine white porcelain "made by Johann Friedrich Böttger, under the patronage of August the First, Elector of Saxony." In 1710 the Meissen porcelain works were

TUREEN MADE AT SÈVRES IN 1759
Bayerisches National-Museum, Munich

POLISH GENTLEMAN AND LADY
Group made at Meissen
Bayerisches National-Museum, Munich

The Potter

set up in one of the Elector's castles, and the manufacture of the world-famous Dresden china was begun.

Poor Böttger's discovery brought him little luck. The Elector . . . was as secretive about his china-making as he had been about his gold, or as the Chinese were with their wares. Workmen engaged in the work were imprisoned in the castle and made to swear that they would keep the secrets of the craft " till the tomb should seal them." Böttger himself was virtually a prisoner while he supervised the factory and pursued, along with his studies in china-making, the secret of gold-making. By 1716 he had perfected the art of porcelain, so that his dishes were technically as perfect as those of the Chinese.[1]

No efforts on the part of Augustus, no precautions on the part of those whom he employed, could keep the secret thus curiously discovered. Within fifty years factories had sprung up in Austria, Russia, and France, and true porcelain, as distinct from the old glazed earthenware, was produced in abundance. The works at Meissen continued to flourish until 1756, when the Seven Years War broke out and Frederick the Great sacked the place.

Already in the seventeenth century the county of Staffordshire was one of the important centres of the English ceramic industry. In 1730 the thirteenth and youngest son of a Staffordshire potter, Thomas Wedgwood, was born at Burslem and received the name of Josiah. Most of little Josiah's relatives were potters like his father, some of them master-potters, some of them mere journeymen. His eldest brother, Thomas, was already established in the family calling when Thomas senior died, leaving his youngest boy fatherless at the age of nine. Schooldays now ended for Josiah and he began work with his brother at Burslem, soon becoming expert at the art of 'throwing' on the wheel. At the age of fifteen he was bound apprentice, but, owing to ill-health following a violent attack of smallpox, he was not able to do heavy work, and thus, by mere chance, got an opportunity to study all the different processes of his craft. The intelligent lad began to experiment with new methods on his own account, but his brother did not

[1] M. F. Lansing, *Science through the Ages*, p. 48 (Harrap).

The Book of Craftsmen

encourage his enterprising spirit, and refused, when the time of his apprenticeship was over, to take Josiah into partnership with him. After working at two other potteries, the indomitable Josiah, at the age of twenty-eight, took the lease of a small pot-works at Burslem, at an annual rental of £10, and set up in business for himself.

It was not long before perseverance and intelligence began to bring their reward. The works had to be enlarged, more houses had to be built for the workpeople, and more kilns had to be made. Josiah Wedgwood had noticed many annoying little defects in the crockery of his time—plates were of unequal thickness, or lop-sided and irregular, so that if piled one upon another they toppled over; spouts dribbled; lids did not fit; handles were of such awkward shapes that one could not get a good grip on them. These things he set himself to remedy, and with such success that within a few years he was sufficiently prosperous to subscribe a sum of £500 towards the construction of new roads linking up the Staffordshire district with London and other parts of the country. By an amusing turn of the wheel—Fortune's wheel, not the potter's wheel—his elder brother Thomas had been fain to take service at Josiah's works, and was glad to be received into partnership by the junior whose early efforts he had so short-sightedly discouraged. Exactly ten years after he had launched forth as a master-potter Josiah Wedgwood opened his great new works between Burslem and Stoke-on-Trent. Under the mistaken impression[1] that the ancient Etruscans had been skilful makers of vases, he called the works and the village which sprang up near them 'Etruria.' He had been appointed potter to Queen Charlotte in 1762, and as a compliment to her he gave the name of 'Queen's Ware' to the cream-coloured china for which he took out a patent in 1763. But he was never satisfied with what he had done, nor even with what he was doing: his active mind seemed to be fixed rather upon what he wanted and hoped to do.

Wedgwood designed and manufactured not only all sorts of

[1] See page 17.

The Potter

ornamental and useful ware: he made clever imitations of jasper, agate, and other semi-precious minerals, and from these he fashioned life-sized busts, vases, candlesticks, inkstands, chessmen, seals, and medallions ranging in size from small ovals to be set in finger-rings to large plaques for decorating walls. Popular enthusiasm for the antique vases brought to England by Sir William Hamilton, English Ambassador in Naples, turned Wedgwood's energies in another direction, and he set about copying and adapting these very beautiful classical models. Then came into existence the type of ware usually associated with his name—dull-surfaced, with a background of blue, greyish-green, or purplish-black against which graceful, pure white figures of a Greek or Roman type are modelled in low relief.

WEDGWOOD JASPER VASE
Imitating the ancient Greek.

During all these busy years Wedgwood had been hampered by the weakness of his right leg, the result of his early sufferings from smallpox. Courageously, he determined in his thirty-ninth year to have the troublesome limb amputated. In those days, when methods of surgery were crude and cruel, and anæsthetics unknown, this was a really heroic decision. Happily, the patient made a good recovery, and was able to resume his crowded and vigorous life, directing the works at Etruria, encouraging the cutting of canals and the making of new roads and bridges, experimenting with fresh clays and glazes, laying out his gardens, writing papers for the *Philosophical Transactions* of the Royal Society, and entertaining his friends at the handsome house he had built for himself on the outskirts of Etruria[1]—a house still standing, though no longer used as a private residence.

Josiah Wedgwood died in 1795. A monument to his memory was erected in Stoke Church, with a portrait bust by Flaxman,

---

[1] Etruria is a suburb of Hanley.

The Book of Craftsmen

the well-known sculptor of the period. His epitaph declares that he "converted a rude and inconsiderable manufactory into an elegant art, and an important part of national commerce."

Many famous people in foreign lands were numbered among the patrons of the Wedgwood potteries. Catherine, Empress of Russia (Catherine the Great), possessed a complete Wedgwood dinner service specially made for her, with a little green frog on the back of each dish and plate. There was, however, no lack of fine china on the Continent. France was justly proud of the beautiful objects which came from the royal porcelain factory at Sèvres. Louis XV's silversmith, Duplessis, designed some of the large vases made at Sèvres, which accounts for their rather massive outlines and the heavy richness of their moulded ornaments.

It would take too long to describe in detail all the various kinds, colours, and shapes of porcelain and pottery produced in Europe after Böttger's discovery became known. The habit of drinking tea and coffee encouraged the manufacture of teapots and teacups, coffee-pots and coffee-cups. The earliest type of teacup had no handle, and it was necessary for the tea-drinker to balance his cup daintily upon the tips of his fingers. In those days people spoke not of a *cup* of tea, but of a *dish* of tea!

It was in the eighteenth century that fashionable folk on either side of the Channel were seized with a violent craze for collecting china. It is a craze that has never wholly died out, and it broke forth with fresh fury in the nineties of the last century when blue china became all the rage; *Punch* represented enthusiasts affectionately patting their favourite specimens as if they had been living pets, or tearfully declaring that they had nothing left to live for when a rare piece was broken.

The first English works where porcelain—as distinct from miscellaneous pottery—was made stood at Bow. Quaint and charming little figures were made by the Bow potters, and by their imitators and rivals, the potters of Chelsea. Distinguished sculptors did not think it beneath their dignity to provide designs for the Chelsea factory, and poor gentlewomen with a talent for fine brushwork

FIGURES MADE AT DERBY AFTER THE STYLE OF CHELSEA
About 1775.
Victoria and Albert Museum

BRISTOL CHINA FIGURES
About 1770.
Victoria and Albert Museum

The Potter

painted gaily-hued fruits and brilliant posies on the cups and saucers made there. Potteries sprang up at Worcester, Bristol, Derby, and elsewhere, sometimes borrowing patterns and ideas from London, sometimes from China or Japan, sometimes thinking out perfectly good ideas of their own.

Popular demand created a supply of coloured earthenware or porcelain figures of well-known public characters. James Quin, the actor, was seen impersonating Shakespeare's fat knight, Sir John Falstaff; John Wesley preaching from a canopied pulpit; John Wilkes, M.P., that raffish champion of popular liberties, squinting as violently as he did in real life; and that good-looking soldier Field-Marshal Conway gazing proudly at nothing. Innkeepers wanted Toby jugs, those jolly jugs in the form of portly old gentlemen in red waistcoats and three-cornered hats: cottagers wanted white dogs with golden bells hanging round their necks to stand on either side of the mantelshelf. Early settlers in Australia seem to have taken some of these china dogs out with them to their new home on the other side of the world, for the Sentimental Bloke, in Mr C. J. Dennis's amusing book of that name, remarks, when he describes how he went to pay a call at a small house in Sydney,

TOBY JUG

> Two dilly sorter dawgs made outer delf
> Stares 'ard at me frum orf the mantelshelf;

nor is that staring breed extinct in England even now.

CHAPTER II
THE WORKER IN METALS

IT is quite easy to imagine how, in the dawn of human life upon this planet, the first men obtained clay for their pots, flint for their scrapers, and wood for their fires. These things, so useful, so necessary, lay all ready to his hand. But it is not so easy to imagine how he got possession of metals, which are for the most part embedded in what are called 'deposits,' far below the surface of the earth. Probably he chanced upon some lumps of ore uncovered by a landslide or by a flood, or dug into an outcrop where the mineral was less deeply buried: and then, finding new uses for this new substance, proceeded to dig systematically for it.

Copper seems to have been the earliest mineral discovered by man. Three thousand years before the beginning of the Christian era the ancient Egyptians were working great copper mines on the Sinai peninsula, and a flat copper celt[1] of Egyptian workmanship found upon the floor-level of a prehistoric dwelling in Crete proves that copper tools and weapons were exported to the Ægean in the remote past. The next stage was the discovery of tin. Then—perhaps by mere accident—man learned that by alloying tin with copper he could produce a metal more serviceable to him than either—the metal described in the English Bible as 'brass,' but now commonly called 'bronze.'

Copper abounded in the Near East, and was mined and smelted there long before iron or gold were known. Its use spread to Greece, Crete, Italy, Sicily, Portugal, and Spain. Bronze, properly so called, makes its appearance in Asia Minor[2] about 2200 B.C. Objects fashioned from this metal were unearthed at Hissarlik by

---
[1] A chisel-edged primitive weapon.
[2] Professor Eliot Smith thinks it may have been in Northern Persia.

The Worker in Metals

a German scholar called Heinrich Schliemann. His is a wonderful story of determination and endurance. Born in 1822, the son of a poor pastor in Mecklenburg-Schwerin, he was first a grocer's assistant, then a cabin-boy, then a book-keeper. Through all his struggles he never ceased to pursue his hobby, the study of Greek and of the Homeric poems which were the glory of Greece. He taught himself seven or eight languages, and pored over every

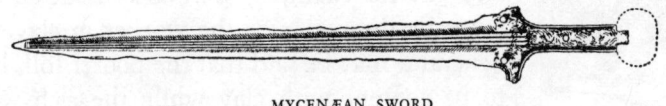

MYCENÆAN SWORD

book he could lay hands on which dealt with Homer, and Homer's heroes, and the immortal story of the siege of Troy. Finally, fulfilling the dream of his youth, he betook himself to the Troad, and began to excavate what he firmly believed to be the site of Troy.

He dug deep into the ground, and was rewarded by finding not one ancient settlement but *nine*. It was in the second layer from the bottom that the very early bronze objects were found. The seventh layer contained the remains of Homer's Troy, girt by a curtain-wall of ashlar[1] masonry. Later Schliemann excavated the site of the ancient city of Mycenæ, where he discovered a hoard of magnificent gold ornaments.

Let us now return to the first makers of bronze, and to that period of human history known as the Bronze Age.

The knowledge of the discovery of bronze spread by way of the trade-routes on land and sea which even these far-off peoples knew and followed. It meant that tin and copper were now equally important, and where there were big deposits of tin—as in Spain and Cornwall—the enterprising traders and seafarers of the ancient world found their way. At a later date a long and fierce struggle raged between the Carthaginians, who controlled the tin traffic, and the Romans, who desired to control it. It was a struggle in which Rome triumphed.

[1] Masonry made of hewn and shaped blocks of stone.

The Book of Craftsmen

Bronze proved serviceable for many purposes. Axe-heads, spear-tips, swords, razors, chisels, hammers, bowls, jars, kitchen utensils, helmets, shields, lamps, were among the useful things made of this metal; and among merely ornamental things were rings, brooches, bracelets, necklaces, and statuettes. You will notice that some of these things, lamps, bowls, and jars for example, were also made in old times by the potter or the worker in clay. In general it may be said that the poorer folk had to be content with clay while the rich were able to obtain the more rare and costly bronze: but it is of interest that the potter and the metal-worker frequently paid each other the highest form of compliment—imitation. The metal-worker would imitate the lamp or the jar made by the potter: the potter—this is especially true of those who fashioned the red Samian or Aretine ware—would copy, as closely as he could, the embossed designs, the decorative handles, the other details of the metal-worker's finest handiwork.

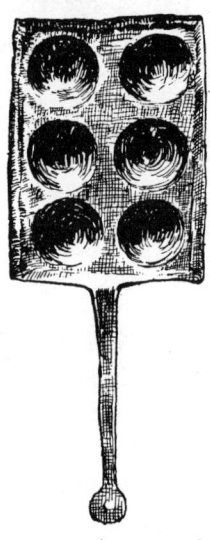

BRONZE 'BUN-TRAY'

The Greeks used bronze—which they called *chalkos*—extensively, and some of the designs invented by their craftsmen were very beautiful. They made frames for chairs and tables of bronze, often with feet in the form of lions' paws; they made three-legged stands for bowls or jars, and the jars themselves had handles in the form of sphinxes, human figures, grotesque masks, or satyrs. Mirrors were made of highly polished bronze, as the process by which a piece of glass can be turned into what we call a 'looking-glass' had not then been invented.

The Celtic inhabitants of Britain and Ireland were skilful workers in bronze, which they ornamented with discs or bosses of coloured enamel. The seafarers of Scandinavia understood its use, both for domestic and warlike purposes. Among the most beautiful of the Ancient British exhibits in the British

The Worker in Metals

Museum is a bronze shield decorated with studs of red enamel. This shield is oblong: another form was circular, with a boss in the centre.

The Bronze Age was a period of great activity and enterprise among the more advanced peoples of the world. The necessity for finding fresh supplies of copper and tin spurred the more adventurous sea-trading nations to penetrate into oceans hitherto unknown; and these metals, either in their crude state or blended and fashioned, became a medium of exchange between various races to whom the idea of minting coins had not occurred.

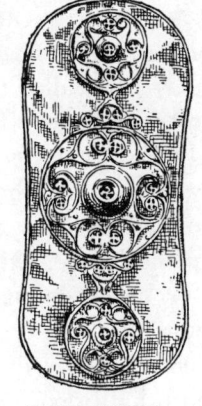

EARLY BRITISH SHIELD
British Museum

There was another metal, however, which the heart of primitive man desired even more intensely than copper, tin, or bronze—and this was gold.

Now gold is not intrinsically—that is to say, *in itself*—the most precious metal in the earth. It is not the most scarce; it is not the most difficult to find, or to separate from its surrounding substance. But because civilized men agree in setting a higher value upon this metal it has become the recognized king of them all. Uncivilized men do not share this delusion about gold: and the Spanish invaders of Mexico and Peru, countries where gold was then extremely plentiful, were amazed to see the natives handling golden vessels as carelessly as in other lands pots and pans of humble iron would have been handled.

Why should the inhabitants of so many far-scattered countries in the ancient world have come to set such a store by gold? It seems likely that it was because of a fanciful connexion between that metal and the golden-coloured sun, so often adored as a god. The sun was the life-giver, at whose warm touch the grey winter world awoke, and the green grain ripened into yellow corn, and the vines bore purple fruit. Small wonder that men worshipped

The Book of Craftsmen

him! Small wonder that they prized the metal which in colour and brightness resembled his disc and his rays! They did not only prize it; they believed that it had mysterious magical properties—hence its frequent use for crowns and sceptres, sacrificial vessels, and priestly ornaments. In the ancient kingdom of Sumer the gods were called the Lords of Gold. The Egyptians were fashioning ornaments of gold as early as 3500 B.C., and at Naga-el-Der in Upper Egypt a hoard of worked gold was discovered dating from 3300 B.C. This hoard consisted of ten egg-shaped beads, twenty-four models of snail-shells, and a small figure of a gazelle. Vast quantities of gold were obtained from the Sudan, and from Nubia —so called because in the language of the ancient Egyptians the word for gold was *nub*. The Celtic tribes of Britain and Ireland decked their arms with golden bracelets and their horses' harness with half-moons of beaten gold. It was with a golden sickle that the ancient Druids used to cut the sacred mistletoe from the oak-tree at the time of high festival. Much of the gold used by Celtic goldsmiths came from Ireland, and was of a lovely pale daffodil colour.

In the far distant past miners were often slaves or criminals, desperate and friendless men at the mercy of their masters and their gaolers. Picks made of stags' horns were much used, but quite often the bare hand was the miner's only tool. The clay found in ancient mine-workings bears the finger-prints of hundreds of hands with the thumbs developed to an unusual size by hard toil.

The Indians and the Chinese were sinking shafts and digging tunnels five thousand years ago, and according to a Greek myth Cadmus, the famous sower of the dragon's teeth, opened up gold and silver mines on Mount Pangæus, in Thrace—the same mountain where Orpheus was said to have charmed the wild beasts with the sweet music of his voice and his lyre.

Owing to its royal and sacred character, gold was in great favour among the proud princes of Egypt, Babylonia, and Assyria. The

The Worker in Metals

kings whose bones were discovered recently in the mysterious death-pits beneath the ruins of the city of Ur, in Mesopotamia, bore with them to the grave helmets, and daggers, and drinking-vessels of finely worked gold, and their queens wore wreaths of beaten gold foliage in their black hair. In one grave the skeleton of a little girl was found wearing three separate garlands of gold. Half-moons of gold had hung from the child's ears and necklaces of gold and semi-precious stones had encircled her neck. With her in the earth had been laid a miniature set of two bowls and a tumbler in silver and a plain cup in gold, perhaps because she had loved and played with them while she lived, perhaps for the use of her childish spirit in the world of shades.[1]

GOLD VASE
From a royal grave at Ur.

When the tomb of King Tut-ankh-Amen of Egypt was opened the number and magnificence of the golden objects within it dazzled and overwhelmed the discoverers. The King's coffin was enclosed in a sarcophagus of gold, supported at the four corners by four golden goddesses with arms outstretched as if in supplication, and there was a golden mask over his face. In the treasure-chamber adjoining the tomb there were unimagined wonders in the way of goldsmiths' and jewellers' work, including a marvellous golden throne, on the back panel of which there appear embossed likenesses of the young King himself and his youthful consort.

It seems strange that it should have been so, but the Age of Iron came later than the Age of Bronze. One would have imagined that a crude metal would have become known at an earlier date than an alloy; but it was not so. The ancient Egyptians called iron ' the stone of heaven ' and the Greeks called it *sideros*, ' from the stars,' which suggests that the first form in which these peoples

---

[1] D. M. Stuart, *The Girl through the Ages*, p. 20 (Harrap).

The Book of Craftsmen

encountered iron was meteoric iron—iron fallen from interstellar space. In India the metal was known and worked as early as 1500 B.C. At Kutub, near Delhi, there is a huge iron column twenty-three feet in height, and weighing seventeen tons, which —as its inscription shows—was erected in the ninth century before Christ. The ancients knew some method of preserving iron from rust, but in some instances, such as the Kutub column and the bolts and nails in a Viking ship discovered at Oseberg, the absence of rust is due to the unusual purity of the iron. (It must be remembered that, unlike gold and tin, iron is not found pure in its natural state. It is usually found mixed with clay or rock —iron *ore*—and can only be separated from the ore by the action of intense heat—one of the reasons why it came late into human ken.)

TUT-ANKH-AMEN'S GOLDEN THRONE

Owing to the tendency of iron to perish by rust, fewer objects have survived from the Iron Age than from the Age of Bronze. Sometimes bronze and iron would be used by some ancient people at the same period of their history, as in Babylon under Nebuchadnezzar II in the sixth century B.C., when the bolts of the city gates were of iron. It must not be imagined that in the Age of Bronze no metal other than bronze was known, nor in the Age of Iron no metal other than iron: these terms indicate the period during which one substance or the other came into general use and was widely distributed among the more intelligent peoples of the globe. There are still some races, such as the aborigines of Australia and

The Worker in Metals

the Polynesians of Oceania, who have never 'off their own bat' discovered how to mine or smelt metals.

The Hebrews of Biblical times employed both bronze ('brass') and iron, and among the wrongs done by the Philistines to the Israelites was the forcible carrying off of the Israelitish smiths. Ezekiel speaks of an iron pot, and in the Book of Ecclesiasticus we

MEDIEVAL BLACKSMITHS AT WORK
The tools of the smith, and his methods of work, altered little between Biblical and medieval times.

get this vivid glimpse of just such a Jewish worker in iron as might have made such a pot:

> The smith also sitting by the anvil, and considering the iron work, the vapour of the fire wasteth his flesh, and he fighteth with the heat of the furnace: the noise of the hammer and the anvil is ever in his ears, and his eyes look still upon the pattern of the thing that he maketh; he setteth his mind to finish his work, and watcheth to polish it perfectly.[1]

As the moon is to the sun so is silver to gold, the one richly glowing, the other pensive and pale, the one warm crimson or flaming yellow, the other soft grey or glimmering blue. Silver was known among the ancient Egyptians at an early period, and was

[1] Ecclesiasticus, xxxviii, 28.

The Book of Craftsmen

much prized by the Greeks, the Etruscans, and the Romans. In the eighth and seventh centuries B.C. the Etruscans—of whom we heard something in the first chapter of this book—made extensive use of silver, not only for trinkets, table-vessels, and ornaments, but also for the toilet accessories, mirrors, ointment-pots, and combs, placed in the grave with dead Etruscan ladies. As it was believed that these silver objects would be handled by the ghost of the departed they were made very light and thin, so that they should not be too heavy for the shadowy fingers to lift up. The same belief led the Greek goldsmiths to make funeral diadems of flimsy golden foliage, and armlets of gold-leaf as thin as the leaf of a tree.

During the Dark Ages, that dim and stormy period separating the collapse of the Roman Empire from the rise of a new Christian civilization in the West, silver and gold continued to be employed for both sacred and ordinary purposes. Silver was used for the votive tablets hung by suppliants in the temples of Roman and of Celtic divinities: it would also appear to have been used for the headdress of the high priest in certain cults, and it forms the diadem of a prehistoric lady who was discovered at

GOLD EARRING WITH FIGURE OF CUPID AS PENDANT
Ancient Greek.
British Museum

El Argar in Spain. A magnificent hoard of silver vessels was unearthed some years since upon a mound known as the Traprain Law, in Haddingtonshire. From the fact that each of these vessels, whether cup, salver, bowl, platter, or jar, had been hacked through with a heavy blade, it has been concluded that this was the plunder of a band of Scandinavian pirates, homeward bound, who had been alarmed or surprised in the very act of breaking up the silver for melting, and had hastily buried it, meaning to return and dig it up again some day. Why they did not return we shall never know.

The taste of the ladies of ancient Greece and Rome for elaborate jewellery encouraged the craftsmen of those lands to invent new

The Worker in Metals

and wonderful designs. Greek earrings were often decorated with tiny winged figures of Eros, the god of love; and apparently the pious worshippers of the goddess Venus in the island of Cyprus thought that even a divine being might take delight in an offering of delicately wrought gold. The foam-born goddess had a famous temple on the island, at a place called Paphos, and on the site of that temple was discovered a long golden pin of the shape used by Greek women to hold up their hair. This trinket, ornamented with bulls' heads and tipped with a large pearl, was a votive offering given to Venus by some long-ago worshipper who wanted some favour from her, and hoped to win it by the very human gift of a golden hairpin.

Since the discovery of the New World by the Spaniards in the fifteenth century a great part of the Old World's supply of silver has come from Mexico and Peru, but the ancients drew most of their silver from Spain itself. An historian of the first century B.C. declares that the metal was first accidentally discovered by some Pyrenean shepherds, who set fire to a forest among the mountains, and so melted the ore in the veins of the rocks.

The rise of Christianity brought new tasks to the metal-worker. He learned to make the sacred vessels used in the celebration of Mass, chalice, paten, ciborium, and pyx; he fashioned candlesticks and lamps, censers and incense-boats; he wrought reliquaries and shrines to hold the bones of saints and martyrs, or even to hold objects which had once been

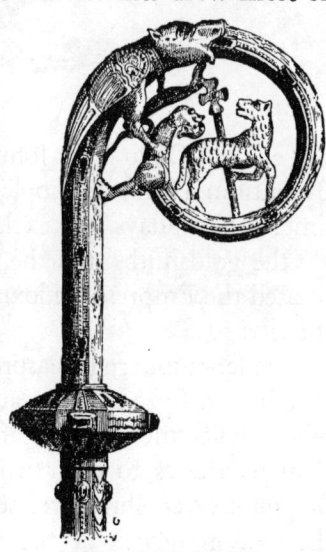

GILDED BRASS CROZIER
Medieval French.

theirs. He it was who made rings for the thumbs and fingers of popes and prelates, clasps for their prayer-books, golden adornments for their diadems and mitres. Often it was he who made the

The Book of Craftsmen

crook-shaped top of the crozier or pastoral staff, though this might be of ivory, or even of wood. On the other hand, the Fathers of the Western Church, notably St Cyprian, St Clement, and St Jerome, were particularly anxious that their women-converts should give up wearing golden rings on their fingers and in their ears, and golden tags on their sandals! And one of the Fathers of

CHALICE OF ARDAGH

the Eastern Church, St John Chrysostom, preached eloquently at Byzantium (Constantinople) against the luxurious habits of the time. "Nowadays," he exclaimed, "our admiration is all reserved for the goldsmiths and the weavers!" These bold words so displeased the Empress Eudoxia that she banished the preacher from the city.

The far-rumoured treasures of the monasteries and churches of Britain and Byzantium, Gaul and Spain, were among the inducements which moved the Scandinavian sea-robbers of the ninth and tenth centuries to quit their craggy homelands and steer their dragon-prowed ships over seas as yet to them unknown. Among the treasure-hoards of the Vikings exquisite glassware from the Near East and golden vessels of Celtic or Anglo-Saxon origin are still to be found. The Norsemen had skilful metal-workers among themselves. We have already seen that their smiths forged a particularly pure variety of iron. The warriors wore heavy bracelets

SAXON JEWELS FOUND AT PRITTLEWELL

The 'saucer' is of bronze, into the bottom of which a decorated plate set with garnets is cemented; the whole of the metal-work was gilded on its exposed face.

From the originals in the Southend-on-Sea Museum

The Worker in Metals

of gold, and the hilts of their swords were sometimes set with garnets, while their wives and daughters sported necklaces and girdles of coloured stones set in fine gold filigree. The great drinking-horns from which these hardy seafarers quaffed deep draughts of mead had rims of gold, bronze, or silver, and it is interesting to remember that among the nine accomplishments of the well-educated Viking was working as a smith. The Saxon invaders of Roman Britain, though inferior in culture to the people they overwhelmed, sported very gorgeous jewellery. In 1930, at Prittlewell, near Southend-on-Sea, some beautiful ornaments were discovered in a pre-Christian Saxon burying-ground. These included a pair of brooches set with garnets; from the two gilded bronze discs there hung a pendant of coloured stones.

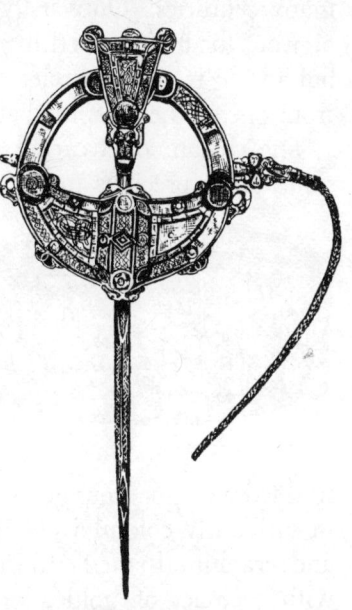

THE TARA BROOCH

Ireland, as we have said before, was one of the principal gold-producing countries of the prehistoric period, and Celtic Christianity created some of the loveliest pieces of workmanship in bronze, silver, gold, and enamel-work in the world. Some—but all too few—of these marvels still exist. Among them are the Ardagh Chalice, the shrine of St Patrick's bell, the Tara brooch. The chalice is composed of six different metals—gold, silver, bronze, brass, copper, and lead; it is ornamented with exquisite chasing and filigree work, and with bosses of amber and of blue enamel. The brooch is of a metal known as ' white bronze ' and bears seventy-six different designs. A boy digging potatoes discovered the chalice, while a little peasant girl picked up the brooch on the seashore.

The Book of Craftsmen

According to tradition, it was Pope Gregory the Great who gave to the Langobardic Queen Theodelinda the diadem afterwards famous in history as the Iron Crown of Lombardy. With this the Emperors of the Holy Roman Empire were crowned for many centuries. Outwardly it does not look as if it were made of iron, for it is encased in gold, emeralds, sapphires, and rubies: but inside is a thin circlet of iron said to have been hammered from one of the nails used at the Crucifixion.

The custom of wearing diadems or garlands of gold, or of some other precious metal, is a very ancient one. The Romans rewarded successful naval commanders with golden circlets decorated with the prows of ships. Charlemagne's crown as Emperor of the Franks was composed of eight panels of gold, four large and four small, connected by hinges. The large ones were studded with gorgeous gems, while the small ones bore little figures in brilliantly coloured enamel representing prophets, patriarchs, and seraphim. In medieval Europe monarchs were usually crowned with a circlet of gold adorned with conventional foliage. The kings of France sported the fleur-de-lis; the kings of England wore golden strawberry-leaves or trefoils until the fifteenth century, when they too adopted the fleur-de-lis; about the same time two intersecting arches were added to the diadem, giving it the form familiar to British eyes upon the heads of living sovereigns. The sceptre, as an emblem of kingship, dates back to Homeric and Biblical times. Early sceptres were often of ivory mounted in gold.

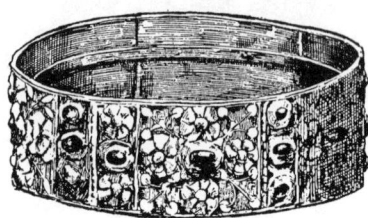

THE IRON CROWN OF LOMBARDY

Let us turn now from kings and queens, prelates and princes, all of whom were likely to encourage the goldsmith, and think of that humble but much more useful craftsman, the worker in iron.

At first sight it would seem as if the most obvious use to which man would put metal would be for tools and implements. Well,

The Worker in Metals

it *was* put to that use at a very early period, but not always in the way that we should expect. Prehistoric folk had fish-hooks of bronze before they had metal picks or spades, and prehistoric cultivators and flint-miners continued to wield picks made from the horns of deer long after the secret of bronze had been discovered and the knowledge widely diffused.

Among the earliest agricultural implements invented by mankind was the plough; but the ancient Egyptians made theirs entirely of wood, and the ancient Greeks were not much more enterprising. The Romans, a practical breed, and a nation of farmers and craftsmen, introduced the iron ploughshare. The Roman smith also made horseshoes—to our minds the most natural thing for a smith to do; and he made the iron framework in which the thick green glass of Roman windows was fixed.

In Anglo-Saxon England the smith was a man of many accomplishments. Early in the eleventh century Ælfric, Abbot of Eynsham, wrote for the use of his pupils in the monastery school a little book of *Colloquies* which tells us a great deal about the craftsmen of the time.

> The cobbler's boy can do many useful things as well as making and mending shoes: he has learnt how to make bottles of leather, purses, spur-straps, and bridles. . . . The blacksmith points out that without *his* aid not only would the ploughboy have no ploughshare and the fisherman no hook, but the tailor would lack a needle and the cobbler an awl.[1]

We shall return to the blacksmith presently—but now let us take a look at another worker in metal, the bell-founder, or, as he was called in medieval England, the 'bellyeter.'

The maker of bells has used bronze in his work for nearly one thousand years—indeed, in some parts of the world, for *more* than one thousand years—but gold and silver and copper have often been employed for the same purpose. The great, thundering bronze gongs of the ancient Chinese temples and the tinkling bells

---

[1] D. M. Stuart, *The Boy through the Ages*, p. 117 (Harrap).

The Book of Craftsmen

hung round the Chinese pagodas were the first cousins of the chimes which rang from Christian belfries to call good folk to their prayers. Of Aaron, the Jewish High Priest and brother of Moses, we read that God, giving His commandments concerning the vestments of the High Priest, said:

> Thou shalt make the robe of the ephod all of blue. . . .
> And beneath, upon the hem of it, thou shalt make pomegranates of blue, and of purple, and of scarlet, round about the hem thereof; and bells of gold between them round about.
> A golden bell and a pomegranate, a golden bell and a pomegranate, upon the hem of the robe round about.[1]

From the most distant past bells, gongs, and cymbals have been associated with the ceremonials of religious worship, and to this day the Patriarch of Babylon carries a pastoral staff upon the knob of which hang little tinkling bells: but the peoples of the antique world found other uses, quite practical and unsacred, for such objects. The Greeks had things called *kodones* ('tinkling things'), with which to give signals or commands to soldiers in camp or garrison—something like the bugles of to-day in purpose: the Romans had a large bronze bell to announce the hour when bathing might begin; this they called the *aes thermarum*, the hot-bath bell!

At the dawn of Christianity a curious tug-of-war went on in the minds of the first Christian leaders. On the one hand they wished to break clear away from paganism and all pagan practices; on the other hand most of their converts, and often they themselves, were steeped in pagan lore, and found it difficult to detach themselves entirely from the past.

The adoption of bells by the Christians had probably some connexion with the passage in the Book of Exodus quoted above; but the Children of Israel did not hang bells *outside their temples*, nor did *they* use them to call the people to prayer, whereas the pagans *did*. The Emperor Augustus caused bells to be hung round the roof of the temple of Jupiter Tonans,

[1] Exodus xxviii, 31, 33, 34.

THE SHRINE OF ST PATRICK'S BELL
By permission of the National Museum, Dublin

FROM GHIBERTI'S SECOND BAPTISTERY DOOR
Photo Alinari

SALT-CELLAR MADE FOR FRANCIS I BY BENVENUTO CELLINI
Wolfram photo

The Worker in Metals

Jupiter the Thunderer, in Rome, and it has been suggested that when the conversion of Constantine made Christianity the official religion of the Roman Empire the Christians, on taking over the sacred buildings of the older faith, took over the bells with them.

In the Celtic Church bells were at first hand-bells, and were regarded as very holy objects. One which belonged to St Patrick, the Apostle of Ireland, is mentioned in the Annals of Ulster as early as the year 552, within a century of the Saint's death, and still exists. It is six inches high, five inches broad, and six inches deep, and it was rung at the Eucharistic Congress in Dublin in 1932. The rich bronze shrine which holds this bell was made, the Irish inscription on it tells us, between 1091 and 1105. These bell-shrines, to which I have already alluded, were fairly common in Celtic Christendom, and some of those which survive are objects of great beauty, adorned with exquisite metalwork and set with enamels and precious stones.

The particular kind of bronze used in making bells was also employed for a variety of other purposes—so much so that in medieval Latin the bell-founder was called an *ollarius*, or a 'potmaker.' He made domestic utensils, skillets, ladles, saucepans, and bowls, of metal. A bronze jug bearing the arms of Richard Cœur-de-Lion was discovered not long ago in Palestine, near the site of a Crusaders' stronghold. Bronze also was used to make three magnificent double doors of the Baptistery at Florence. The first doors were made in the fourteenth century by Andrea Pisano, the second and third by a most skilful craftsman called Ghiberti, who devoted more than twenty-five years to the task. Michelangelo said of Ghiberti's last doors that they were worthy to be the Gates of Paradise.

The passing of years often separated crafts into various branches, as we shall see when we come to the workers in leather and in wood. In the case of the metal worker these branches included the jeweller, goldsmith, silversmith, coppersmith, brazier, blacksmith, whitesmith (or tinsmith), cutler, bell-founder, ironfounder, swordsmith, and armourer. These last two we shall meet

The Book of Craftsmen

later on. Spoons and knives were in use as eating implements from the earliest times, and were fashioned from bone and flint long before metals were known. Later the coppersmith made the humbler and the silversmith the more elegant table furnishings.

A MEDIEVAL BELL-FOUNDER
From the Tunnoc window in York Minster.

Forks were introduced into England from Italy in the sixteenth century, and at first people who were not accustomed to them found great difficulty in steering their way to their mouths. The earliest type was two-pronged and very sharp.

Bells tended to grow larger during the Middle Ages. The small bells of the Celtic Church developed into enormous fellows like the one at Rouen which weighed 36,364 pounds. Special belfry towers had to be built to house these giants.

The making of bells was an elaborate process, and is illustrated in a magnificent window in York Minster—a window in memory of a bell-founder of the City, Richard Tunnoc by name. The medieval bell was an object of affection as well as of veneration. When it was hung in its tower it was christened with almost as much ceremony as if it had been a baby. Sometimes it received the name of the donor, sometimes that of some appropriate archangel or saint. Gabriel was the godfather of many bells . . . When the godfather was a mere mortal his name was apt to cling to the bell in a shortened and familiar form, and so we have Great Tom of Oxford, called after Cardinal Wolsey, and Bell Harry at Canterbury, the gift of Henry VIII.[1]

Bell-metal was not used only for domestic utensils: it formed the basis of many elaborate works of art, such as the Gloucester Candlestick given by Peter, Abbot of Gloucester, to the great church over which he ruled. Dating from somewhere about the year 1110 this candlestick, probably one of a pair, swarms with grotesque figures and scrolls inscribed with Latin texts; its gilt surface is still bright, but of the precious stones which once studded

[1] D. M. Stuart, *Men and Women of Plantagenet England*, p. 99 (Harrap).

The Worker in Metals

it hardly any now remain. Other uses to which bell-metal was put included mortars for chemists, scales for wool-staplers, and seals for merchants.

The seal-cutter was one of the most delicate-fingered of workers in metal. Among the ancients seals were often engraved upon semi-precious stones and set in rings called signet-rings, but later both the very large seals used by kings, prelates, cities and states, and the smaller ones used by individuals, were of metal. Abbeys and universities, cathedrals and colleges, frequently chose to adorn their seals with figures of the Virgin Mary, or of some patron saint, standing under a fretted canopy. London had St Thomas Becket, himself a Londoner, sitting in the middle of London Bridge: a seaport town, such as Winchester in Sussex, would be very likely to have a ship on its seal; a wool-trading town, such as Boston in Lincolnshire, would have a wool-pack. A king's seal, of course, bore an image of the King, either on horseback or sitting on his throne. Royal and noble ladies occasionally adorned their seals with stately little images of themselves.

SEAL OF WINCHELSEA

CAST BRONZE MEDAL OF GIULIA ASTALLIA
By an unknown medallist, probably of Mantua. End of fifteenth century.

From the craft of the seal-cutter it is only one step—and that not a long one—to that of the medal-maker and the coiner. The medal is the twin brother of the coin. Although the custom of rewarding merit by the gift of a special medal, such as the Royal

The Book of Craftsmen

Humane Society's medal or the Victoria Cross, is comparatively recent, medals were struck to commemorate historical events quite far back in history. In medieval Italy the medal-worker was often a skilled artist, whose head-and-shoulder portraits are as lifelike as any piece of painting or sculpture could possibly be. The English seem always to have been fond of marking historic turning-points by the designs on seals and medals. Thus, Oliver Cromwell's Great Seal bore on one side a map of the British Isles, the Channel being marked 'the British Sea' and swarming with (presumably) British ships, while on the other was seen the House of Commons sitting, all in high-crowned hats of the true Roundhead shape.

A medieval gentleman who could not write his name must have found a signet ring helpful when he wanted to sign a letter or a legal document. English merchants borrowed from the Flemings the habit of sealing business documents with a personal device, not a coat of arms, which was as binding as a written signature. There was another kind of ring which he firmly believed could be even more helpful, if the occasion arose. This was a ring set with a toadstone, supposed to be an infallible protection against poison. The toadstone was actually the fossilized tooth of a fish, but in those days it was thought to grow in the skull of a toad. It is to this belief that Shakespeare refers in *As You Like It* when he says:

GOLD RING WITH MERCHANT'S MARK
Sixteenth century.

> Sweet are the uses of adversity,
> Which, like the toad, ugly and venomous,
> Wears yet a precious jewel in its head.[1]

Poisoners sometimes slipped tiny grains of fatal venom from rings into wine-cups, or injected a poisonous drop into the hand of an enemy by means of a hollow setting and a hidden needle.

[1] *As You Like It*, Act II, Scene i, lines 12–14.

54

The Worker in Metals

Unfortunate people who had reason to fear that they might be objects of interest to would-be assassins strove to protect themselves not only by wearing toadstones, but also by having the names of the Magi, Caspar, Melchior, and Balthazar engraved on their rings. Betrothal rings often bore sentimental remarks. One thirteenth-century English gold ring is inscribed:

Pensez de li par ki sui ci.

TOADSTONE RING

It is French, but very bad French. The giver of the pretty trinket *meant* to say *Pensez de lui par qui je suis içi*—"Think of him through whom I am here." A Puritan wedding-ring bears the rather stern and sober couplet:

As God decreed,
So we agreed.

One of the most remarkable of all the metal-workers of Italy—a land always famous for the skill of its craftsmen—was Benvenuto Cellini. The son of a Florentine musician who desired that his son should follow his own calling, Benvenuto strongly objected to practising the flute, "the odious flute, the abominable flute," as he called it. The boy's heart was set upon learning to work in gold and silver, and finally, in the year 1515, when he was fifteen years of age, his reluctant father bound him apprentice to a goldsmith.

His fiery, proud, and energetic character led the young man into many brawls and quarrels, in which he proved himself to be as strong with his fists and as quick with his dagger as he was skilful with his tools. Before his twenty-first birthday he was established in Rome, making candlesticks, salvers, medallions, and rings for cardinals and princes, and exquisite pieces of jewellery for fair ladies. He enjoyed the patronage of Pope Clement VII, an artistic though a somewhat timid pontiff, to whom he rendered loyal service during the siege of Rome by the Constable of Bourbon. According to Cellini's own story, he himself fired the shot which killed the Constable. In the course of his adventurous

The Book of Craftsmen

career he found himself more than once in prison: on one occasion for killing a rival goldsmith, on another for having spoken disrespectfully of the Pope's taste in art. He was a great braggart, and if you believe everything he tells you about himself you will come to the conclusion that there was never a more skilful craftsman, a more doughty swordsman, or a handsomer fellow than Benvenuto Cellini. Yet he has not boasted too wildly of his own handiwork, for some of it remains, and we can judge for ourselves of its excellence. He was employed by many of the famous men of his time, and might have come over to England to help to make the bronze screens in Henry VII's chapel had he not taken a dislike to Pietro Torrigiano, the King's principal sculptor, on hearing him brag that he had broken Michelangelo's nose with his fist!

FORGED IRON GRILLE
Fifteenth-century French workmanship.

Cellini went to France in 1537, and did some fine work for that splendour-loving monarch François I. He made silver figures of heathen gods, gorgeous salvers and salt-cellars, and drew designs for fountains and gateways. One of the salt-cellars he made for the French King is surmounted by finely modelled figures of Venus and Neptune. This is regarded as his greatest surviving work. Returning to Florence, he was employed by Cosimo de' Medici, Duke of Florence, for whom he produced the bronze figure of Perseus holding the gorgon's head, which is still one of the treasures of the city. When the Grand Duke saw the wax model of the Perseus he annoyed Cellini by expressing doubts as to whether it could *possibly* be cast in bronze. The process of casting *did* prove to be unexpectedly difficult, and at the first attempt Perseus lacked the toes of his right foot.

The Worker in Metals

The iron-worker of medieval Europe had almost as great a variety of tasks to tackle as his forerunner in Anglo-Saxon times. He made clips to hold rushlights, tips for ox-goads, clasps for purses, hooks for butchers, spits for cooks, coffers for the safe storing of money or jewels: he made lace-like screens for shrines and for royal tombs. He collaborated with the harness-maker when he supplied stirrups, and bits, and buckles, and with

HINGE FROM ST ALBANS ABBEY
English, twelfth century.
Victoria and Albert Museum

the armourer when he made those gilded spurs which were strapped on the heels of the newly dubbed knight. Another worker in metal was the locksmith, whose earliest known productions go back to ancient Egyptian times. The Romans had " door-fastenings of diverse colours made of brass and ivory." Medieval locks and keys, at first of bronze but later of steel, were intricate and ornamental rather than secure. Wherever Henry VIII went he took with him a lock fourteen inches long by eight inches wide, which he caused to be screwed to his bedroom door. Bolts and hinges were also objects of beauty right up to the eighteenth century, and it often happened that the signboard of an inn would swing from a bracket of beautiful iron scroll-work.

The Book of Craftsmen

As the centuries passed and man's inventive gifts got ever wider opportunities new tasks never ceased to confront the worker in metal. After the invention of printing he had to learn to found type. The earliest printed books, both in Asia and in Europe, were made from *wooden* blocks: metal type was first used towards the middle of the fifteenth century. We cannot deal here with the development of machinery in general, which is a different branch

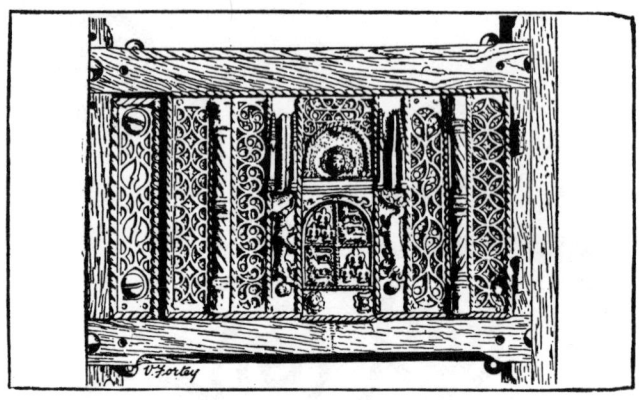

BEDDINGTON LOCK
From the "Encyclopædia Britannica," 14th edition

of our subject, and a very fascinating one. But we must say something about that 'daughter' of iron called steel. The 'father' is a grim fellow, rough, dark, and strong; the 'daughter' is brilliant, supple, and keen, but her strength is not less than his. To produce steel, iron has to be combined with carbon and subjected to violent extremes of heat and cold. The Chinese, that resourceful and inventive people, were making something very much like steel in the fifth century B.C.; Aristotle, the great Greek philosopher, describes a method of melting and refining iron in order to change it into steel; but the Indians were the most skilful steel-makers of the ancient world. Their steel—called *wootz*—was produced from iron mingled with chips of wood and heated for three or four hours in small crucibles. The necessary carbon was obtained from the charcoal thus brought into existence.

The Worker in Metals

The Arabs were among the most expert of the medieval workers in steel, as we shall see when we begin to think about arms and armour, and it was from Damascus that steel needles were first brought to Nürnberg in Germany as late as 1370. Curiously enough, it was not realized by anyone until 1781 that the quality of the steel depended upon the amount of carbon in it. So much

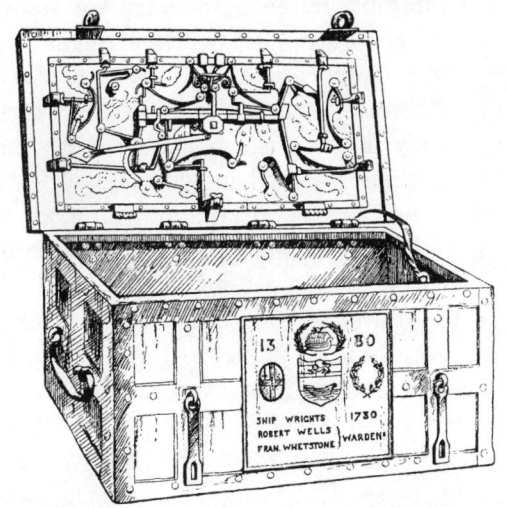

AN EIGHTEENTH-CENTURY MUNIMENT CHEST WITH COMPLICATED LOCKS
Guildhall Museum

faulty steel had to be rejected under the earlier process of manufacture that it was a wasteful and costly business, and the product was too expensive to come into general use. If you want to hear how an Englishman called Henry Bessemer revolutionized the whole industry by his new method of refining steel you must read *Pioneers of Invention*, by William and Stella Nida.

After the opening up of the great coal-mines in England, Scotland, and Wales, the centre of the iron and steel industry shifted from the weald of Sussex and the Forest of Dean to the coal-fields of the west and the north. When charcoal was an important ingredient the dense woods of the weald tempted charcoal-burners and iron-smelters to settle there, and the now green and tranquil

The Book of Craftsmen

county of 'Sussex by the Sea' was the Black Country of medieval England. Old fire-backs and fire-dogs may often be seen stamped with a buckle—the device of a noble Sussex family called Pelham, upon whose estates a great deal of iron was smelted—and in some of the fine old churches of the weald there are iron tombstones!

Talking of tombstones reminds me to tell you something about a branch of the metal-workers' art which attained much beauty in England during the Plantagenet period. The difficulty and expense of transporting masses of heavy stone, alabaster, or marble over long distances made the English craftsmen cast about for some equally durable but more easily handled material for monuments and tombs: and so they took to fashioning figures of lords and ladies, prelates and kings, from a sort of bronze called 'latten,' which was gilded, and sometimes enamelled as well. The earliest surviving example of a gilt-bronze effigy is that of Queen Eleanor of Castile in Westminster Abbey. Two London craftsmen, Nicholas Broker and Godfrey Prest, were responsible for the double tomb of Richard II and Anne of Bohemia, which included the life-sized effigies of the King and Queen, twelve little saints and angels, two lions for the King's feet, and an eagle and a leopard for the Queen's, as well as a number of brilliantly enamelled 'escutcheons' or heraldic shields. The process employed was one known as the 'waste wax' process, by which a layer of wax was first modelled over a core of roughly hewn timber and then gradually replaced by molten metal.

In England and—though to a less degree—in Flanders another branch of the metal-workers' craft developed during the fourteenth and fifteenth centuries. This was the making of monumental brasses, flat figures incised on a sheet of brass and embedded in a slab of stone. A great many of these old brasses still exist, in spite of the habit of the Cromwellian troopers of tearing them up and melting them down for use as bullets. Some people make a hobby of going round ancient churches and taking rubbings of the brasses, with the aid of sheets of special paper and lumps of a sort

The Worker in Metals

of black wax called heel-ball; and in this way a most interesting collection of historic pictures can be gathered together. The brass effigy does not try to show you the exact features of the person it commemorates—the faces of such figures are usually too regular, calm, and perfect to be true to nature—but it *does* show you most faithfully the sort of armour a knight would wear at that time, the sort of gown and headdress his lady would don, the sort of vestments a priest would be robed in, the sort of clothes a merchant would choose. Much of our knowledge of medieval costume is drawn from this source, and some of these ancient brass men and women are really works of art. The earliest English brass is that of Sir John d'Abernon, in Stoke d'Abernon Church, Surrey. Dating from 1277, it is life-sized, and Sir John's shield is adorned with enamel of a beautiful blue colour.

SIR JOHN HARSYCK AND
HIS WIFE
From a brass of 1384.

You may have noticed that I have mentioned rather often that objects of gold, bronze, or silver were decorated with coloured enamels. Now, since the material used by the enameller is molten glass, you may think we ought to include *him* in a chapter on glass-workers. But I don't think we should. Because, you see, the usual foundation for enamel is metal, and it was the metal-workers of bygone days who brought the art of enamelling to its highest pitch of beauty. Egyptians and Greeks, early Britons, and ancient Romans, all practised the art, and have all bequeathed us lovely examples of their skill. In the East, in China and Japan, India and Persia, it was understood far back in the mists of time. Some of the Oriental enamellers had very quaint ideas, as when they fashioned little figures of camels, or horses, or sheep, sprinkled with rosebuds or dappled with scrolls of green and silver.

The Book of Craftsmen

Gorgeous enamels were produced in Byzantium by the method known as *cloisonné*, or ' enclosed.' When this method is used the pattern is outlined in fine gold and the coloured portions are thus kept from overlapping or running into each other. The enamellers of Germany and France in the Middle Ages seem to have preferred the *champlevé* process. A plate or disc of metal—usually copper—had the design so deeply cut into it that a thin dividing line kept the molten colours from mixing. At a later date yet another process came into vogue. A metal surface was covered with white, non-transparent enamel; upon this the colours were delicately applied with a kind of brush known as a ' hair-pencil,' before being fired in a kiln like porcelain. It was this variety of enamel that was made at Battersea in the eighteenth century.

DETAIL FROM ENAMELLED CASKET
Limoges, end of twelfth century.

We have already mentioned, in Chapter I of this book, how the daily habits of mankind have influenced craftsmanship, invention, and even discovery. The introduction of tobacco inspired the worker in clay to model pipes; it inspired the worker in metal to make elaborate pipe-racks of bronze or iron, with a socket for a candle in the centre and a receptacle for paper spills on either side. When fashionable gentlemen—and even ladies!—began to take snuff beautiful snuff-boxes appeared, many of them made of gold or silver-gilt, and many of them decorated with patterns, pictures, or medallions of enamel. People collected snuff-boxes, just as they collected teacups, or carved ivories, or painted fans. One pretty box might have a classical subject, the " Judgment of Paris " or the " Death of Patroclus "; another would have a portrait, perhaps

The Worker in Metals

of the reigning monarch, or perhaps of some much-admired beauty of the day. A sportsman might have a favourite horse or hound on his snuff-box lid, a scholar might have gods and goddesses, a courtier might have a king.

Byzantium was the great centre of the enamellers' art in the earlier Middle Ages; later the loveliest of the *champlevé* enamel

SIGN OF THE ELEPHANT INN, BRIXEN
An exquisite example of sixteenth-century craftsmanship in the Brenner Pass.

was produced in the French city of Limoges. In the fifteenth and sixteenth centuries the metal-workers of Germany and the Tyrol were among the most skilful of their calling. In Nürnberg every apprentice had to qualify as a master of his craft by making three objects of great excellence, of which one must be a richly ornamented cup. Among the productions of this ancient city were many gruesome instruments of torture, but it is more pleasant to dwell upon the delicate and intricate ironwork used for peaceful, or cheerful, or solemn purposes. In the Tyrol crosses of iron with scroll-work as delicate as the fronds of a fern were set at the head of graves; and outside inns were signs made entirely

The Book of Craftsmen

of iron, looking like a silhouette against the sky. One such sign is adorned with a chubby elephant, the beast from which the inn takes its name, and above is a little sportsman taking aim with his musket at an anxiously leaping chamois!

SEVENTEENTH-CENTURY IRON CROSS
From a grave in the Austrian Tyrol.

In the Franciscan Hofkirche at Innsbrück, in the heart of the Tyrol, are to be seen at least two examples of the handiwork of one of the greatest of the Nürnberg ironworkers, Peter Vischer. These are the fine bronze images of Theodoric, King of the Goths, and Arthur, King of Britain, which form part of the monument of the Emperor Maximilian I. The Emperor planned his own

The Worker in Metals

tomb during his lifetime, and he desired that it should be surrounded by forty bronze mourners, all of high degree, and each holding a candle in his hand. Unfortunately, the plan was never carried out as he had intended, and, curiously enough, he does not sleep his last sleep in the place of his choice, but in the church of St George Neustadt, at Vienna. For eighty years people tinkered with his monument, and even at the end of that period much remained to do. Some of the effigies adorning it are stiff and pompous, but King Arthur is one of the finest images ever wrought by Peter Vischer. The mythical but far-famed King of Britain stands with the visor of his helmet raised and one hand resting on his sword. He wears the armour of a fifteenth-century knight, and on his shield sprawl the leopards of Plantagenet England!

Peter Vischer and his five sons worked in wood and in stone, as well as in bronze, but it is as a worker in bronze that we are thinking of him now. Like the della Robbia family of Florence, the Vischers of Nürnberg might almost be called a craft-clan.

CHAPTER III
THE WORKER IN WOOD

Wood must have been one of the earliest, if not the very earliest, of the natural substances taken for his use by primitive man. The boughs of a tree would give him fuel for his fire, a shaft for his axe, a paddle for his canoe; the trunk would give him the canoe itself. The lake-dwellers of what is now called Switzerland supported their thatched huts upon wooden piles, and drank from wooden goblets. The people of neolithic England, earlier than 2000 B.C., had pickaxe handles of beech and clubs and oars of oak. What else they and other races of the ancient world may have fashioned from wood we can only surmise, because owing to the perishable nature of wood very few things made from it so long ago have survived to our own times. The bronze blade of a knife, the bronze tip of a spear, may still exist, but in almost every instance the wooden handle has mouldered away. The hearthstones, even the rubbish heaps, of Stone Age huts remain, but the walls of turf and wood and the roofs of wicker vanished long ago.

So we may imagine our far-off ancestors in the Ages of Stone, Bronze, and Iron fashioning many wooden objects for many different purposes, though not as yet showing much skill in carving, or jointing, or fitting together. The rise of a great civilization in the valley of the Nile did not bring with it any general advance in the woodworker's art, as timber was scarce in Egypt. The same is true in Mesopotamia when the Sumerian city-states emerged from the mists of dawn. Splendour-loving Pharaohs sent expeditions to adjacent countries where there were forests, and entered into trading agreements with rulers who could barter cedar and fir in exchange for turquoise and copper and gold. We have all heard

The Worker in Wood

of the Cedars of Lebanon, and of Hiram, King of Tyre, who sent "cedar trees and carpenters and masons" to build a house for David, King of Israel. But already timber was growing scarce in Palestine, and as the years passed stone, clay, and metal took its place more and more.

The Egyptian craftsman, being one of the 'cleverest ever,' made the best of his rather poor materials, and did wonders with rough planks of sycamore and tamarisk. The Egyptian sculptors and carvers made statues of gods and men, and models of men, and beasts, and boats, all out of wood. One of the most famous existing works of art is the wooden statue of an overseer or steward, dating from some four thousand years before our era began, which stands in the Museum at Cairo. It is amazingly vigorous and vivid; the glass eyes have an uncanny glint, the left foot is thrust forward as if to take an energetic stride, the left hand is clasped resolutely round the wand of office.

More graceful are the many figures of young girls, some of them playing harps, some carrying loaves or wine-jars on their heads; more amusing are the models of ploughmen and oxen, seamen and ships, granaries and field-labourers, soldiers marching with shields on their arms and bakers kneading dough in troughs.

Allusions to wood as a building material are very frequent in the Old Testament, and we hear also of images and idols, and of the trees whereof they were made. In Isaiah xliv, 13, 14, we read:

> The carpenter stretcheth out his rule; he marketh it with a line; he fitteth it with planes, and he marketh it out with the compass, and maketh it after the figure of a man, according to the beauty of a man; that it may remain in the house.
>
> He heweth him down cedars, and taketh the cypress and the oak . . . he planteth an ash, and the rain doth nourish it.

And in the *Wisdom of Solomon* we get a vivid glimpse of a craftsman at work:

> Now a carpenter that felleth timber, after he hath sawn down a tree meet for the purpose, and taken off all the bark skilfully round about,

The Book of Craftsmen

and hath wrought it handsomely, and made a vessel thereof fit for the service of man's life;

And after spending the refuse of his work to dress his meat, hath filled himself;

And taking the very refuse among those which served to no use, being a crooked piece of wood, and full of knots, hath carved it diligently, when he had nothing else to do, and formed it by the skill of his understanding, and fashioned it to the image of a man;

Or made it like some vile beast, laying it over with vermilion and with paint colouring it red . . .

And when he had made a convenient room for it, set it in a wall, and made it fast with iron. . . .

Then maketh he prayer for his goods, for his wife and children, and is not ashamed to speak to that which has no life.[1]

From both these quotations it is clear that the carpenter of ancient Israel was a woodsman as well, and felled the timber from which he obtained his raw materials.

The earliest piece of carpentering mentioned in the Bible is, of course, Noah's Ark, but nobody can tell exactly of what wood it was made, as the meaning of the Hebrew word ' gopher ' is uncertain. It was a boat-builder's as well as a carpenter's job, and we know that the strange craft was caulked inside and outside with pitch. There is no doubt as to the meaning of ' shittim-wood,' of which another sort of Jewish ark, the Ark of the Covenant, was made—it was acacia-wood. This ark or tabernacle was an oblong chest lined with gold, about three feet nine inches in length and two feet three inches in breadth, and in it were the Ten Commandments inscribed upon two tablets of stone. Covered first with a curtain of badgers' skins and then with a blue cloth, it was carried in procession upon staves of shittim-wood passed through the rings attached to it for that purpose.

The Babylonians and the Egyptians also had arks, supposed to be the actual habitations of divine beings, and as such regarded with the utmost reverence. Cedar-wood was used in the palaces of the princes of Israel. In the *Song of Songs* Solomon is made to say: " The beams of our house are cedar and our rafters of fir ";

[1] Wisdom of Solomon, xiii, 11–17.

WOODEN STATUE OF EGYPTIAN OVERSEER
Photo Mansell

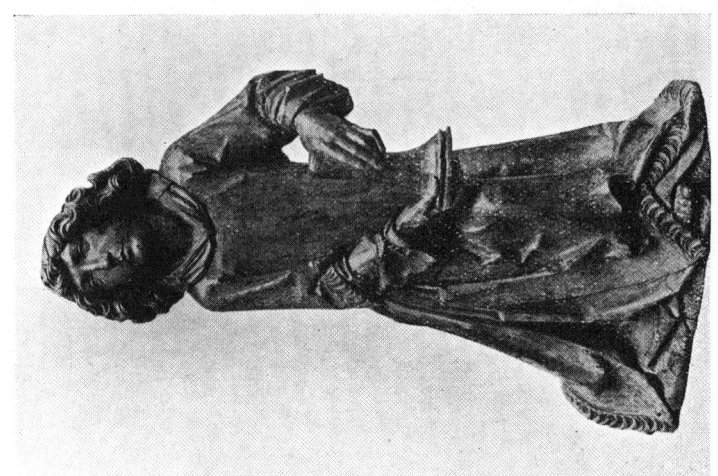

WOODEN FIGURE OF EGYPTIAN GIRL
PLAYING THE HARP

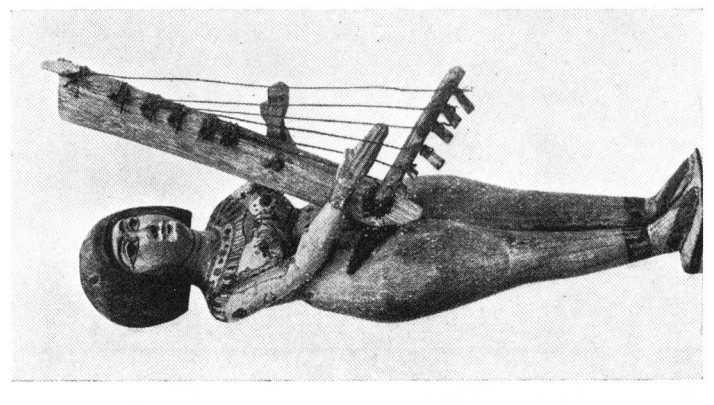

ANGEL CARVED IN WOOD
German, fifteenth century.
Victoria and Albert Museum

The Worker in Wood

and Jeremiah speaks of a wide house with large chambers " ceiled with cedar and painted with vermilion."

Another purpose for which Egyptians, Babylonians, and Israelites used wood was the building of the chariots which played so great a part in their military history. Among the Egyptians

> the chariot was a thing of marvellous beauty, made of tough, shining wood strengthened with leather thongs and plates of metal, and decorated in gorgeous colours. It was so light that one man could carry it, and yet so strong that it would bear two men throughout the surge and stress of battle. At the side hung the bow-case and the quiver, the first pointing forward and the second back; both were beautiful with figures of lions, and with fine inlaid work like a glorified draughtboard of black and scarlet, or blue and gold.[1]

AN EGYPTIAN CHARIOT

As we have already seen, the earliest type of boat was a canoe scooped out of a tree-trunk and propelled by a single-bladed paddle. No boats are mentioned in the Old Testament—the Israelites were not a seagoing people, and their great river, the Jordan, was not easily navigable. The ships to which we find allusion come from far places, from " Tarshish and the Isles," from Kittim, now called Cyprus, and the coast-line peopled by those hardy sea-rovers the Phœnicians. King Solomon's ' navy of ships ' was manned—and probably built also—by the men of Tyre. The Egyptians were skilled boat-builders at a very remote period, and rough sketches of vessels with both sails and oars are found upon their ancient jars

[1] D. M. Stuart, *The Boy through the Ages*, p. 42 (Harrap).

The Book of Craftsmen

and vases. A stone carving dating from about 3000 B.C. shows a ship with a rounded hull rising well out of the water at each end; on either side are thirteen oars, and she is steered by means of three large paddle-like blades at the stern. The mast consists of two spars

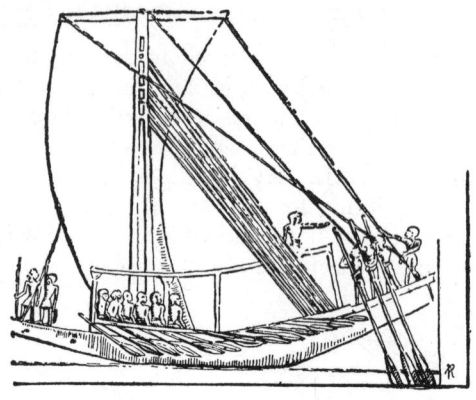

AN EGYPTIAN BOAT
About 3000 B.C.

lashed together at the top: the sail, high and narrow, has a yard at the head and probably a boom at the foot.

The Egyptians built their boats of short, narrow pieces of wood, each pinned sideways to the next. They gave them no keel, and depended for strength on thick sides and strong fastenings.[1]

A human eye was usually painted on the upright post at the extremity of the bows.

This ornamental eye is still found in many parts of the world, particularly on the Chinese ships which we call 'junks.' The Λ-shaped mast is another ancient Egyptian feature that can now be seen in the East. For instance, the ships of the Irawadi river in Burma have a mast and sail that are very like those of the Nile vessels of five thousand years ago.[2]

The Greeks, too, were seafarers and boat-builders in the very dawn of time; so were the non-Greek inhabitants of the marvellous island of Crete, who traded with Egypt. In the Piræus, one

---

[1] R. and R. C. Anderson, *The Sailing Ship*, p. 20 (Harrap).
[2] *Ibid.*, pp. 23–24.

The Worker in Wood

of the three fortified ports of ancient Athens, as many as three hundred ships would sometimes be lying at anchor. They were of many different forms and colours. Most common were the single-masted ships, built of long, tough planks, oak-, pine-, alder-, or poplar-wood, their hulls painted blue or crimson, their sterns ornamented with a fish's head, or a bird's, or, if the vessel came from Egypt, a lotus-flower. Unseasoned or 'green' wood was used for the curved parts of the vessel, 'dried' or seasoned wood for the straight parts, deck-planks, masts, etc. The Greeks did not rely only on their solitary linen sail hung from a crossbeam of fir and lashed with oxhide ropes; each of the larger ships carried a crew of rowers—twenty, fifty, or even a hundred, who plied shovel-shaped oars fastened to the gunwale with loops of leather. Greek and Roman ships were 'carvel-built'—that means, built of planks joined edge to edge: later came the 'clinker-built' craft of overlapping planks.

The peoples of the antique world used wood for many purposes in much the same way as we should use it to-day. The Greeks seem to have been particularly fond of chests and coffers, for storing clothes, weapons, and valuable possessions. Like the Egyptians and the Babylonians they made idols from the branches or trunks of trees. In the Parthenon, the great temple dedicated to the patron goddess of Athens, there was a mighty image of ivory and gold, but the citizens regarded as more holy the ancient effigy, a mere formless stump of olive-wood, which they preserved in the smaller temple of the Erechtheum and draped every four years with a newly woven robe of saffron yellow and sea-purple. Greek children bounced on see-saws formed from a plank balanced on a log, and Greek schoolboys scratched their lessons on wax tablets mounted in wooden frames.

Quite apart from the use of wood as a material for idols, the people of the distant past regarded trees as sacred, the dwellings of divine beings whose goodwill it was important to win. A living tree sometimes formed part of a human habitation, as in the palace of Odysseus on the island of Ithaca, and in the hut of

The Book of Craftsmen

Hunding in the Germanic legend of the Rhinegold. As late as the fifteenth century trees were believed to be haunted by fairies. Jeanne d'Arc and her youthful playmates used to dance at midsummer round a fairy-tree on the outskirts of her native village of Domrémy.

A VIKING SHIP

Wood, as well as ivory, brass, and bone, was fashioned into musical instruments in these far-off days. It formed the sounding-board of the harp, the hollow body of the lute, and the delicate framework of the seven-stringed lyre. The Arabic word *úd* means 'wood,' and also 'a lute.'

For very many years—enough years to form quite a big section in a history-chart—man continued to make of wood just those things which we have mentioned, and which you can guess for yourself: tools and implements, doors and roofs, ships and chariots, images and idols, musical instruments and children's toys, chests and coffers, pens for sheep and stalls for cattle, oars and paddles, benches and beds.

The character of the wood, and the manner of its hewing and carving, would depend, of course, upon the place where the parent-tree grew and the period in history when it was annexed by the craftsman for the purposes of his craft. In the East cedar and olive, sandal and teak, in the north oak and fir and pine were the most common. It is interesting to realize that the woodworker's outlook on life varied little from century to century until near the end of what are usually called the Dark Ages, somewhere about the tenth and eleventh centuries after Christ.

The Worker in Wood

During this period the Scandinavians were among the most skilful boat-builders in Europe, and their clinker-built vessels,

CARVED OAK CHEST
Thirteenth century.

with fourteen or sixteen rowers on either side and a golden dragon at the prow, were seen as far from their own shores as Paris and Constantinople. Medieval boats were also clinker-built, with

CARPENTERS SAWING WOOD
Fourteenth century.

a single mast and one very large sail; the poop, topcastle, and forecastle were often carved, and sometimes painted in gay colours.

In England during the Anglo-Saxon period Christian churches were built of timber, and even when our " rude forefathers "

The Book of Craftsmen

adopted stone as a building material they planned their churches as if they had been using tree-trunks for pillars, walls, and towers.

Christianity stimulated the woodworker as well as the worker in metal. He had to learn how to make pulpits, lecterns, chancel-screens, pews, choir-stalls, alms-cupboards, desks for monkish scribes, shelves for their books, long tables—refectory tables—and long benches for their use at meal-times.

Speaking of the worker in metals we have already remarked how, as the centuries passed, different crafts tended to split up into various branches. This was especially true of the woodworker's craft in the Middle Ages. There were carpenters in ancient Rome, in the far-off days of Numa Pompilius, when the craftsmen of the city-state banded themselves into guilds. In medieval England the useful calling of the carpenter might be practised by the members of either of two separate divisions. The carpenter, strictly so called, tackled the heavier sort of woodwork, such as door-posts, roof-beams, stakes for fences, scaffolds for the spectators at tournaments, platforms for the players in the mystery-plays, of which more presently.

The joiner undertook the lighter and smaller jobs, and produced window-frames, bargeboards for gables, stools, shelves, clothes-pegs, distaffs, platters.

CARVED PEW-END
Fifteenth century.

In the days when most houses were built of wood the carpenter had more to do with house-building than had the mason. His tasks were almost as multifarious as those of the smith; for he, or his 'opposite number,' the joiner, might have to make a gibbet for a felon, a palisade for a tournament-ground, a coffer for a damsel's dower, a perch for her bridegroom's hawk, a trestle-table for a banquet, a pew for a church, or a beam for a barn.[1]

---

[1] D. M. Stuart, *Men and Women of Plantagenet England*, p. 103 (Harrap).

The Worker in Wood

The worker in wood who had a skilful hand and a ready imagination went one step beyond the carpenter and the joiner, and became a wood-carver. Many of *this* fellow's productions were veritable masterpieces. Some of them were quaint rather than beautiful: some of them were both.

An interesting example of church carving in the Middle Ages is afforded by the brackets known as 'miserere seats' still to be seen in many great cathedrals. *Miserere* is the Latin for 'Have mercy!'

A MISERERE SEAT (UNDER-SURFACE)

and the name is understood when we know to what use these brackets were put. In the choir-stalls of the great medieval monastery churches there were hinged seats for the monks: but during long hours of chanting and praying the brethren had to stand up instead of sitting down, and the seats at such times were turned up against the back of the stalls. However, out of 'mercy' to the monks a miserere bracket was put under each flap, so that they might support themselves upon these and thus take some of the weight off their weary feet.

The under-surface of the flaps gave the sculptor in wood, sometimes the monkish occupant of the seat, a chance to exercise his skill, his imagination, and—very often—his sense of humour. An immense variety of designs is found in miserere seats. Some are quite serious: portraits of kings, queens, and saints, or episodes from sacred history and legend; others are decidedly quaint, such as Satan wheeling Judas Iscariot away in a wheelbarrow, three rats hanging a cat, or a fox dressed as a bishop preaching to a flock of geese. Here you see a specimen from Exeter Cathedral—St George,

The Book of Craftsmen

not on horseback for once in a way—spiking the dragon through the 'tummy' with his good blade.

Statues of saints were often made of wood, painted and gilt. In the abbeys and churches of medieval England you would always see the Virgin Mary with the Christ-Child in her arms, carved as nobly as the craftsman knew how to do it. And you would often see St Michael trampling triumphantly upon Satan in the form of a horrible scaly monster; and St George, on horseback, driving his long spear through an indignant dragon; and St Martin dividing his cloak with the beggar; and St Catherine with the wheel upon which she was martyred; and St Barbara with the model of a church-tower in her hand; and St John the Baptist dressed in a sheepskin. Some of these figures were very stiff and unlifelike, partly owing to the general ignorance of the structure of the human body; others were graceful and charming, and as knowledge of anatomy increased the stiffness vanished and the curves of the muscles, the proportions of the limbs, became natural and convincing. Intense religious feeling on the part of the carver often made up for his lack of anatomical lore. This is especially noticeable in the figure of Christ on the Cross which was seen so often in medieval churches. The earliest type of Crucifix, whether in wood, metal, or stone, shows the Saviour upright, His feet side by side, each foot transfixed by a separate nail, and draperies on the body reaching below the knee. Slowly the treatment of this solemn subject became more realistic. The head was made to lean wearily towards one shoulder, the feet were crossed and held by one nail, the elaborate garment gave place to a loin-cloth. The Tyrolean crucifix of the thirteenth century in our illustration belongs to the period midway between these two methods. Its stiffness certainly does not lessen its pathos.

The first recorded example of an English sculptor studying from a living model is to be found in the Chronicles of the Abbey of Meaux in Yorkshire, where we are told that in the days of Abbot Hugh (1339–1349) a new crucifix was set up in the Lay Brothers' choir,

TYROLEAN CRUCIFIX CARVED IN WOOD
Thirteenth century.

A CHINESE LANTERN IN CARVED WOOD
Nineteenth century.

AN EXAMPLE OF
POLYNESIAN WOOD-CARVING

The Worker in Wood

whereon the sculptor carved no specially goodly or notable lineament save upon Fridays when he himself fasted upon bread and water. Moreover he had a naked man before him, to look at, that he might learn from his shapely body and the better carve the crucifix.

Another, and much less solemn, task which the wood-worker might have to approach was carving the grinning head for a

OAK CRADLE FROM CHEPSTOW CASTLE
Traditionally said to have belonged to Henry IV, and used by his son (afterwards Henry V). Fifteenth century.
Reproduced by gracious permission of His Majesty the King

jester's bauble. Another would be to make shields for knights either in friendly tilts or in battle: another would be to rig up the ' toile,' the screen of timber covered with tapestry, which ran down the centre of the sanded lists, to prevent the rival horsemen from meeting ' head-on.' Yet another would be to erect the scaffolding upon which, every summer, the members of the various craft guilds acted miracle-plays, representing episodes in sacred history; and not the scaffolding only, for a kind of rough scenery was needed—gilded turrets for the gates of paradise, and a dreadful, red-painted arch for the entrance to Hell, an ark for Noah, a throne

The Book of Craftsmen

for Herod, a manger in which to lay the Baby Jesus. Cradles were almost always of wood. The humbler sort were mounted on rockers, but the cradles of royal and noble babies had slots at each side through which cords were passed, so that attendants might alternately pull and let go, thus causing the infant to sway rhythmically to and fro, and—one hopes—inducing him to fall

NOAH BUILDING THE ARK UNDER THE DIRECTIONS OF AN ANGEL
From a thirteenth-century manuscript.

asleep. There is just such a cradle, dating from the fifteenth century, in the London Museum. It is made of oak, with panels of 'linen-fold' carving, and a carved falcon keeps guard over it.

Geoffrey Chaucer, the first of all the great English poets, has given us a glimpse of the daily life of a carpenter in the town of Oxford in the reign of Edward III. We gather that the worthy fellow, whose name was John, had a house so large that he was able to take in a lodger, a clerk called Nicholas. From the peep which we get of the clerk's bedroom we conclude that John's was a comfortable and clean dwelling. Sweet herbs were strewn on the floor; there were shelves for books at the top of the bed, and there was a chest covered with a green mat. Chaucer does not describe the carpenter's everyday raiment, but he tells us all about the carpenter's wife, who wore a girdle of striped silk, a white

The Worker in Wood

apron, an embroidered smock, a black silk collar, and a silken fillet round her head. Nicholas plays an impish trick on poor honest John when he persuades him that a second Flood is about to overwhelm the world. John, believing that his learned lodger, a student of astrology, has had a revelation direct from the stars, proceeds, at his instigation, to hang three kneading-tubs upon the gable of his house, so that when the waters rise he and his wife and Nicholas

ST JOSEPH WORKING AS A CARPENTER
From a fresco in Carpenters' Hall, London.

may be saved. The simple fellow made three ladders with his own hands, so that they might climb up to their refuge; and he stocked each tub with bread, cheese, and good ale. But, of course, it was all a rather cruel and foolish hoax, what we should now call a 'leg-pull,' and poor John was left looking very stupid in his tub when the Flood failed to materialize.

Although the carpenters of ancient Rome had formed themselves into a guild in the dim dawn of Roman history, it was not until the fifteenth century of the Christian era that the carpenters of London received a grant of arms from the king's heralds. Theirs was a very powerful fraternity, and the hall where they met was one of the few which survived the great Fire. They have preserved a quaint series of frescoes dating from the early Tudor period. These consist of four panels. The first shows Noah receiving God's commandments to build the Ark: the second shows

The Book of Craftsmen

King Josiah giving orders for the repair of the Temple at Jerusalem, and that silver (*i.e.*, silver coins) should be paid " unto carpenters and builders and masons, to buy timber and hewn stone. Howbeit," adds the author of the Second Book of Kings, " there was no reckoning made with them of the money that was delivered into their hands, because they dealt faithfully." This tribute to the honesty of their forerunners in Biblical times seems to have pleased the London carpenters. The next panel in their Hall shows St Joseph working as a carpenter with our Saviour as a little boy carrying chips of wood in a basket. The last shows Christ preaching in the synagogue at Capernaum on the occasion when the hearers asked each other in wonder, " Is not this the Carpenter's son ? "

Three different medieval guilds in London were associated with the worker in wood. Over and above the Carpenters' there were the Joiners' and the Turners', of whom we shall speak presently. The first and main purpose of these ancient trade guilds was to regulate each craft, protect the interests of the craftsmen, and look to their welfare both in this world and the next; but they also protected the general public by punishing any dishonest and incompetent members, and by encouraging honourable dealing and skilful workmanship. Sometimes this last branch of their activities brought the guilds into collision with each other.

There was a subdivision of the Joiners' Company known as the ' Fusters,' and these supplied wooden pommels and cantles to the saddlers. It is recorded that in 1309 " the Fusters, having resorted to the woods at night, and with unseasoned wood made saddlebows, which after they had called in the aid of the Painter to colour their imperfect work they sold to the Saddlers, these last refused to pay for the same." Here we have an interesting return to the old Biblical idea of a carpenter who himself went into the forest in quest of his raw material.

Like the other City guilds, the Carpenters were hospitable, and gave sumptuous banquets in their painted Hall. Accounts were carefully kept, and here is an example for the year 1438:[1]

[1] Money had then more than ten times its present-day value.

The Worker in Wood

	s.	d.
Beadle's wages	36	8
A labourer for 5 days' work	2	0
Washing for tablecloths for a year	2	0
Wages of a cook for a year	12	0
A whole sheep, except the shoulders	1	8
Two hundred eggs	1	6

It is curious that for a whole year's work a cook should receive only six times as much as a labourer did for five days': but perhaps the cook was employed only 'off and on,' when his services were needed.

The joiners placed themselves under the patronage of St James: the patron saint of the turners was St Catherine. This last craft dealt principally in wooden cups and platters, in wooden measures such as were used for weighing corn, spices, and sugar, and in wooden bowls. A turner would have to collaborate with a goldsmith to produce one of the beautiful 'mazer' bowls, made of maple-wood mounted in silver, silver-gilt, or gold, which were so much prized by rich men in the Middle Ages. The turners did not, however, make wooden casks for holding wine, beer, or water. Those were made by the coopers, who, in 1396, applied to the Lord

COOPERS AT WORK IN THE SIXTEENTH CENTURY

Mayor of London for an ordinance restraining members of their craft from converting old oil or soap tuns into casks and barrels. One could imagine that if such a thing were done the effect upon the flavour of the fluid would be anything but agreeable! Baths were not used very frequently in the old days,

The Book of Craftsmen

but the coopers made the wooden tubs in which people *did* take a dip from time to time.

A MAZER BOWL

In the reign of Edward III the London guilds were reconstituted, and, dropping their old name, were transformed into the City Companies, practically as we know them to-day. This King gave these companies a right which they continued to exercise till the passing of the Reform Bill in 1832—the right of electing members to represent them in Parliament. He also made a law that each artificer should choose his 'mystery,' and, having chosen it, practise no other. The word 'mystery' has completely lost its ancient meaning. In the old days it meant a handicraft or art into the 'mysteries' of which an apprentice had been admitted—in fact, a skilled occupation. For example, the man who *chopped* wood did not belong to a 'mystery,' but the man who *carved* it did.[1]

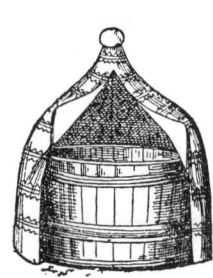

A MEDIEVAL BATH-TUB

In the open-air miracle plays performed every summer by the various trade guilds it very often fell to the Carpenters to enact the building of the ark by Noah—an appropriate episode!

Most of the medieval craftsmen, masters of their several 'mysteries,' worked with their apprentices on the actual premises where the goods they produced were sold; almost every shop had its 'workshop,' either within it or at the rear. A typical fourteenth- or fifteenth-century shop would occupy the front ground-floor portion of the house, open to the

[1] D. M. Stuart, *England's Story*, Part II, p. 435.

The Worker in Wood

street, windowless, but closed at will with stout shutters of wood. At the back might lie either the workshop itself or a store-room for surplus merchandise. A jutting upper storey, consisting of one or two rooms, served as a dwelling for the merchant and his

FOURTEENTH-CENTURY SHOPS AT NEWCASTLE-UPON-TYNE

family, while the apprentices slept upon truckle-beds or mere pallets under the counter of the shop below.

According to the natural bent of the citizens the guilds of a city would be more or less powerful. In Flanders the weavers were among the most wealthy; in England the mercers, woolstaplers, and leathersellers flourished. In France the goldsmiths seem to

The Book of Craftsmen

have borne away the palm, and one of them, Jacques Coeur of the city of Bourges, became an influence in French history and a friend of Charles VII, King of France. Jacques Coeur took as his motto "Nothing is impossible to valiant hearts," but the King whom he served, the same King who left Jeanne d'Arc 'in the lurch,' proved ungrateful, and the once-wealthy goldsmith died in exile, a comparatively poor man.

In Siena the silk-workers were perhaps the most prominent of the guilds which took part in the traditional pageant and horse-race round the cathedral square every summer; in Florence the picturesque banners of the various confraternities were brought forth upon every occasion of public ceremonial, and those who dealt in gold, silk, and drugs were among the most important.

Chaucer has left us a lively picture of a London 'prentice in the fourteenth century. This particular youth was a victualler—we shall hear more about his craft in a later chapter—gay as a gold-finch, brown as a berry, with neatly combed black hair. We may take him as typical of his class, and he might just as well have been a carpenter or a cordwainer as a victualler. Evidently his was an indulgent master, for we are told that

> At every bridal he would sing and hop,
> Better he loved the tavern than the shop.
> For when that any riding[1] was in Chepe[2]
> Out of the shop thither would he leap,
> And till he had all the sight y-seen
> And dancèd well he would not come again.

Well, we will now return to our friend the worker in wood, after neglecting him for a paragraph or two. No, we have not *really* been neglecting him: we have been thinking about things connected with the daily life of *all* medieval craftsmen, and he belongs to that great, many-coloured multitude.

Changes in fashions, as usual, led to developments in craftsman-ship. Elsewhere we talk about furniture, and how its shapes and

[1] Procession, pageant.   [2] Cheapside.

The Worker in Wood

colours and purposes altered as the centuries passed: here we must stick to the ordinary carpenter, joiner, and carver in wood.

A change in taste can be seen in the woodwork of the late fifteenth century all over Europe. The earlier designs were often suggested by the delicate, lace-like tracery of the stonecarver, and many panels and other flat surfaces took on the appearance of

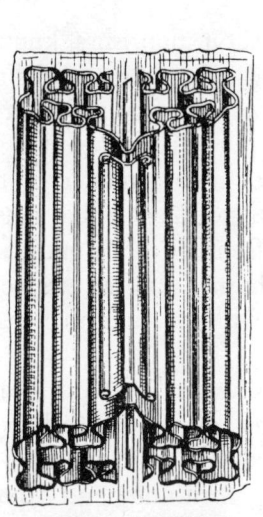

LINEN-FOLD PANEL

CARVED DOORS SUGGESTED BY STONE TRACERY

church windows. This architectural style of design remained in favour from the thirteenth to the fifteenth century, when the revival of classical learning led men's minds towards the decorative ideas of the ancient Romans—or, at least, what they imagined those ideas to have been! So the fretted pinnacles, the complicated tracery, the angular 'linen-fold' patterns, the stiff birds and beasts of heraldic art, all gave way to scrolls and masks, heads of Cæsars, figures of allegorical virtues or pagan deities.

In the East, where the craft of the wood-carver had been practised from immemorial times, no such changes were to be seen, because men's minds were not moved by great intellectual

The Book of Craftsmen

upheavals. The screens, pulpits, and window-panels of the mosques, the woodwork of the houses, in Egypt and in Asia Minor, in Moorish Spain and in Arabia, continued to follow the traditional lines. The Koran forbade the representation of the human form or of any living creature, so the designs were rather monotonous. Sometimes it seemed as if the carver were imitating basket-work, sometimes as if he were influenced by the weaver of carpets or of brocades.

Geometrical curves, elaborate interknit flourishes known as 'arabesques,' and adaptations of actual foliage formed the stock-in-trade of the Islamic craftsman. The woods he used were, for the most part, box, cypress, cedar, and pine. These he often inlaid with ivory, or with mother-of-pearl, or with a mosaic of tinted bone. In India also the woodcarver handed on to his sons and grandsons the ideas he had received from his great-grandfather. There, however, the introduction of human figures was not forbidden, and Indian carvings swarmed with gods and men, as well as with elephants and tigers.

In Polynesia, especially among the Maoris of New Zealand, wood-carving reached the rank of a fine art at a very early period. Maori houses were—and are—decorated inside and out with most elaborate wood-sculpture, the coiling, writhing, and squirling designs serving very often as a background or a framework to some grotesque figure in whom the sculptor personified the god of good luck or of prosperity. Canoes and canoe-paddles, window-frames and boxes, were also adorned with patterns of wonderful delicacy, often produced with stone tools only. According to a Maori legend the art of carving was brought to the world of men from the deep-sea habitation of the Ponaturi, the sea-fairies, by a man whose son the Ponaturi had stolen to form the gable-ornament of their home. This man—whose name was Rua-pupuke—changed himself into a fish, dived to the rescue of his child, and destroyed the fairy palace, all but the four side-posts, the ridge-post, and the door and window-frames, which he brought back with him to dry land!

In the Far East the Chinese and the Japanese had, through many

The Worker in Wood

generations, attained to great skill, especially in handling hard woods like ebony: and they had invented a characteristic and very clever method of beautifying the surface of wooden objects. This was with the aid of a sort of varnish called 'lacquer,' made from the juice of a tree, the *Rhus vernicifera*. The Chinese excelled at *red* lacquer, which they could carve in wonderful designs, with sprawling dragons, bristling fir-trees, and curly waterfalls: the Japanese brought to perfection a beautiful *golden* lacquer, in which powdered gold is introduced.

The lacquering process is not a quick or an easy one. Several coats of ordinary lacquer are first applied; then one coat of powdered earthenware, mixed with water. After each coat the surface is polished with a whetstone. Then come two or three more coats of lacquer, with friction, and applications of charcoal and water, between each. Finally the outer coat of the very finest lacquer is laid on, and then polished with the powdered ashes of deer-horn.

MOSQUE PULPIT

The ancient connexion between the carpenter's and the ship-builder's craft was continued right down to the period when iron-built vessels began to replace the old 'wooden walls.' The shipwrights of London formed themselves into a brotherhood, under the patronage of St Simon and St Jude, as early as 1260.

The Book of Craftsmen

Owing to the din rising from their yards along Thames-side and the complaints of the London citizens, they were compelled to move to Ratcliffe and Wapping, then lonely districts far beyond the city's boundaries. As vessels became more ornate, the woodcarver, as distinct from the shipwright, had more and more to do with them. He had to provide the rich scroll-work, the proud figurehead, the panelling in the captain's cabin, the ornamental

THE ROYAL CHARLES
Built in 1655, and first called the *Naseby*.

part of the poop and the forecastle. Henry VIII's famous *Henri-grace-à-Dieu*, launched in 1515, was a floating mass of carving and gilding; but she was difficult to steer, and rolled heavily in rough water. If the credit of founding the modern British Navy belong to the Tudors, it should not be forgotten that no dynasty ever did more to make it efficient and powerful than did the Stuarts. It was in the reign of Charles I (you will remember that Parliament objected to his ship-money tax) that the first English three-decker was launched at Woolwich. This was the *Sovereign of the Seas*, a 1637-tonner, carrying sixty-four guns. A fascinating task which the seventeenth-century shipwright-woodcarver sometimes had to tackle was making an accurate model of the ship which his master had designed and proposed to build. These models were often things of real beauty, complete in every detail, with rigging, cannon, flags, and figureheads. The grave officials of the English

The Worker in Wood

Admiralty must have felt something of the delight of small boys when they had to inspect such perfect playthings.

To this period in English history belongs one of the most remarkable woodcarvers whose work remains to bear witness to his skill—Grinling Gibbons. A very worthy gentleman, Mr John Evelyn, in high favour with King Charles II, happened to be walking one day near his home at Sayes Court, Deptford, when, looking in at the window of a solitary thatched cottage, he saw a young man hard at work. This young man was carving in wood a copy of a large picture of the Crucifixion by the Venetian painter Tintoretto. Evelyn had seen the original picture in Venice, and had brought an engraving of it home with him to England. Let Mr Evelyn tell us in his own words what happened next.

> I asked if I might enter; he opened the door civilly to me, and I saw him about such a work as for the handling, drawing, and studious exactness I never had before seen in all my travels. I questioned him why he worked in such an obscure and lonesome place: he told me that it was that he might apply himself to this profession without interruption, and wondered not a little how I had found him out. I asked if he was unwilling to be made known to some great man, for that I believed it might turn to his profit. He answered he was yet but a beginner, but would not be sorry to sell off that piece. On demanding the price, he said a hundred pounds. In good earnest the very frame was worth the money, there being nothing in nature so tender and delicate as the flowers and festoons about it, yet the work was very strong: in the piece were more than a hundred figures of men, etc. I found he (Gibbons) was likewise musical, and very civil, sober, and discreet in his discourse. There was only an old woman in the house. So, desiring leave to visit him sometimes, I went away.

Mr Evelyn did not forget the young man, and at the first opportunity he told King Charles about his discovery, with the result that a few weeks later Grinling Gibbons was invited to bring his masterpiece to Whitehall, the vast, rambling old palace where the King was then sojourning. Evelyn told the King that Gibbons had arrived, and his Majesty asked where the carving was.

> I told him in Sir Richard Browne's (my father-in-law) chamber,

The Book of Craftsmen

and that if it pleased his Majesty to appoint whither it should be brought, being large and heavy, I would take care for it. " No," says the King, " show me the way. I'll go to Sir Richard's chamber." Which he immediately did, walking along the entries after me. No sooner was he entered, and cast his eye on the work, but he was astonished at the curiosity of it, and having considered it a long time, and discoursed with Mr Gibbons, whom I brought to kiss his hand, he commanded it should be immediately carried to the Queen, to show her.

Charles, a sincere if indolent lover of the fine arts, readily promised his patronage to Evelyn's young *protégé*, whom he later employed to do much of the carving at St George's Chapel, Windsor, as well as in the royal apartments at Whitehall. Another powerful patron of the young woodcarver was Sir Christopher Wren, the great architect to whom was entrusted the planning of the churches built to replace those destroyed by the disastrous Fire of 1666. In many of the dusky old churches, hidden away in odd corners of the busy modern city, you will find pulpits, galleries, lecterns, and choir-stalls heavy with garlands of carved fruit, or cheerful with groups of chubby cherubs, from the hand of Grinling Gibbons. It was a hand employed not only upon work for palaces and churches; Betterton, a famous tragedian of the period, engaged Gibbons to do the carved ornamentation for the theatre which was opened in 1671 at Dorset Gardens, Whitefriars. This theatre stood on the south side of Fleet Street, and had a staircase leading down to the Thames for the convenience of patrons who came to the performances by boat instead of by coach. Think for a moment, and you will see that all these places and things had something to do with the worker in wood. First there was the theatre itself, with its rows of benches, with its boxes and balustrades, with its wooden stage, and with its scenery mounted on a framework of wood. Then there were the wherries on the river, bringing gallants from upstream to see the play, and there were the oars with which the wherrymen rowed. The very steps up which the playgoers climbed were more probably of wood than of stone.

Eleven years after their first encounter in the lonely thatched

CARVING AT PETWORTH BY GRINLING GIBBONS
Showing his use of classical designs and his skill in representing flowers and foliage.

LACE CRAVAT CARVED OUT OF LIMEWOOD BY GRINLING GIBBONS

THE GREAT DOOR OF THE CLOSE, CANTERBURY CATHEDRAL

Carved by Grinling Gibbons between 1660 and 1663.

The Worker in Wood

cottage Mr Evelyn was still befriending Grinling Gibbons, and we find the woodcarver writing to him to ask if he will speak for him to Sir Joseph Williamson, so that the woodwork of the house of Sir Joseph's stepson, Lord Kildare, might be entrusted to him. The letter ends: " and I shall for Ev're be obliaged to You. I wold speack to Sir Josef my sealf but i knouw it wold do better from you. Sir your must umbell sarvant G. Gibbon."

From this it is clear that Grinling did not shine as a speller! But his lack of skill is more easily understood when we realize that he was born in Holland, and probably learned Dutch before he learned English. This remarkable man worked in stone and bronze as well as in wood, and produced the statue of Charles II in Roman attire which stands in front of Chelsea Hospital. So deft was he in his own particular craft that he sometimes amused himself—and his patrons—by imitating a lace cravat so perfectly that it seemed as if the thing were woven instead of carved. He used various woods—oak for church panels and mouldings, limewood for fruit, flowers, and garlands, boxwood or pearwood for small medallions.

Of all the crafts in which man has learned to excel none, I think, has changed so little with the passing of years as the craft of the worker in wood. We still need planks and beams, boats and oars, handles and poles, panels and frames, boxes and carts, and wheels for the carts; and all these things—with many, many more—he still makes for us. And this not counting chairs and tables, which are to have a chapter all to themselves!

Wood-sculpture went somewhat out of fashion in the nineteenth century, but there has been a revival of interest in it lately. Especially in Scandinavian countries, sculptors are using wood more and more, making the natural veinings of the timber suggest the surface of the model's hair, or the texture of his muscles, or the wool of his garments. Even though steel and concrete have replaced wood in many industries it is impossible to imagine a world in which men would no longer go to the great forests for their raw material, and no longer fashion from the tree-trunks various objects of beauty and utility for their daily needs.

CHAPTER IV
THE WEAVER

IF you find yourself with a bundle of silks or a loose clump of string in your hands, what do you do? Supposing you do not want at the moment either to thread a needle or tie up a parcel, the chances are that you will start twisting the stuff into a sort of mesh. That was what primitive people did in the very dawn of human life on earth. They used vegetable fibres, or sinews of the beasts they had slain, and with these things they made nets and snares long before it occurred to them that they might clothe their bodies with anything more elegant than the skins of those same beasts.

Then—nobody can tell exactly when or where, but somewhere infinitely long ago—this process was carried a long step forward, and people began to spin and to weave.

There is sometimes a certain confusion between these two verbs, so closely connected and yet describing quite different actions. The old jingle beginning " when Adam delved and Eve span " was quite correct in its suggestion that you spin first and weave afterwards. Spinning is the process by which fibrous substances, such as flax or wool, are twisted into yarn: weaving is the process by which the threads of yarn are fashioned into linen or cloth. (We shall talk about silk and cotton later.) Spinning is an occupation clearly suited to women rather than to men, and from the verb comes our English word 'spinster'! Curiously enough, certain races of men who have excelled in making nets and ropes, such as the Otaheitians of the South Seas, have failed to carry the idea further, and so have remained ignorant of the art of weaving—an art practised by the Swiss lake-dwellers of the Stone Age, and by many other primitive people both in Asia and in Europe.

The Weaver

Flax was one of the first substances employed for the purpose. The fibres, separated from the soft parts of the stems, combed and dried, were spun into yarn and then woven upon a rough sort of loom. The sound of the word 'spinning' suggests the sound of the moving spinning-wheel, yet this useful invention belongs to a comparatively late period in history, and for many generations the industrious womenfolk of Egypt and Greece, Europe and Asia, had only a spindle and a distaff with which to twist the necessary threads for the loom. The flax—or, it might be, the wool—having been combed and prepared, was wound loosely round the distaff, which the spinner either held in her left hand or thrust through her girdle. The threads were wound on to the spindle, a smaller, tapering rod, after its twirling motion had given them shape. To make the spindle rotate more easily when as yet it carried but little yarn weights of stone or metal were fixed to it: as it grew heavier, this weight—known as a whorl—would be removed. Spindle-whorls are frequently discovered upon the sites of Iron Age and Bronze Age settlements. Constant manipulation of the spindle and the shuttle served to develop the bones and muscles of women's right arms, as was observed when the skeleton of a young girl of the late Stone Age was unearthed upon the Essex coast in 1910.

> About this girl Sir Arthur Keith has told us quite enough to make us feel that she was a real person. She had a slender neck . . . her face was oval, her hands and feet were small. Except that her teeth met edge to edge, instead of overlapping in the characteristic modern European fashion, she might have been a girl of our own day. The bones of her right arm were so well developed that she must have used that arm with considerable industry and vigour, probably spinning, weaving, and grinding corn. " Whether a lady of high degree or merely a handmaiden, she had her daily round of specialized toil," says Sir Arthur Keith.[1]

Presently we will consider the different materials used by the spinners and weavers of the remote past; now we will think

---

[1] D. M. Stuart, *The Girl through the Ages*, pp. 14–15 (Harrap).

The Book of Craftsmen

chiefly of the two earliest—flax and wool. Modern botanists recognize about a hundred and fifty varieties of the flax-plant, and from its Latin name—*linum*—our English word 'linen' is derived. When the great Swedish botanist Linnæus classified all the well-known plants of his time—the eighteenth century—and gave them the Latin names which they still bear, he called the type of flax commonly employed for linen-making *Linum usitatissimum*— the most usual or ordinary flax: but a different type, the *Linum angustifolium*, or narrow-leaved flax, is found in the Swiss lake-dwellings of the Stone Age, whence come some of the earliest known examples of the weaver's craft.

Nobody can tell exactly in what country or at what period the first loom was set up and the first swift shuttle sent flying; but we have a very fair idea of what they would look like, and it is possible to draw an imaginary picture of the type of loom in use in the early Iron Age. It would consist of a wooden framework supporting the 'warp,' the threads running downward; these threads were kept stretched by means of loom-weights of stone or clay, and such weights are frequently found among the ruins of prehistoric homes. The threads passed to and fro across the warp and intertwined with it are known as the 'weft,' and were handled with the aid of a shuttle. From this simple structure developed the looms upon which the ancient Egyptians were able to weave the most delicate linen and the ancient Chinese the most exquisite silk: it is the direct ancestor of the modern power-loom, which shows traces of its descent even to-day.

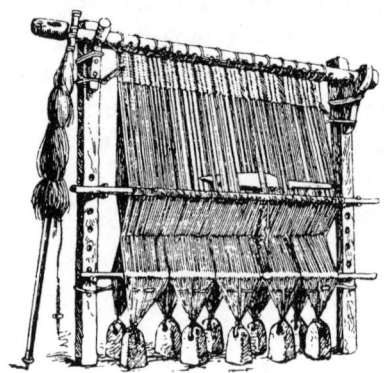

PRIMITIVE LOOM AND SPINDLE

Of all the peoples of the ancient world the Egyptians were the most skilful weavers. We know from the lifelike pictures painted

The Weaver

on the walls of Egyptian tombs that robes of transparent, gauzy fabrics were worn by rich men and their wives; priests sported pleated kilts of fine linen, and many yards of a special sort of material were required for wrapping the mummies of the dead. In the grave of King Zer, who lived and died about 5400 years

EGYPTIAN COTTON ROBES

before Christ, there were discovered mummy-bands so finely woven that there were a hundred and sixty threads of warp and a hundred and twenty threads of woof to the inch. By the time of King Tahutmes IV (1414 B.C.) the weavers of Egypt had mastered the art of producing patterns of various colours, and of making, with the aid of shorn-off loops of thread, a surface resembling velvet or plush. Each Egyptian temple of any importance

The Book of Craftsmen

maintained a staff of weavers, whose handiwork was sold for the joint profit of the ruling sovereign and the priests of the temple. Those warlike and luxury-loving rivals of the Egyptians, the Babylonians, were also notable weavers, and from the fact that many of their floors are paved with coloured tiles closely resembling tapestry designs it has been concluded that potters, masons, and architects were willing to borrow ideas from the textile worker.

If you go to a big museum and ask to be allowed to see some examples of ancient weaving you will be directed to what is known as the Department of Textiles. The word 'textile' comes from the Latin *texere*, to weave, and we shall probably use it quite a lot in the course of the present chapter. Except the craft of the potter, there is hardly any craft so ancient or so widely distributed as that of the weaver. Even some primitive peoples who do not weave garments are known to weave sails for their canoes and mats for their huts. Obviously the Eskimo cannot learn to weave, since neither flax nor wool, silk nor cotton, is available to him, but Arabs and Red Indians alike have mastered the art, using various raw materials, sheep's wool and goat's hair among them.

The earliest type of loom, as we have seen, consisted of a framework upon which the threads of the warp were stretched perpendicularly with the aid of weights. This type was universal through the Near and the Far East. A later development, perhaps not unknown to that inventive people, the Chinese, was the horizontal-warp loom, from which all the elaborate western models have been developed.

Allusions to spinning and weaving are found in Homer and in the Bible. We shall say something about the ancient Greeks very soon; in the meantime let us see what the Bible has to say about this ancient craft.

In the thirty-fifth chapter of the Book of Exodus we are told how when the Tabernacle was being built God chose certain men to make the various adornments for it. This chapter tells us

The Weaver

something about several different arts and crafts, and the last six verses are so interesting that I must quote them in full:

> And Moses said unto the children of Israel, See, the Lord hath called by name Bezaleel the son of Uri, the son of Hur, of the tribe of Judah;
> And He hath filled him with the spirit of God, in wisdom, in understanding, and in knowledge, and in all manner of workmanship;
> And to devise curious works, to work in gold, and in silver, and in brass,
> And in the cutting of stones, to set them, and in carving of wood, to make any manner of cunning work.
> And He hath put in his heart that he may teach, both he, and Aholiab, the son of Ahisamach, of the tribe of Dan.
> Them hath He filled with wisdom of heart, to work all manner of work of the engraver, and of the cunning workman, and of the embroiderer, in blue, and in purple, in scarlet, and in fine linen, and of the weaver, even of them that do any work, and of those that devise cunning work.

Here we see the influence of the belief held by many primitive people that man was taught all his knowledge of craftsmanship by some divine Power or some more than mortal Being. We saw this in the case of the Maoris and their woodcarving, and we shall see it again among other races.

You will remember that the staff of Goliath's spear was "like a weaver's beam," and the same simile is used of the spear of an Egyptian slain by Benaiah, one of King David's "mighty men." Job exclaims in his despair, "My days are swifter than a weaver's shuttle." In the story of Samson we hear how Delilah, hired by the Philistines to betray the Jewish Hercules, fastened seven locks of his hair to the pin of her loom-beam, and he, thanks to his great bodily strength, escaped, carrying off the beam and the web with him.

Most famous of all Biblical allusions to weaving and spinning are those to be found in the thirty-first chapter of the Book of Proverbs, where the virtuous woman, whose "price is far above rubies," has her portrait traced.

The Book of Craftsmen

> She seeketh wool, and flax, and worketh willingly with her hands. . . .
> She layeth her hands to the spindle, and her hands hold the distaff. . . .
> She is not afraid of the snow for her household: for all her household are clothed with scarlet.
> She maketh herself coverings of tapestry; her clothing is silk and purple. . . .
> She maketh fine linen, and selleth it; and delivereth girdles unto the merchant.[1]

This last statement reminds us that in the world of the ancients most of the spinning, weaving, and embroidering was done by women in their own homes—a state of affairs which some idealists of our own time would like to see restored.

The mention of 'scarlet' and 'purple'—two terms often used interchangeably in Hebrew and in Greek—brings us to the question of dyeing. Crude dyes made from the juice of mosses and herbs were discovered in very distant days, and are still used in many parts of the world. I myself know a Scottish lady, whose home is in a remote island of the Hebrides group, who spins and weaves the wool of her own sheep, and dyes it with beautiful colours made from lichen. Some plants, such as indigo and madder, have been used for countless generations to impart various tints to linen and cloth: but perhaps the most famous source of textile colour in history was not a plant but an animal, a tiny shell-fish called the murex. This shell-fish was found in large numbers off the coast of Phœnicia, and as early as the fourteenth century B.C. an Egyptian papyrus describes that part of the seaboard near the Phœnician city of Tyre as being "richer in fish than in sands." We hear a great deal about this once famous and flourishing city in the twenty-seventh chapter of the Book of Ezekiel; about her ships, with masts of cedar and oars of oak, and sails of "fine linen with broidered work from Egypt"; and about the merchandise she exported to other centres of civilization. From the list of her exports it is clear that the Tyrians rivalled the Egyptians

[1] Proverbs, xxxi, 13-24.

The Weaver

as weavers, dyers, and embroiderers, for we read of "purple, and broidered work, and fine linen," and one glowing verse exclaims:

> These were thy merchants in all sorts of things, in blue clothes, and broidered work, and in chests of rich apparel, bound with cords, and made of cedar, among thy merchandise.[1]

It may have been by mere chance that some intelligent Tyrian

THE DYER
He belongs to the sixteenth century, but his ideas would be very similar to those of his forerunners in classical and medieval times.

discovered that the murex, crushed and mingled with water, would dye white fabrics purple, blue, or red. When you remember that the colour purple is formed of blue and red mingled you will understand how at one end of the colour-scale the Tyrian stain looked blue and at the other red. 'Tyrian' came actually to *mean* purple in the ancient world: and owing to the costliness and beauty

[1] Ezekiel, xxvii, 24.

The Book of Craftsmen

of materials dyed by the Tyrian process purple came to be the characteristic wear of kings. 'Born in the purple' meant 'born of royal blood,' and to 'don the purple' or 'assume the purple' meant to succeed to a throne—or to usurp one!

The women of ancient Greece were skilful both with distaff and loom. In addition to woollen and flaxen fabrics they made a gauzy material called *byssos*, spun from the silky threads of the pinna shell. Like all the nations of the antique world the Greeks had myths and legends connected with weaving and spinning. There was, for example, the legend of Arachne, daughter of Idmo, a dyer of Colopho, who was so skilful in her craft that she challenged the goddess Athena to a trial of skill. The goddess, not unnaturally, proved victorious, and poor Arachne, as the result of her presumption, was changed into a spider —an insect which in the Greek language bears her name to this day!

GREEK WOMAN SPINNING

Among the quaintest figures in Greek mythology were the Three Fates—Clotho, Lachesis, and Atropos. They spun the lives of mortal men, Clotho wielding the distaff and Lachesis the spindle, while Atropos cut off the thread of each life at the appointed time. They had their counterpart in the Norns of Scandinavian mythology—the Three Sisters who were supposed to sit under the undying ash-tree Yggdrasil weaving the woof of human events. The Fates were imagined as aged women weaving chaplets of white wool studded with narcissus flowers. According to some ancient poets they were the keepers of the records of the gods!

We hear quite a lot about weaving and spinning in the two great epic poems of Homer—the *Iliad*, telling of the siege of Troy,

The Weaver

and the *Odyssey*, describing the wanderings of Odysseus. Hector, "the tamer of horses," son of Priam, King of Troy, requests his mother, before he goes forth to battle, to make an offering to the goddess Athena on his behalf. "Go thou," he says, "to the temple of Athena—and the robe that seemeth to thee the seemliest and the best in thy dwelling lay thou upon the knees of the lovely-locked Athena." And we are told how his mother went to her perfumed chamber where were stored her embroidered robes, "the work of Sidonian women," and took out the one that lay beneath all the rest, and was the richest and the largest of all, and Theano the priestess laid it upon the carven knees of the goddess.

Helen of Argos, like the housewife in the Book of Proverbs, "appointed handiwork for her maidens." When Achilles sojourned in the house of Priam before the funeral ceremonies over the body of Hector the old King ordered his serving-maids to set a bedstead under the portico, "and cast fair shining rugs thereon, and to spread coverlets, and to lay thick mantles over them"; and the golden urn in which the ashes of the hero were gathered was draped in purple.

When Chryseis the priest strives to ransom his captive daughter from the besieging Greeks before the walls of Troy King Agamemnon of Argos received him churlishly, and said, "I will not set her free. Nay, long ere she grow old, in my palace at Argos she shall ply the loom far from her native land."

The *Odyssey*, a much more romantic and eventful epic, contains many more allusions to spinning and weaving. When Athena, disguised as an old man, arrives at the house of the long-absent Odysseus she is welcomed by the hero's young son Telemachus:

> ... on a chair, outspreading the cover of linen, he set her:
> Richly adorned was the chair, and below for the feet was a foot-stool.

And when Telemachus decides to assert himself and turn out the numerous suitors contending for the hand of his mother Penelope, he thus addresses that astonished lady:

The Book of Craftsmen

"Now to thy chamber return and attend to thy own occupation,
Ever the loom and the distaff, and order thy maiden-attendants
Busily keep to their tasks: we men will attend to the talking."

Perhaps the most famous loom in all literature is the loom of Queen Penelope, which she used as a device to stave off her suitors:

Rearing a spacious loom in her hall she betook her to weaving,
Working a broad and a delicate web.

To the suitors she spoke thus:

"Princes, who sue for my hand—since dead is the god-like Odysseus—
Patiently wait, though eager to hasten my marriage, till fully
Woven this web. . . ."
Thus did she speak—
Thus then all of the day at the spacious loom she was weaving:
During the night she unravelled the web with her torches beside her:
Three long years with her secret device she befooled the Achaeans.[1]

But of course "god-like Odysseus" was *not* dead at all, and after long wanderings in far lands he won home to his island kingdom of Ithaca.

In the course of those wanderings Odysseus was cast ashore on the island of Phœcia, where the young daughter of the King of the island was the first to welcome him. Her name was Nausicaa, and she had risen early the same morning to drive a mule-wagon full of "men's raiment, and robes, and shining coverlets" down to the river to be washed. We are told that her mother, Queen Arete, busied herself "spinning yarn of sea-purple stain," and, in addition to grinding corn and keeping the palace clean, spinning and weaving would be among the principal duties of the fifty handmaids of this industrious Queen. Nausicaa herself would assuredly be skilful with distaff, shuttle, and needle, and the embroidered cloths upon the benches in the palace-hall would many of them be the work of her hands.

The finest woollen stuffs and the most delicate linens came from Ionia, the coast-lands and islands of western Asia Minor, but the

[1] Translated by H. B. Cotterill.

The Weaver

young girls of Athens were taught the craft of the weaver almost as soon as their little fingers were strong enough to hold and control the shuttle. The Greeks did not believe in giving their daughters the same sort of intellectual training that they gave their sons. Spinning, weaving, and cooking were the accomplishments considered most suitable for girls.

To Athenian maidens who were skilful at the loom there might come a most exciting reward. Every four years a procession passed through Athens, starting outside the city boundaries and ending at a temple called the Erechtheum on the flat-topped cliff of the Acropolis, and in it certain highly favoured daughters of noble Athenian families took part. This procession formed the climax of the great Panathenaic festival instituted by a semi-mythical King of Athens, called Erechtheus, in honour of Athene Polios, the divine protectress of the city-state which bore her name. She had her own magnificent temple, the Parthenon, on the summit of the cliff, and she had to share the Erechtheum with Poseidon[1] and with Erechtheus himself, but it was felt that the smaller and more ancient temple was more closely associated with the "grey-eyed goddess." The archaic wooden image of her which stood there could not compare for splendour with her mighty statue of ivory and gold in the Parthenon, yet men held it more holy, and every four years, at the close of the Panathenaic festival, it was garbed in a new *peplos*, or mantle, of saffron-yellow and sea-purple, woven by certain young girls of her own city. These girls, known as *ergastinai*, or workers, dwelt within the precincts of the Erechtheum, under the care of the priestess of Athene, while they were engaged upon their important task, and when the *peplos* was finished men bore it to the Acropolis slung upon the yard of a wooden ship mounted on wheels.[2]

We have been speaking more of linen than of woollen fabrics, more of flax than of fleeces. Dwellers in hot countries like Egypt and Mesopotamia would naturally need light and thin fabrics, but people whose climate varied with the seasons would need warm clothing. Thinking of their marble statues of gods and goddesses, athletes and heroes, we are rather apt to think of the ancient

---

[1] The Sea-god, the same whom the Romans called Neptune.
[2] D. M. Stuart, *The Girl through the Ages*, p. 52 (Harrap).

The Book of Craftsmen

Greeks as a people who wore few and scanty garments—if any. In practice it was only the Spartans who went about meagrely clad in all weathers. In other parts of the Grecian archipelago and on the Ionian mainland sheep were bred, and woollen yarn was spun; woollen fabrics were woven from a very early period, and blankets, mantles, and rugs were made from these fabrics. Arcadia, Thessaly, and Sicily were famous sheep-breeding centres. The wool-merchants of Arcadia took Hermes, the messenger of the gods, as their patron: the shepherds of Sicily chose Pan, the goat-footed, pipe-playing divinity, as theirs. Our old friend the metal-worker had to make huge shears to clip off the loose ends of the woven wool, and the worker in wood, tubs for the fuller who freed the fabric from grease.

GAULISH SHEARMAN

In the Near East goat's hair was also spun and woven, as it is to this day. From this tougher and more elastic substance tent-cloth was made, and ship's cables, and even a sort of rough raiment for seafarers. The Jews of Old Testament times were skilful weavers both of goat's hair and of sheep's fleeces. 'Sack-cloth' in the Bible means goat's-hair cloth, which was always rough in texture and dark in colour.

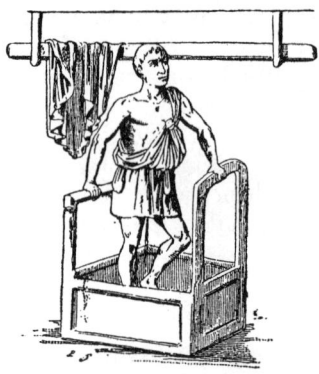
GAULISH FULLER

When the Romans took the place of the Greeks as the foremost nation of the antique world they gradually abandoned their originally thrifty and simple manner of life and adopted all sorts of luxuries, including rich linen, silken and woollen stuffs. In the

The Weaver

early days the Roman ideal of a good wife was very similar to the ideals of the Hebrews and the Greeks: she must be industrious, and, besides cooking, she must busy herself with distaff and shuttle. Woollen stuffs were used to make the principal garments of both men and women. The *toga*, the characteristic garb of the free-born Roman citizen, was of wool, and so was the *palla*, the long outer mantle, of his wife. Of wool also was the *paenula*, a cloak worn by either sex in cold weather. For a long time the Romans were content with these plain and serviceable clothes, but after the Second Punic War (218–202 B.C.) Rome became the mistress of the Mediterranean and was thus brought into contact with older and more luxurious civilizations than her own.

As Rome's dominions spread east and south, and new, gorgeous merchandise began to pour into her markets, Roman ladies ceased to ply the old, homely crafts of spinning and weaving. They also demanded finer fabrics for their own use than the woollen and linen cloths that had satisfied their mothers and grandmothers. Caravans from the Far East brought them a fine, delicate, and costly substance spun not by human hands but by caterpillars, and then wound into reels and woven upon looms, and made into *silk*. China was the land whence silk first came, and in the Chinese language *Sze* means a silkworm. The Greeks called the Chinese people *seres*, the people providing silk, and the Romans called silk *sericum*.

According to Chinese tradition it was a royal lady, Se-ling-She, principal Queen of the Emperor Hwang-te, who, about the year 2640 B.C., first reared silkworms and fashioned silken stuffs from the delicate floss which they spun. To this Queen was attributed the invention of the loom, and her memory has been kept green through many succeeding generations. Sticks of sweet-scented incense are still burned before her *joss*, or image, on a certain day in the ninth month of the year. When China was still an Imperial State the Empress and her ladies always used to worship at the shrine of Se-ling-She on that day, and ceremonially collect

The Book of Craftsmen

mulberry leaves, feed the palace silkworms, and wind off some cocoons of silk.

Realizing the importance of the silk industry to their subjects, one Chinese Emperor after another issued edicts for its encouragement and protection. The secret was carefully preserved even when silken fabrics were exported in great quantities to the markets of the Near East and thence to the Levant, Greece, and Rome. Roman writers were in much doubt as to the nature and origin of the material in which proud Cæsars and magnificent ladies delighted to drape themselves, and one theory was to the effect that silk grew upon trees! Not until the centre of Roman imperialism had shifted from the Tiber to the Bosporus was the jealously guarded monopoly broken through. This befell in the reign of the Emperor Justinian, in the middle of the sixth century after Christ, when two Persian monks, who had gone to the Far East as Christian missionaries, conveyed some silkworms' eggs out of China concealed in a hollow bamboo staff. The eggs were duly hatched out in Constantinople, and the monks, who had mastered the technique of silkworm breeding while in Pekin, fed the little creatures upon mulberry-leaves, and watched over them till they had spun their shimmering cocoons. From this small beginning developed the vast silk-trade of the Near East.

THE EMPEROR CONSTANTINE IN CONSULAR ROBES

Charlemagne, the famous Emperor of the Franks, had the princesses, his daughters, taught to weave silk, and wealthy folk in every part of his domains imitated him in encouraging their womenkind to learn this craft.

Byzantine silks were seen in England for the first time at the

CHINESE BROCADE OF THE EIGHTEENTH CENTURY
With trees, barges, bridges, sedan-chairs, pagodas, and people.
Victoria and Albert Museum

The Weaver

coronation of Eleanor of Aquitaine in 1154, when the officiating clergy were robed in such marvels of coloured tissue as sober English eyes had never beheld before. Soon these tissues, brought from Damascus, Byzantium, and Baghdad, and even from far Cathay, were used to make gowns and tunics for lords and ladies, as well as copes and chasubles for priests.

BYZANTINE BROCADE
Twelfth century.

Henry III is said to have been the first English king to wear the silk called 'baudekin.' The name —when we understand it—tells us whence this silk came. *Baldacco* is the Italian for 'Baghdad,' and it was from that many-domed city on the Euphrates that the great glittering bales were brought, over many perilous miles of sand and sea, to be made into garments for the King and Queen of England. Samite and sarcenet came respectively from Constantinople and from the land of the Saracens. Sendal, another favourite fabric, came from Sindhu, or India.[1]

Before we think about the weavers of medieval Europe let us pause for a moment and think about another ancient craft closely associated with weaving—needlework and embroidery. The first use to which mankind put their bone needles and fibre threads was to sew garments together, but at a very early date clever fingers began to trace patterns in stitchery for the beautification of robes and hangings. The Egyptians were skilful embroiderers, and we hear quite a lot about 'needlework' in the Old Testament. When Jericho fell one of Joshua's captains was so much charmed by the "goodly Babylonish garment" which he saw among the spoils that he saved it from the general destruction of Canaanitish splendours —an act of disobedience for which he paid with his life. In

[1] *England's Story*, Part I, p. 287 (Harrap).

The Book of Craftsmen

Exodus we read of the veil of the Tabernacle, "of blue and purple and scarlet, and fine twined linen of cunning work," and we find this commandment, "Thou shalt make an hanging for the door of the tent of blue and purple and scarlet and fine twined linen, wrought with needlework." The High Priest was to have " a girdle of needlework," which sounds as if it might have been very beautiful indeed.

In the Book of Judges Sisera's mother confidently anticipates the return of her warlike son, laden with spoil:

DARIUS AND ATTENDANTS

> Have they not sped? have they not divided the prey; to every man a damsel or two; to Sisera a prey of divers colours, a prey of divers colours of needlework, of divers colours of needlework on both sides, meet for the necks of them that take the spoil?[1]

Very gorgeous must the King's daughter of Psalm xlv have looked in her clothing of wrought gold, her raiment of needlework; and we know from ancient Assyrian carvings that the kings of Assyria went lion-hunting clad in tunics richly embroidered.

The Greeks adorned their houses with rugs, curtains, and cushions wrought in elaborate and lovely designs, and the women of Sidon, the Phœnician city, were famous for their skill with the needle.

Coming to the Scandinavian peoples of Europe in the early ages we find that high-born ladies made hangings adorned with the heroic life-stories of their national heroes. In France, when the education of girls took a great forward step under the enlightened rule of some of the Merovingian princes, every young damsel of gentle birth learned embroidery as part of

---

[1] Judges, v, 30.

The Weaver

her training. One Frankish lady embroidered an altar veil with verses of her own composition! Princesses of Byzantium wore cloth-of-gold adorned with borders representing warriors engaged in combat, and petticoats of Indian shawl-stuff with patterns similar to what came many centuries later to be called " Paisley pattern."

A BYZANTINE EMPRESS

Pious women throughout Christendom delighted to use their needles for the glory of God by embroidering vestments and altar-hangings. So skilful did English-women become in this particular art that the finest Church embroidery was known in the Middle Ages as *opus Anglicanum*. A masterpiece of this work was produced in the thirteenth century. It is known as the Syon cope, because it belonged to a nunnery at Syon, near Isleworth, and is covered entirely with figures of saints, archangels, and apostles, and scenes from the life of Christ. The chief colours are tawny brown, gold, green, and blue. "This last tint," we are told, " appears rather startlingly upon the hair and beard of more than one apostle!"

Of course it was not upon Church embroidery only that the ladies of medieval England exercised their long white fingers. They devised wonderful—and sometimes quaint—decorations for their own gowns. We read in a thirteenth-century chronicle how the gentlewomen gathered in their " bower " after supper would discuss " needlework, frilled work and open work, scalloped work and wool-work, diaper-work and German and Saracenic stitchery." Sometimes to beautify their dresses they cut heraldic monsters out of highly coloured stuffs and sewed them on: Queen Philippa of Hainault had a mulberry coloured dress sprinkled with golden squirrels.

The Book of Craftsmen

Now let us leave these industrious and resourceful ladies and return to their humbler contemporaries, the men and women who wove and spun the fabrics from which those rich garments were fashioned.

As is the case with so many other handicrafts, weaving did not stand alone. The weaver could not produce the finished product all by himself. He needed the aid of the dyer, the fuller, the tenter-

THE SYON COPE

man, and the shearman. To obtain blue, green, and purple the dyer used a great deal of the plant called *Isatis tinctoria*, familiar to us by its English name of 'woad'—the same plant with whose juice the ancient Britons were wont to stain their naked bodies. To obtain scarlet he turned to a curious little insect, the female of the *Coccus ilicis*, once believed to be not a beast but a berry. When the woollen stuff had been dyed the turn of the fuller came. He took the cloth and scoured it with the clay known as fullers' earth, thus removing all the animal grease remaining in the wool. Then he laid it in a vat full of water and he and his assistants trampled upon it until the desired degree of suppleness was reached. In the thirteenth century an ingenious device was introduced by which a wooden bar was made to do the work hitherto performed by human feet. This contrivance was kept in motion on the principle of a mill, and when water-power did not

The Weaver

happen to be available man-power, or even *woman*-power, was employed.

On the outskirts of most medieval towns in England were fields called ' tenter-grounds,' where the newly fulled cloth was taken to be stretched and dried. London's tenter-grounds were situated

AN EMBROIDERED CARPET
Fourteenth century.

where the busy streets of Whitechapel run to-day. Unscrupulous tenter-men would weaken the cloth by stretching it to excess, using a powerful lever so that a piece thirty yards in length was extended to thirty-five yards. In vain were edicts issued and royal decrees sent forth: the practice continued, and the tenter-men refused to mend their ways.

After the cloth had been stretched it was combed all over with the prickly heads of teazles (*Dipsacus fullonum*) to draw out the

The Book of Craftsmen

loose ends. Then the shearman took his sharp shears and trimmed the shaggy surface, and made it smooth and neat. Finally the cloth was rolled into bales, and carried on pack-horses to the warehouses of the merchants, or stowed in ships and sent overseas to be bartered or sold.

The rougher variety of English cloth was called 'burel,' or 'borel,' and was brownish or greyish in colour. Henry II clad his

A WOMAN WARPING WOOL

foot-soldiers in 'burel' during the Irish campaign of 1172, and charitable rich folk were wont to purchase many bales of this cloth for gifts to the poor and needy. Fine cloth of bright scarlet, purchased at Lincoln in 1182 for the use of the royal household, cost 6s. 8d. an ell, or about £7 a yard in modern money. In the wardrobe accounts of Henry III we read of " blues of Beverley, scarlets and greens of Lincoln, and blues of Stamford." One no longer speaks of ' Beverley blue,' but the phrase ' Lincoln green ' is not quite obsolete even now. Edward III, probably instigated by his good Queen, Philippa of Hainault, encouraged Flemish weavers to come and settle in England. His purpose was to counteract the habit of the English weavers to hamper trade by reducing their output. In his anxiety to remedy this state of affairs the King temporarily suspended that clause of Magna Charta which decreed that dyed and russet woollen stuffs should be two ells in width from selvage to selvage.

All this time, and for long after, weaving was done upon hand-

The Weaver

looms in the homes of the weavers, when it was not carried on by the womenfolk of large households. Matrons of the prosperous mercantile class were proud of their skill with distaff and shuttle, and Chaucer's Wyf of Bath was so well versed in cloth-making that she "passèd [*i.e.*, surpassed] them of Ypres and Gaunt."

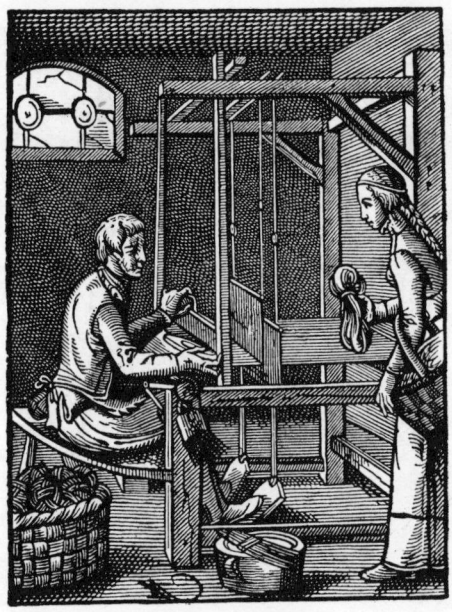

WEAVING A TAPESTRY

These two Flemish cities, Ypres and Ghent, were famous all over Europe for the excellence of their linen and woollen stuffs, which they began to produce as early as the tenth century. A separate but kindred industry was that of tapestry weaving, which flourished in the fifteenth century at Arras and Tournai, and later at Brussels and Lille. The Dukes of Burgundy were bountiful patrons of the tapestry-weavers working in their dominions, and foreign princes, including the kings of France and England, were glad to purchase Flemish or Burgundian arras-cloth (it took its English name from one of the places where it was made) for the adornment of their palace-halls.

The Book of Craftsmen

Scenes from Holy Writ, chivalric legend, and ancient history were represented on arras-cloth. In 1368 one Huchon Barthélemy, a money-changer, received nine hundred golden francs for " a piece of tapestry work showing the Quest of the Holy Grail." Charles V of France possessed an awning for his royal barge made of tapestry

A FRENCH TAPESTRY
Fifteenth century.

" wrought with towers and fallow deer." The Abbot of the Monastery of St Florent at Saumur hired two laymen to make him two large tapestry hangings " of admirable quality, representing elephants," while the Prior, not to be outdone, ordered a red carpet adorned with silver lions.

The weaving of carpets was practised in the Near and Far East long before the craftsmen of the West learned how to do it. Eleanor of Castile, wife of Edward Longshanks, is said to have introduced examples of this art into England for the first time in history.

The Weaver

WEAVING CARPETS IN PERSIA

The Fullers and the Shearmen of London joined together early in the reign of Henry VIII to form the powerful Clothworkers' Company, whose badge, rather appropriately, is a ram with a fine woolly fleece. At an earlier date the Shearmen had a quarrel with

The Book of Craftsmen

the Dyers as to who should ride first in processions through the City, and the Lord Mayor decreed that " the Dyers should lovingly and charitably follow the Fellowship of Shearmen without any further strife or debate." Older than any of these were the Weavers, to whom a Charter was granted by Henry I, William the Conqueror's book-loving son. Their guild was involved in a squabble with King John, who suppressed it with a relentless hand: but it revived under his milder son and successor, Henry III, and exists, in a modified form, at the present day.

SPINNING-WHEEL

Until the middle years of the eighteenth century the woollen trade of England depended entirely upon the spinning-wheel and the hand-loom. The spinning-wheel had been introduced in Tudor times, when it marked a great advance upon the ancient and primitive distaff and spindle: other and greater forward movements were now at hand. Men were asking themselves whether it might not be possible to produce more and better linen or woollen cloth with a smaller expenditure of human labour. A French naval officer called de Gennes invented " a machine for making linen cloth without the aid of a workman," but nobody was enterprising enough to put his theory into practice. Then, in 1733, John Kay, of Bury in Lancashire, thought of the fly-shuttle. His invention received this name from its rapidity of movement, and was destined to have far-reaching results. Thirty years later another landmark in the history of textile manufactures loomed up. This was the Spinning Jenny.

One day, when one of his numerous children had happened to knock over a spinning-wheel James Hargreaves, carpenter and

The Weaver

weaver, noticed that the wheel continued for a time to revolve horizontally, while the spindle revolved vertically. This set him thinking. Then he began to experiment. And finally he put together a machine—nicknamed the Spinning Jenny—upon which

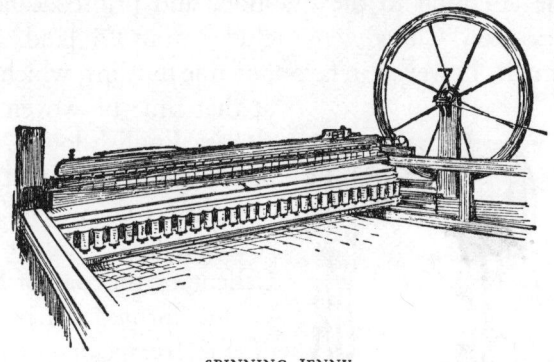

SPINNING JENNY

twenty or thirty threads could be spun in the time formerly needed to spin one thread only. The other weavers of the neighbourhood broke into the house of their too-inventive comrade and smashed up his apparatus, fearing that if the Spinning Jenny came into general use unemployment would follow and wages would fall.

The thread spun by Hargreaves in the new way was suitable for the weft only: it was not strong enough for the warp. (You will remember that early in the present chapter I explained the meaning of the terms 'warp' and 'weft.') Full development could not be given to Hargreaves' idea until Richard Arkwright, barber and wigmaker of Bolton, turned his attention to the subject. It must not be for-

COTTON GIN

gotten that by this time the raw material of the weaver was quite as likely to be cotton as it was to be flax or wool. In 1610 the Earl of Salisbury had petitioned King James I and VI to

The Book of Craftsmen

continue a grant for the reform of abuses in the manufacture of "cotton such as groweth in the land of Persia, being no kind of wool." To protect the new English industry of cotton-spinning laws were passed by successive sovereigns. George I's Ministers gave some attention to the question, and printed calicoes from India, Persia, and China were excluded from England. An exception was made, however, in favour of fine muslins, which could not at that time be woven upon the clumsy English looms. (It is interesting to realize that the word 'muslin' comes from Mosul, in Mesopotamia: 'calico' is from Calicut, on the coast of Malabar.) Cotton formed the basis of one of the cottage industries of the period before factories came into being.

ARKWRIGHT'S SPINNING MACHINE

In 1768 Arkwright set up a mill at Nottingham worked by horses: three years later he set up another mill at Cromford in Derbyshire, where power was supplied by a water-wheel. Furious mobs destroyed his machines, but he persevered, and lived long enough to introduce steam-power at his Nottingham mill in 1790. By 1788 there were already one hundred and forty-three cotton mills worked by water-power in the United Kingdom, forty-one of these being situated in Lancashire, where the moist climate was less likely to make the cotton threads snap than the drier air of the south-eastern counties would have been.

Among the numerous inquisitive strangers who visited Arkwright's mills was a country clergyman, the Reverend Edmund Cartwright. He was so much interested that he abandoned his

The Weaver

pet hobby of verse-writing and set to work experimenting with an improved form of power-loom. Despite its shortcomings, Cartwright's invention was the direct ancestor of the power-loom of modern industry.

Now comes on the scene a boy called Samuel Crompton, the son of a poor widow who eked out a meagre livelihood by weaving in their cottage home. Samuel helped his mother in her work,

CROMPTON'S MULE

and also earned a few extra shillings by playing the fiddle in the local theatre. He was constantly hampered by the snapping-off of the tips of the yarn, and he began to wonder whether he could not combine the principles of Hargreaves' spinning jenny and Arkwright's spinning frame so as to prevent this snapping. After five years of hard toil he completed his machine, which came to be known as the Mule, because just as the mule is the offspring of the horse and the ass, this machine was the offspring of those invented by Hargreaves and Arkwright.

> Master-spinners, eager to learn his secret, besieged Crompton's house. The principle of the thing was so simple that any expert could have grasped it at one glance, but the inventor was too poor to protect himself by taking out a patent, so he was obliged to mount guard over his precious machinery night and day. Finally he

The Book of Craftsmen

arranged to divulge the secret to a group of manufacturers, but they did not deal fairly by him, and he never received the rewards due to his ingenuity and his perseverance. Thanks to him, most of the fine muslins so much in demand for ladies' caps, aprons, and scarves were soon woven in England instead of being imported from the East.[1]

French inventors early turned their attention to the problem of reproducing *patterns* accurately and rapidly with the aid of the hand-loom. Three ingenious Frenchmen, Falcon, Vaucauson, and Jacquard, grappled with it during the eighteenth century, and it was the last of the three whose name has stuck to the machine which evolved from their separate labours.

As this is a book about craftsmen rather than about inventors we must not say too much about machinery, which became more and more complicated as the years passed, or about chemistry, which led to the introduction of so many wonderful new colours, or about fashions in fabrics, patterns and dyes, which have had such far-reaching influences now that the markets of the Old World and the New, the East and the West, receive each other's commodities and react to each other's needs. It is enough to pause for a moment and realize how far man has travelled since the days when with bone needles he sewed together mats roughly plaited from the fibres of the blue-blossomed flax.

[1] *England's Story*, Part III, p. 806 (Harrap).

CHAPTER V
THE SCULPTOR AND THE BUILDER

WHEN we say 'sculptor' we think first and foremost of a man who carves images out of stone; and that is the kind of sculptor we are going to talk about in this chapter. His brother-craftsmen, the carver in wood and the maker of images in metal, have already appeared upon the scene. His forerunner, the shaggy fellow of the cave period who chipped flints, must be allowed to cross the stage now, though he did nothing *but* chip, and never attempted to carve.

Flint was a most useful material to prehistoric man, especially in south-eastern England, south-western France, and Scandinavia,

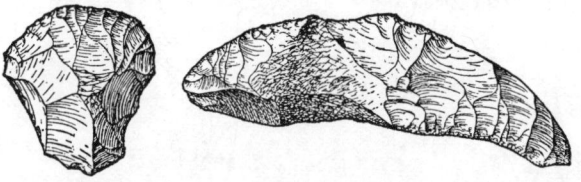

FLINT AXE AND SCRAPER

where it abounds. On the sites of long-vanished centres of the flint-chipping industry enormous quantities of chips are still found, some of them flawed or imperfect fragments, rejected by the workman, others fine examples of his craftsmanship. Flint-miners of the Stone and Bronze Ages used picks made of deer's horn, and spades made from the shoulder-bones of oxen. They knew how to sink shafts and cut tunnels through the flinty deposits lying in seams of chalk. At Weeting, in Norfolk, there are the remains of an elaborate system of flint mines known locally as Grime's Graves. You can still see faint traces of human habitations near these mines, perhaps marking the site of the hut occupied by some

The Book of Craftsmen

foreman or overseer, and you can still follow the line of an ancient embanked track-way which must have been a scene of great activity between 3000 and 1500 B.C.

The earliest chippers of flint lived in caves; after a time their

ENGRAVING OF CERVUS CLAPHUS

successors learned to make themselves little huts of stones, willow-boughs, and turf. Far away, by the banks of the Nile and the Euphrates, men of the same far-off time were chipping a very similar stone called 'chert' and building little huts of clay, thatched with reeds from the river-bed.

Though primitive man did not at first *carve* stone, he *did* sometimes make incised—or 'cut'—patterns on flat surfaces. These patterns often represent horned animals, such as reindeer or

The Sculptor and the Builder

the now extinct breed of large and powerful wild cattle. Presently the idea of carving entered into the craftsman's mind. Some of the most ancient carved objects known to us are uncouth and clumsy rather than beautiful. Human figures are often represented as being very podgy and awkward, though figures of animals are sometimes quite true to nature. Statues carved by a neolithic sculptor often look like drawings scribbled by a modern baby—two dots representing the eyes, and a few vague scratches doing duty for nose and mouth. Yet these same people, so childish in this particular art, were all the time groping towards the finer workmanship which their descendants of the Bronze Age duly attained. Some of the flints of the Stone Age are masterpieces in their own simple way; some of the designs scratched on pieces of bone are full of vigour and beauty.

NEOLITHIC MENHIR
It exhibits traces of human form.

One of man's first instincts was to build a home not only for himself but for the god or gods upon whose goodwill he believed the prosperity of himself and his tribe depended, and thus the temple came into being. He also built a habitation for the souls of his dead kinsfolk, and thus came into being the tomb that resembled a dwelling-place.

Sometimes it happens that there is some doubt as to the exact purpose of a very ancient erection. A case in point is Stonehenge, that grim assembly of giant stones on Salisbury Plain. To-day it consists of an encircling ditch and the remains of four groups of two different kinds of stone. The outer circle is of sandstone boulders with lintels; an inner circle is of blue-coloured stone brought from Pembrokeshire; inside this is a horseshoe of five great sandstone boulders in groups consisting of two uprights and one horizontal stone; and within this horseshoe is an oval of the blue-coloured stones enclosing a recumbent slab of sandstone

The Book of Craftsmen

known as the altar-stone. The outermost circle is one hundred feet in diameter, and the average height of the boulders above the ground is thirteen-and-a-half feet, each weighing about twenty-six tons. The inner circle of blue stones has a diameter of seventy-six-and-a-half feet. Some of the fallen stones have been set up again; others still lie full length on the turf.

Now whether, as some learned men suppose, this was a temple built in honour of the sun-god, or whether, as other equally learned men suppose, it was the burial-place of some powerful chief, it is certainly a monument to the enterprise and perseverance of the tribe who hauled and hammered those heavy stones and heaved them into position. The labour of bringing the blue-tinted boulders from Pembrokeshire must have been very great, and nobody can tell exactly how the thing was done. The task of arranging them in exact circles and ovals must have demanded much care and skill, yet nobody can tell with what instruments and with what tools the task was carried out.

Meanwhile, far from the greeny-grey, grassy uplands of the West, mankind had progressed much further along the paths of art and architecture. The people of ancient Egypt, of Babylon and Sumeria, whom we have already met as skilful weavers, dyers, and workers in metal, built for themselves and their gods most goodly habitations.

In Akkad and Sumer, the northern and southern parts of Babylonia, four thousand years before Christ, houses were built of clay bricks and roofed with reed-thatch. Many of these houses were two storeys high, and all were windowless where they faced the street. Light and air were admitted by casements opening on a central courtyard. In addition to sleeping- and living-rooms, kitchens and—sometimes—bathrooms, every fair-sized dwelling would have its own private chapel, where the gods were duly worshipped and where members of the family, especially children, were buried, so that in death they might not be laid far from the scenes familiar to them in life. Temples were of great splendour, and had doors of wrought bronze, while the characteristic terraced

THE TOWER OF BABEL RECONSTRUCTED

LIFELIKE FIGURES OF MAN AND HORSE FROM THE FRIEZE OF THE PARTHENON

ROMAN MARBLE RELIEF OF THE THIRD CENTURY

Showing the cart used to carry images of gods to and from the circus during ceremonial performances.

British Museum

The Sculptor and the Builder

tower, called a 'ziggurat,' probably gave to the Old Testament scribe the idea of the Tower of Babel.

To the west of Babylonia, in the land of Egypt, houses were built of clay bricks, or, more rarely, of stone. The country houses of the wealthy classes had delicious gardens, with paved fish-ponds and shady groves of palms and fig-trees; those in the great cities

THE TOWER TEMPLE OF UR

were, like the Sumerian houses, built round central courtyards, and without windows in the outer walls. Throughout the East roofs tended to be flat. Sharply sloping roofs were needed in countries where heavy falls of rain or snow had to be prevented from breaking down the house-tops. On either side of the street-entrance to the Egyptian house was a column with an oval tablet bearing the name of the occupier; along the top ran a ledge from which gaily coloured streamers hung on days of public rejoicing. The inside walls were painted with a great variety of charming designs. Birds and fishes, palms and papyrus-reeds, were skilfully introduced, also human figures, and even humorous scenes representing animals in unexpected positions, such as cats dining with flocks of geese or hippopotami sitting at table!

The Book of Craftsmen

Now let us leave the builder of houses for a little while, and return to his fellow-craftsman, the carver of statues. Both in Egypt and Babylonia the art of sculpture was understood from very early times, but the Egyptian sculptor was the greater artist. The Sumerians produced quaint rather than pleasing objects, and the Babylonian fondness for gigantic figures of heavily bearded kings and wide-winged bulls did not tend to what we should now consider beauty. Some of the Egyptian work was really lovely. You will remember that the wood-carvers of that wonderful land were master-craftsmen. The stone-carvers were master-craftsmen too.

ASSYRIAN KING WITH CAPTIVES

Much of the handiwork of the Egyptian sculptor had to be planned on a scale far larger than life-size. Sometimes he had to tackle enormous surfaces of limestone or other rock, as at Abu-Simbel in Nubia, where the warlike Pharaoh Rameses II, hewn out of the cliff, towers over the desert and seems to gaze with his vast, vacant eyes at the far-off horizon. Sometimes the sculptor had to handle strange, hard stones, with strange, hard names—diorite, obsidian, basalt, schist, and quartz. He made images of gods and goddesses, some of them most weird to behold, and of kings and their families, merchants, scribes and priests, soldiers, captives and peasants. Upon huge slabs of stone in tombs and temples he carved scenes of war and peace; upon mighty obelisks and monuments, set up to record the triumphs and conquests of some proud Pharaoh, he carved inscriptions in the picture-script of his race—that script which seems so quaint to us, with its owls and serpents, pot-hooks and papyrus-reeds.

The statues hewn by the most skilful sculptors at the best period of Egyptian art are unrivalled, even by the finest work of the

The Sculptor and the Builder

Greeks, for their truth to nature. Four thousand years before Christ a craftsman in the Nile delta carved the diorite statue of King Khafra which is now in the Cairo Museum. The King sits erect on a throne guarded by lions, a hawk with wings outstretched protecting his head. He wears the ceremonial head-dress, the artificial chin-beard, and the pleated linen kilt which formed the recognized costume of a Pharaoh of that time. His expression is serene and aloof, as of one who feels himself to be of a different breed from the rest of the human race.

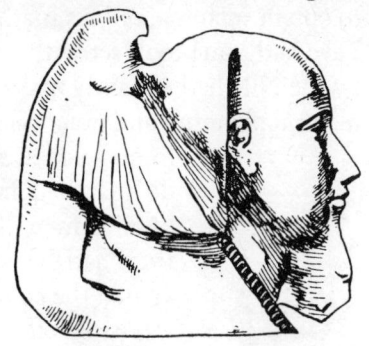

HEAD OF KING KHAFRA

It was during the Fourth Dynasty, the Dynasty to which Khafra belonged, that the Great Pyramid was built by his predecessor, King Khufu. Khafra himself built the second Pyramid, and his successor, Menkama, the third. So skilful were Khufu's masons that they were able to fit the huge blocks of stone together without using any cement. The Great Pyramid has an error of less than ·6 of an inch on its side of 9069 inches, or 1 in 15,000, and its corners are square to 12 inches.

There is no doubt as to the purpose for which these mighty masses of squared stone were piled up. They were tombs—the tombs of the sovereigns who caused them to be built. Let us look at the Great Pyramid. The smooth surface of the original has long vanished—a surface so smooth that the most nimble monkey could hardly have climbed upon it. Now we see huge blocks of stone which may be scaled with much effort and with the help of native guides. The finely worked outer stones were, many of them, removed to Cairo by the Moslem conquerors of Egypt in the seventh century A.D. and used to build mosques and walls. Even now, when thirty feet of the original summit have vanished, Khufu's monument is one hundred and fifty feet higher than St Paul's Cathedral; the base covers nearly thirteen acres, and each of

The Book of Craftsmen

the three sides is seven hundred and fifty feet in length. Egyptian masons used hammer-heads of black hornstone and tubular drills of bronze. Their saws were of copper, and some experts think that to obtain such marvellous mathematical accuracy of line they must have had some tools set with diamonds. These long-dead dwellers by the Nile had certainly mastered all the main principles of architectural planning and practical construction. They understood how to make an arch, and men who understood how to do that had taken a long forward stride. They knew how to handle gigantic masses of stone as if they had been small blocks of wood. They invented the column and the colonnade.

People often, consciously or unconsciously, borrow ideas from the natural world about them. The Egyptian saw palm-trees and lotus-flowers every day; he gave to his column the lofty, rounded and tapering form of the palm, and adorned the top either with a capital resembling palm-leaves or with one carved in the likeness of the closely furled buds of the lotus. Later we shall find the architects of western Europe imitating the glades of a forest in their rib-vaulting.

Among the countries with which Egyptian merchants and seafarers traded was Crete, an island forming a sort of geographical stepping-stone between the Nile delta and the Peloponnesus. Homer speaks of it as " lying in the wine-dark sea, a fair land and a rich, girdled with water, wherein are men without number and ninety cities." The Cretans were skilful craftsmen, and their chief city, Knossos, has been described by Mr H. G. Wells as " not so much a town as the vast palace of the king and his people." The upper storeys of the Cretan houses were probably built of wood and clay, but the lower storeys were of sturdy, well-hewn stone. The palace itself would have been a marvel in any age. Apart from its great size, its

COLUMN WITH LOTUS CAPITAL

The Sculptor and the Builder

elaborate ground-plan, the gaily coloured frescoes adorning its walls, its lighting, ventilation, and drainage systems were far in advance of anything attempted in Europe until well into the nineteenth century. The Cretan craftsman, too, borrowed designs from his surroundings; he depicted cuttle-fish and flying-fish, swallows and seaweed, and made stencilled patterns with the aid of wet sponges! The wonder-palace of Knossos was sacked and burned by foreign foemen somewhere towards the year 1400 B.C., but the fame of its complicated courts and corridors, and the faint memory of the bull-fights which were the favourite amusement of its kings, persisted in the mind of the ancient Greeks and gave rise to the legend of the Minotaur, the monster who dwelt in the centre of a vast labyrinth and was slain by Theseus.

Cretan sculptors seem to have excelled rather at figures in low relief, only partially detached from their background, than at figures carved 'in the round.' They also invaded the domain of the potter, and made vases and lamps, substituting pale yellow alabaster or deep red gypsum for his clay. Egyptian influences were strong, and some of the carvings discovered in Crete were obviously brought from Egypt. There was, however, one race dwelling within the reach of such influences which steadfastly resisted them, and that was the Children of Israel, among whose sacred laws was the stern commandment: " Thou shalt not make thee any graven image." Moses, the great law-giver, went further, for besides declaring that it was the will of God that His people should *not* make graven images he told them to break down such images when they were made by *other* nations, and destroy them with fire.

We do not hear very much about the craft of the sculptor in stone when we try to learn something of the daily life of the Jews of old. Nor did architects and builders find many opportunities among this people, who lived for so many years in tents and whose natural prejudice against cities was increased by the fact that their powerful idolatrous neighbours were city builders and city-dwellers. Babylon, with its brilliantly coloured walls, its gigantic statues and stately streets, its paven quays and lofty palaces, was a

The Book of Craftsmen

bitter memeory; and of Egypt, the land of artistic marvels, the descendants of Pharaoh's victims thought only as a land of bondage. When we *do* read of houses in the Old Testament they are usually built of wood—fir, pine, or cedar. Like all Eastern houses, they had flat roofs, upon which people would sit " in the cool of the evening." Sparrows sat there too, as we know from Psalm ci.

Just as Egyptian ideas affected Crete, Cretan ideas affected the Greeks, who lived within the zone of their seafaring ventures.

LION GATE, MYCENÆ

Two cities in the northeastern Peloponnesus, Tiryns and Mycenæ, where wonderful buildings and treasures of antique art have been unearthed, were planned and erected quite in the Cretan manner. The size of the blocks of stone forming the outer walls suggested the legend that giants and not men had first placed them in position. At Mycenæ the chief gateway was guarded by two carved lions: they still keep guard there, though they have lost their heads, and have no longer the gold vessels of King Agamemnon to protect. How skilful were the masons of prehistoric Greece we may guess from the vaulted tomb hewn out of the hillside, believed at one time to be the tomb of Agamemnon himself. The vault is nearly one hundred and fifty feet in height and diameter, and is lined with neatly shaped and fitted blocks of stone which were probably faced with brazen plates or brightly coloured tiles. At Tiryns the walls reach a thickness of fifty-seven feet and contain whole galleries and chambers. Within this mighty citadel was a palace,

The Sculptor and the Builder

with store-rooms for provisions, and with separate living-quarters for men and women.

By the seventh century B.C. all these ancient centres of primitive civilization were already in ruins, and the Greeks were raising up important city-states destined to be the inspiration of succeeding generations and the wonder of after-years. Egyptian art had long passed its golden age when the golden age of Greece began to dawn. The earliest known examples of Greek sculpture are rough images of the gods, fashioned out of wood or stone. Then in the sixth century we have what is called the 'archaic' or 'beginning' period, when the sculptors had learned to represent the human form with some accuracy, but without the grace and vigour of nature. Early statues of Apollo and Minerva bear upon their faces a peculiar, prim smirk, sometimes known as 'the archaic smile.' It was during this period, 600–500 B.C., that two still-famous schools of architecture came into being, the Doric and the Ionic, of which we shall have more to say later.

The fifth and fourth centuries B.C. were the greatest in the history of the Greek people, more especially the Athenians. After the defeat of the Persians on land at Marathon and on sea at Salamis the men of Athens, thrilled with patriotic ardour, set about rebuilding their war-shattered city, and raised upon its ruins such marvels as the shores of the Ægean had never beheld before.

Fortunate were the sculptors, able to draw supplies of exquisite marble from the quarry of Pentelicus, near the city, and from two of the islands in the Cyclades group, Naxos and Paros. According to the Roman naturalist, Pliny, the Parian quarries were so deep that even at noonday the quarrymen had to carry lamps, for which reason the Greeks were wont to call this marble *lychnites*, worked-by-lamplight.

The religion of the Greeks taught that bodily perfection was as important as perfection of mind, and most of the statues that have survived the battering of centuries represent gods and goddesses, warriors and athletes, whose calmly regular features and finely proportioned limbs seem to set them apart as models of human

The Book of Craftsmen

beauty. As we see them now these statues are the natural colour of the marble; in the case of the Pentelic marble this is a rather lovely honey shade, owing to the unusual amount of iron in it. We can hardly imagine how Hermes and Pericles, Aphrodite and Apollo, looked when they were faintly tinted, with eyeballs in their now empty eyes and touches of red on their now pallid lips. Still more difficult is it to imagine the great images of gold and ivory which were set up in the temples, to be gazed at and marvelled at by pilgrims from near and far. If we realize that the marble *was* coloured to resemble life we shall find it easier to understand the ancient myth of the sculptor Pygmalion, whose statue of Galatea turned into a living woman.

THREE ORDERS OF CAPITALS
1. Doric. 2. Ionic. 3. Greek Corinthian.

The earliest Greek temples were of wood, with tree-trunks for pillars. Then came the Doric style, in which the severe fluted columns were surmounted by equally severe, unornamented capitals. Then from Asia Minor came the Ionic style, with its more shallow flutings (sometimes even with none), and its more decorative capital consisting of 'volutes,' curving outward and downward like rams' horns, and often enriched with carving in the space between these horns. It has been suggested that one day a Persian wood-carver, shaving the surface of a column with his adze, was struck by the graceful curls of wood, and proceeded to crown his column with a carved imitation of the curls—hence the Ionic capital! Many centuries later, towards the fourth century B.C., a third and even more

The Sculptor and the Builder

elaborate type of pillar was evolved, the Corinthian, which had its capital adorned with acanthus leaves skilfully wrought in stone.

The Greeks built magnificent habitations for their gods, but for themselves they were usually contented with rather shapeless one-storeyed houses of sun-baked, pinkish-white bricks, bricks so brittle that they almost crumbled at a touch.

Let us now leave the Greek archipelago and the fourth century B.C. and transport ourselves to Rome towards the first century A.D.; that is the next stage in the march of human history. More than one Roman poet has left us a word-picture of the typical Roman artisan of this time. He lived often in a low-roofed, sunless attic, at the top of a flight of two hundred steps; its furniture consisted of a mat, a heap of straw, the bare framework of a bedstead, " and a jug with a broken handle." For drink he had vinegar-wine—it does not sound at all good!—and for food black bread, lentils, onions, turnips, salted fish, and sometimes, as a treat, a boiled sheep's head or the smoked head of a pig.

Yet life had its better points. There was work for every man who wanted it; and there were free gladiatorial shows in the arena to amuse him out of working hours. Moreover, it is to Rome that we may trace the origin of the medieval craft-guilds which developed indirectly into the trade unions of our own day. These began in the almost mythical reign of Numa Pompilius, and in the reign of Augustus they were as numerous and as complicated as they afterwards became in the London of the Plantagenets. Of course skilled craftsmen, born free or set free by their masters, lived under much better conditions than did the poor labourers whose attic-homes we have just imagined.

The sculptors of Rome were divided into numerous sections: there were those who specialized in portrait-busts, those who undertook to furbish up old or damaged statues, those who concentrated on tombstones, those—whose workshops clustered round the Temple of Castor—who produced images of gods or guardian spirits, images which were sometimes conveyed in carts to the circus on the occasion of games held in connexion with some

The Book of Craftsmen

religious festival. Then there were those whose part it was to provide eyes of some coloured material to be fitted into the marble faces their colleagues in the first group had carved. The wealthier Romans loved to adorn their town houses and country villas with

ROMAN TESSELLATED PAVEMENT
Discovered in Leadenhall Street, London.

life-sized figures of themselves and their families, or of divine beings, or of fauns and satyrs, or of the reigning Cæsar. The Cæsars themselves, especially the later and more vainglorious among them, were represented in sculpture with the attributes of various gods. For example, that unimpressive Emperor Claudius chose to be depicted as Jupiter, the King of all the Roman gods, with an oaken garland on his head, and an eagle at his feet.

The Sculptor and the Builder

As has been truly said, "The statue is that of a god and the face that of a very puzzle-headed man, dazzled by the light into which he strives to look, and with a comical effort to appear dignified."

Many craftsmen collaborated in the building of a Roman house. Brick was extensively used, and the brickmaker had to supply not only roof-tiles and flat wall-bricks, but also the flues through which warm air was conducted to keep the house cosy in winter. The floors would be inlaid with small chips of various coloured stones, called *tesseræ*, skilfully fitted together. Sometimes the design was stiff and plain, scrolls, cubes, angles, triangles, intersecting ovals and squares; sometimes it was quite ambitious, like the picture of Bacchus riding on a tiger discovered under Leadenhall Street. Then the sculptor had to carve the Corinthian pillars, the cornices and pediments, the little images of the indispensable household gods. The iron-worker, as we have seen, wrought the trellis for the windows into which the glass-worker fitted pieces of thick greenish glass.

Roman sculptors and Roman builders often had to work in lands very far from Rome itself. The sculptor made impressive statues, often larger than life-size, of the reigning Cæsar to be set up in the *fora*, or market-places, of provincial cities throughout the far-flung Roman Empire; he carved ornaments for the villas of governors, military officers, and merchants, tombstones for legionaries, altars for many strange gods. The builder, besides building temples and palaces, houses, markets, and basilicas,[1] played his part in the erection of the great bridges, aqueducts, and

ALTAR OF THE LARES

[1] In Roman times a 'basilica' was a sort of town hall, a centre of local government.

The Book of Craftsmen

viaducts, with which the Romans maintained their long lines of communication.

The extremes of climate which exiled Romans had to endure influenced the planning of their houses. In Africa and Asia they

ROMAN AQUEDUCT AT NÎMES

tried to get as much shade and as little heat as possible; in Britain and northern Gaul they wanted all the sunshine and all the artificial heating they could obtain!

SEVENTH-CENTURY WALL

When the gloom of the Dark Ages descended upon Europe many stately Roman cities were left derelict, for the barbarian hordes who conquered the western world did not care to settle

The Sculptor and the Builder

within city-walls. All arts were practically at a standstill, except the grim arts of war. A faint flickering light of civilization was kept alive by the Christian Church, which encouraged both carvers and masons, but not until the rise of the Frankish Empire in the West did architecture and sculpture come into their own again. In the Near East, Constantinople had seen many-coloured domes

CHINESE GATEWAY

arise at the behest of Justinian, but Byzantine art gave more opportunities to the goldsmith, the weaver, and the worker in mosaic than to the sculptor or the architect.

Meanwhile what had been happening in the Far East? The Chinese had long evolved their peculiar style of architecture, with the steep, angular roof and sharply peaked corners. Some authorities say that this plan was suggested by the form of the tents in which the earlier Chinese people had lived. In any case, the Chinaman did not build his house so that it should endure. It was frequently made of bamboo, the timbers lashed together, instead of being nailed or dovetailed. The roof was often of tiles, but

The Book of Craftsmen

the walls were seldom of stone. The Chinese architect who wanted to plan a building in honour of some divine being—it might be Buddha, or Confucius, or Lao Tze, or some local spirit—was rather apt to think in terms of pagodas, a pagoda being a tower formed of many storeys, each a little smaller than the one below. At Foochow there is a seven-storeyed pagoda built as long ago as the ninth century.

> Though very few really ancient temples or palaces remain in the land, there are many very ancient walls—walls built round cities, and walls built as a barrier against invasion. Most famous of these is the Great Wall of China, which measures, if you include all its windings, about one thousand five hundred miles from end to end, and was begun in the third century before Christ. It is from twenty to thirty feet high, and every two hundred yards stands a forty-foot tower; at the base it is from fifteen to twenty-five feet thick.[1]

During the centuries when Christendom was under the heel of barbarian invaders another type of civilization was growing up in the Near East—the Islamic type. We have already had something to say about Islam in the chapters on the worker in clay and the worker in wood, and you will remember that, as Mohammed forbade his followers to make images of living things, Islamic art developed along lines quite different from pagan and Christian art. The earliest Arab conquerors who invaded North Africa, Egypt, and South-western Europe were nomads, but by the ninth and tenth centuries their descendants were dwelling in magnificent houses, with fountains, and fish-ponds, and gardens, and were worshipping Allah in mosques as beautiful, in their own way, as any Greek temple or Christian church.

The horseshoe arch and the dome are both characteristic of Islamic architecture. Inside the houses of the rich, in Cairo and Baghdad, Granada and Palermo, mosaic was much used for ornament, and ceilings were decorated with fretted sandal-wood inlaid with ivory or mother-of-pearl. Islamic builders made free use of coloured stones and of brilliantly tinted tiles. They usually stuck to

---

[1] D. M. Stuart, *The Book of Other Lands*, p. 14 (Harrap).

The Sculptor and the Builder

the Oriental idea of a central courtyard—hence the *patio*, so characteristic of both Moorish and Spanish houses up to our own time.

When arts and sciences began once more to flourish in Western Europe Charlemagne, the Emperor of the Franks, encouraged sculptors and masons with rich gifts. They carved for him in ivory

GATE OF TEHERAN

and in alabaster stiff, stately images of saints and heroes; they built him mighty palaces, with pillared halls and painted ceilings; but they were imitators rather than creators, and for their inspiration they turned to contemporary Byzantium and ancient Rome.

In England, though the Anglo-Saxons when once Christianized built some fine, sturdy churches and monasteries, their domestic architecture was very rough and simple, and their houses commonly made of wood. For quite a long time after the Norman conquest the houses and shops forming the streets of London City were either partially or wholly built of lath and plaster—hence the many disastrous fires which ravaged the homes of the citizens.

The Book of Craftsmen

The English manor-house in the earlier Plantagenet period was usually planned on very simple lines around a large central hall where the whole household would assemble for meals. The walls would be of stone, the roof of timber. Barns, stables, sleeping-apartments, and outhouses were grouped in a somewhat scrambling, haphazard manner round the hall, and before the time of

HALL OF FOURTEENTH-CENTURY MANOR-HOUSE

Henry III there was very little attempt at beauty of decoration. About that time people who desired to be a little more refined and fashionable than their neighbours took to sheathing their cold stone walls with painted wainscot; glass began to replace wooden slats in the window-openings, and the solar chamber came into being. This was so called because its larger windows admitted more of the sun's light. It was the forerunner of our modern drawing-room. Here the lady of the manor could seek refuge from the clamour of the great hall, and do elaborate embroidery, and play interminable games of chess.

The fortified castle, with moat, drawbridge, portcullis, and outer and inner wards, was a stronghold quite as much as a dwelling-place, and its masonry was stout and crude. The actual building

The Sculptor and the Builder

materials would, of course, depend upon whether there were any quarries in the neighbourhood, and also upon what sort of stone they would afford. Brick, so well known to the ancients and used with such excellent results by the Romans in Britain, was hardly employed at all during the early medieval period. The Roman craftsmen were wont to insert layers of thin red bricks between

CRUSADERS BUILDING A WALL

courses of larger stone, of flint, or of rubble. The French got ahead of the English in reviving brickwork in their domestic architecture, so that it not infrequently happened during the Hundred Years War that a band of English knights, familiar only with stone-built castles and manor-houses, would capture a brick-built French fortress, and would be so much impressed that on their return home they would set about erecting similar buildings for themselves. Then the bricklayer took his place among the craftsmen of the land. In the matter of laying his bricks he was largely influenced by the mason, one of the most conservative of craftsmen, whose methods of setting 'courses' of stones above one another so as to form walls have varied little in four thousand

The Book of Craftsmen

years. Some idea of these methods may be obtained from the quaint little French picture of crusaders constructing a fortress in the Holy Land. You see a pulley with a windlass for raising stones and mortar; you see one busy fellow with a hammer and another with a trowel. A third is testing the straightness of the half-built wall with a plumb-line. Their activities are directed by a very scornful-looking person in a regal head-dress.

It not infrequently happened during the wars between France and England that Englishmen gained not only new ideas but the wherewithal to put them into execution. This he got from the heavy ransoms paid by the French nobles whom he captured. A goodly proportion of this ransom-money must have passed into the rabbit-skin pouches clasped with pewter which hung at the girdles of the masons and the bricklayers. *Their* houses were little better than shacks. Each was made with the aid of four stakes, some willow-wicker, some clay, and, to crown all, some straw, heather, or osier-boughs for thatch. 'Wattle-and-daub' is the name given to this kind of construction.

WINDOW OF CHURCH OF D'AULNAY

Long before men thought of building beautiful—as distinct from strong or serviceable—dwellings for themselves they had learned to make glorious habitations for God. In western Europe churches, especially monastery churches, were often built by monks and priests. It is recorded of St Hugh of Lincoln in the twelfth century that during the erection of the famous Angel Choir he carried a hod like any other labourer, and the monks of Gloucester aided actively in the production of the fine roof of their nave.

The Sculptor and the Builder

But the help of professional masons was also enlisted, and it was they who left upon their handiwork the 'masons' marks' which one may still find here and there in ancient churches.

These marks are of two kinds. The first is the sort of mark

FAÇADE OF SIENA CATHEDRAL

which the stonemason chipped upon the stone before it was carted away, a mark which served the purpose of a signature, and showed by whom the job had been done. Such marks are of great variety, and include rough outlines resembling fishes, suns and moons, twigs and towers. The second sort of mark was used to indicate the position in which the stone was to be placed, and was often a mere notch.

As a skilled craftsman, whose handiwork was constantly in

The Book of Craftsmen

demand, the mason—with whom we must include the bricklayer—enjoyed a better status than did the poor serf tilling the soil. He might rise to be a master-mason, a very responsible post, of which the holder was an architect, a contractor, and a foreman all in one. Whenever what we should now call a 'big contract' was being carried out gangs of masons would be drafted to the spot, and would get to work there, living in a sort of mushroom village of hastily erected huts. They had to be free-born men, not serfs or vassals, otherwise they would not have been able to move about from place to place owing to the feudal law which kept the vassal tied to the soil on which he was born. They had to have some knowledge of reading and writing. Some of the Roman-British labourers working in *Londinium Augusta* certainly had some knowledge of those arts, otherwise how could one of them have scratched on the wet mortar this satirical remark about a fellow-workman—*Augustalis takes a day off every fortnight*!

Compared with modern standards of comfort, the daily life of a medieval labourer in England would seem bleak and wretched enough. He had no minimum wage, no sickness benefit, no bank holidays, no unemployment insurance (though it must be remembered that he was seldom out of work), no cinema, no football matches (except those in which he took part himself), no char-a-bancs, and no tobacco! On the other hand, he was pretty sure of regular employment; his craft-guilds did for him many of the things which the modern trade union does for its members, and even a few, such as looking after his soul in the next world, which it does *not* do. There were no bank holidays, but the feasts of the Church were marked by a rest from toil and by general merry-makings, and such fell more frequently in the medieval year than bank holidays do in *ours*.

That the medieval English craftsman resembled in many respects his descendant and 'opposite number' of twentieth-century England we may guess from the particulars which have been preserved concerning the masons employed at Cambridge five hundred years ago. They were fined if they came late to work,

The Sculptor and the Builder

damaged their tools, quarrelled with their fellows, or idled during working hours. One of them, it is recorded, would never work at all unless he happened to be in a working humour; another, whose name was Robert Goodgroom, was such a stickler for his dinner-hour that never, under any circumstances, would he take up his tools and 'set to' again until the clock should "smyte."

The mason led a less healthy life than the field-labourer, partly because he had to lodge so often in a rickety shack, travel so far through swamps and along perilous roads, and inhale so much

MASONS AND SCULPTORS AT WORK

stone-dust while working. The supply of masons was seldom equal to the demand, and in the fourteenth century the overseers of royal works had the power forcibly to enrol the men whom they needed for the king's service. Some idea of the numbers required for building a castle may be gathered from the roll of workmen engaged at Beaumaris: four hundred skilled masons, one thousand unskilled labourers, two hundred carters, and thirty smiths and carpenters!

During frosty weather tools were 'downed,' and the half-finished masonry would be snugly covered up by turf or thatch. Scaffolding was usually of wicker, and men worked at dizzy heights upon projecting platforms of woven osier. The prepared stone, having been carted, often by oxen, from the nearest quarry, or from the nearest quay, was borne upon shallow wheelbarrows almost like sledges or carried between two men on a sort of wooden stretcher. If we may believe contemporary illuminated pictures

The Book of Craftsmen

the masons of the Middle Ages wore gaily-hued tunics, and worked with their sleeves rolled up and their stockings rolled down.

In the fourteenth century the London builders made a regulation to protect employers from bad workmanship. A mason who had undertaken a contract had to produce six other masons willing to swear that he was a skilful craftsman, and also willing to complete the contract on his behalf if he should leave it unfinished.

Hours varied according to the season of the year, and were longer in summer and shorter in winter, daylight being so necessary to the workers. They were usually allowed twenty minutes for breakfast, an hour for dinner, and a short pause for a drink in the afternoon. But of course the drink would not *then* be the now inevitable cup of tea! Wages were not reckoned by the hour, but by the day, the week, or even by the year. Rates of pay varied. In 1275 a London mason received 5*d*. a day in summer and 3*d*. in winter, larger sums then than now.

TWO STATUES IN CHARTRES

Though little or nothing was done to decorate the interior of even a very great lord's dwelling-place, much was done to make beautiful the interiors of the numerous churches, large and small, which sprang up all over Europe between the close of the Dark Ages and the dawn of the Reformation. In this task the maker of stained-glass windows, the wood-carver, and the stone-carver collaborated.

The sculptor of the medieval period was employed chiefly to carve images of saints and angels for churches or effigies of knights and ladies for tombs; statues were not used as ornaments either in houses or in public places. The custom of erecting a statue to some famous personage did not then exist, and our forefathers

The Sculptor and the Builder

would be much surprised if they could visit our modern cities and contemplate Victorian gentlemen in bronze or marble, complete with side-whiskers, trousers, and elastic-sided boots! The only background against which you would have been likely to see carved people who were neither immortal saints and angels nor dead men and women would be ranged in canopied niches along the façade of some great town hall or guild hall. Such halls were more common on the Continent than in Great Britain, as witness the famous Cloth Hall at Ypres, destroyed in the War, and the still-existing Hôtel de Ville at Brussels.

Each country had its own school of sculpture reflecting the natural genius of the people. Italy was far ahead of the others in technique, and Italian sculptors were producing really lifelike and faithful images at a period when farther north only stiff and conventional dolls were to be seen. There is, however, a certain charm in those doll-like creatures, such as those clustered round the great north porches of Amiens, Bourges, and Chartres. You will remember that in speaking of the Greek sculptors of the primitive period we had something to say about the 'archaic smile.' Now here is *another* archaic smile, appearing and reappearing on the faces of the Virgin Mary and her attendant saints and angels in French religious sculpture of the thirteenth century. French sculptors were skilful in their craft, and they soon learned a more free,

STATUE OF MUSICIAN AT RHEIMS

The Book of Craftsmen

truthful, and natural method of treating their human models; some of the quite early French statues are delightfully living and lively.

LA VIERGE DORÉE OF AMIENS

English sculptors were not so fond of twisting the carved lips into a smirk. They grouped their figures in less closely serried ranks, and gave them a sort of quiet dignity—as witness the west front of Wells Cathedral, sometimes called a Bible in Stone. As we saw when considering the worker in wood, the earliest recorded instance of an English craftsman using a living model was in the fourteenth century at the Abbey of Meaux. English architects, however, like their brethren in France, Flanders, Germany, and Austria, had long drawn their inspiration from Nature—hence those wonderful Norman naves, with their pillars like the trunks of mighty trees, and later that lovely vaulting, with its soaring curves like the mingling of leafless branches high overhead.

In addition to figures for altar-screens, porches, and tombs, the medieval sculptor had to carve lacy pinnacle-tops, or quaint capitals for pillars; he had to carve bosses for the intersecting points of the vaulting, and the stone tracery in which the glazier fitted richly coloured glass. Some of the designs were as unexpected as those on the miserere seats described in Chapter III. In the south aisle of the choir at Wells, for example, near the tomb of a bishop called William de Button, whose relics were reputed to cure toothache, many of the capitals of the pillars are adorned with human faces representing sufferers with agonized expressions and swollen cheeks, some of them nursing their jaws in their

GARGOYLE

The Sculptor and the Builder

hands. In the Temple Church, London, there are carvings of men sneezing, yawning, and grimacing. Queer, curly monsters often writhe and grin round the tops of pillars, or wimpled ladies, or cowled monks, or crowned kings peer down from them. The

NOAH BUILDING THE ARK
Wells Cathedral.

gargoyles, the weird, monstrous figures either used at the terminals of gutters to carry off rainwater from the roofs or as ornaments to the external pinnacles and buttresses, were, as we should now say, 'in a class by themselves.' French sculptors excelled in these 'shudder-making' designs, and one of the most famous of their creations is the demon who sits on the roof of Nôtre Dame de Paris and gazes across the smoky wilderness of the city to the silver gleam of the Seine and the green smudge of wooded hills far away.

The Book of Craftsmen

The stone-carver who worked in Protestant countries after the Reformation in the fifteenth and sixteenth centuries had few saintly or divine models—if any—but plenty of human ones. People took to having images of their children as well as themselves on their tombs, and then rows of dumpy little figures, some of them in swaddling bands, were grouped round their large, impressive parents. The craftsman of the Tudor period excelled in reproducing the elaborate folds of the ruffs which were then worn, and the same desire for realism led him to take great pains with the mats or rugs upon which his models lay, as if in slumber, their hands folded palm to palm. There is a tradition that if a knight was represented with a lion at his feet it showed that he had died in battle; if, on the other hand, he had a hound instead of a lion it meant that he had died peacefully in his bed. No doubt this was often, though not invariably, the case. Here is a picture in words of just such an effigy:

> Grey dust lies on his battered face,
>   The glories of his shield are dim;
> Half vanished are the words of grace
>   Beseeching pity and peace for him
>   Along the purbeck rim.
>
> His hands are folded palm to palm
>   (Some fingers lacking on the right),
> And at his peakèd feet the calm
>   Old lion shows he fell in fight
>   As best became a knight.[1]

The 'purbeck' here mentioned is a variety of dark freshwater limestone thickly speckled with the fossilized shells of the *Paludina carinifera* family, and it was extensively quarried on the Dorsetshire coast at the place from which it takes its name. Before it could be worked upon with a chisel it had to be smoothed with sand and vinegar, after which it took a glossy polish, and looked very lovely.

As we have remarked already, the materials used by the sculptor and the stonemason were, as a rule, brought from the quarries

---

[1] D. M. Stuart, *Historical Songs and Ballads*, p. 72 (Harrap).

HORSESHOE ARCHES IN THE ALCAZAR AT SEVILLE
Photo E.N.A.

TOMB OF CHARLES THE BOLD AT BRUGES
Photo E.N.A.

The Sculptor and the Builder

nearest to the place where they were employed. Sometimes, however, these materials were found in other countries. Such was the fine, cream-coloured limestone shipped to England from Caen in Normandy. Sandstone from the northern and western English shires was carted to districts where there were none, but builders, not unnaturally, were inclined to draw upon the supplies that lay most ready to their hands—flint and chalk in Kent, magnesian limestone in Yorkshire, oolitic limestone in Somerset, Wiltshire, and Lincoln. In Scotland there were rosy-red sandstone, golden-grey limestone, and glittering granite, pink or grey. The Italian craftsman had at his command marbles of many dazzling and delicate colours.

For smaller figures, such as those in altar-pieces and votive panels, English sculptors of the fourteenth and fifteenth centuries turned to the deposits of alabaster found in some parts of the Midlands. Their handiwork, though to modern eyes it seems quaint rather than beautiful, was in much demand, and was even exported to the Continent. After the Reformation the demand and the supply both came to an end, and alabaster was used for large effigies of mortals instead of for small images of saints.

Stone-carvers became fewer and fewer in number as the years passed; they tended to split into two main divisions, the sculptor, who was an artist, and often a famous one, and the monumental mason, whose productions were conventional and standardized. Great sculptors such as Donatello, Michelangelo, and Jean Goujèon do not belong to this book, which treats of the doings of the average craftsman, not of the exceptional genius. As for the monumental mason, a curious change came over the ideas governing his work as the eighteenth century moved on its rather pompous way. Effigies, whether marking actual graves or merely set up as memorials, became more and more stiff and self-conscious. Instead of a figure lying as if asleep or kneeling as if in prayer you find an image standing bolt upright, often with one hand stretched out in a most dignified manner, as if the owner of the hand were making a speech. Upon the faces of these statues

The Book of Craftsmen

there is usually an expression strongly suggestive of Jack Horner's famous "What a good boy am I!" Then, too, it was necessary for the sculptor to drape his subjects in Roman togas, or encase them in Roman armour if he was asked to do so. Occasionally the full-bottomed wig of the period was retained, with comical effect!

Curious, too, was the effect produced by memorial effigies of a very different type in the remote Polynesian island called by the natives Rapanui, and by geographers Easter Island. These images, hewn out of compressed volcanic ash, vary in height from three to thirty-six feet, and are very weird-looking, with their deep, hollow eyes and grim, sphinx-like faces. Strangest of all are those whose heads are surmounted by tall cylindrical hats carved out of red volcanic tuff, quite different in colour from that of which the monuments themselves are made. Many mysteries cling round this remote speck of an island, not the least of them being the mystery as to how the native craftsmen quarried, carved, and transported the stone. We know only that they used stone chisels, and did their carving near the quarry.

As for the builder, whether he worked in brick or stone, the conditions of his life altered far more than the methods of his work after the Reformation broke up all the ancient trade-guilds. Pneumatic drills and travelling cranes have made things quicker and easier in these days, and trade unions have gone some way towards affording to labouring folk the protection once given by their craft-fraternities; but you still see the mortar being slapped with the trowel, the shovel being driven into the earth, the bricks or stones being shouldered on a hod or wheeled in a barrow, just as Pharaoh's overseers saw those things being done in the Thebes of 2000 B.C., or Geoffrey Chaucer, poet and clerk of the King's works, saw them being done at Windsor in the fourteenth century of the Christian era.

CHAPTER VI

THE TAILOR AND THE HATTER

I SUPPOSE that Adam and Eve, when they made themselves aprons of fig-leaves, were the first tailor and tailoress in the world! It is certain that for many centuries after man had begun to make garments wherewith to clothe himself each man was his own tailor, furrier, cobbler, and capper. No doubt the cave-dweller received a good deal of help from the women of his family, who would scrape and prepare the hides used for raiment, and sew them together with needles made from thorns or bones and threads made from animal sinews or vegetable fibres; but the father of the family, who had slain the beast from which the hide had been taken, doubtless had much to do with the fashioning of his own flapping leather tunic. Oddly enough, the making of a man's clothes has almost always been a man's job. The woman spins and weaves; the man cuts out, shapes, plans, and often stitches together. The very word 'tailor' means some one who *cuts*. In French it is *tailleur*, and the verb is *tailler*, to cut: in German it is *schneider*, and the verb is *schneiden*, to cut. And perhaps the shaggy-headed cave-man was quite as particular about the line of his shaggy-fringed cape or jacket as the dandy of later days was about the 'set' of his satin cloak, or the curve of his padded doublet.

The craft of clothing man's body falls into three divisions. He needs a covering for his head—hence the evolution of the hatter, capper, and helmet-maker; he needs a covering for his feet—hence the evolution of the sandal-maker, the shoe-maker, and the cobbler; he needs a covering for his body—hence the evolution of the tailor.

Many long years passed, and people gradually advanced beyond

The Book of Craftsmen

that rough stage of culture in which they used only stone weapons, and wore only the skins of beasts. By slow degrees they invented the various crafts which make life easier and more pleasant. And by dint of practising these crafts they arrived at new methods and new processes which increased the strength, the usefulness, and often the beauty of the things they wrought with their hands.

In an earlier chapter we have seen how the arts of spinning and weaving developed. Now we shall glance at some of the uses to which men put the stuffs spun and woven by women. The earliest use was, naturally, to protect the human frame from heat, cold, or rain. You might think that under a scorching sun it would be better to wear no clothes at all, and a great many savage people in far-off countries still think the same. But other dwellers in torrid zones, such as the Arabs and the Moors, find in their ample cloaks and elaborate headdresses a valuable protection from the blaze of sunshine under which they live.

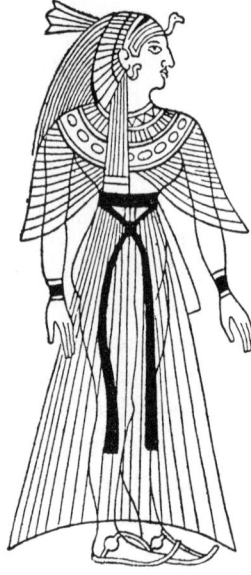

COSTUME OF A LADY OF ANCIENT EGYPT

The ancient Egyptians and Babylonians certainly wore somewhat scanty garments. The Sumerians, their neighbours, preferred rather substantial, blanket-like cloaks with fringed edges. The Egyptians seem usually to have gone about with little or no covering upon their heads, except the kings, who wore diadems, and the priests and scribes, who wore wigs. The men favoured skirts of pleated linen, and the women filmy dresses of stuff so fine that we should call it muslin, or even gauze. Often the linen and the muslin were bleached white; sometimes they would be their natural creamy-tawny colour; or they might be dyed purple, crimson, or blue, or have stiff, angular patterns woven into them. The tailors of ancient Peru must have had good

The Tailor and the Hatter

eyesight and nimble fingers, for their wealthy patrons sported raiment thickly sewn with small, brilliant feathers arranged in geometrical patterns.

There were always, and in all countries, certain differences between a man's clothes and a woman's, but it was not until comparatively late in human history that the distinction arose which has now for many centuries existed in most civilized countries—the difference between the man in his trousers, breeches, knickerbockers, pants, or whatever you choose to call them, and the woman in her petticoat and skirt. This distinction did not begin among the most advanced races, and it is tending to grow less clear nowadays when so many women go in for work and for sport on equal terms with men. Still, speaking broadly, we may say that in the antique world both sexes wore flowing robes, and neither wore anything resembling trousers, while in the modern world, from the end of the Dark Ages down to our own time, men have worn garments defining their lower limbs, while women have worn garments veiling them.

AN AMAZON
Note the Phrygian cap.

So, then, the tailors of Egypt and Babylon, Athens and Rome never had to cut out trousers for their patrons! They might have been sorely puzzled had they been asked to do so, for to cut out pleated kilts, flowing robes, or sweeping mantles must have been comparatively simple, and little or no stitching together was needed.

It was the Scythians, Dacians, Sarmatians, Parthians, and other barbarous or semi-barbarous peoples from whom the Greeks and the Romans learned to wear the leg-coverings later adopted by almost all non-barbarians. Oddly enough, those women-warriors of classical legend, the Amazons, were usually represented in ancient art as wearing trousers " made of the skins of animals " or of " rich and fine tissues, embroidered or painted in sprigs, spots, stripes, checks, zig-zags, or other ornaments," but only when on the warpath. At other times they were believed to wear ordinary feminine attire. One wonders whether they employed men-tailors to make their trousers, or whether they would have thought it beneath their dignity as Amazons!

The Greek tailor's chief task was to make the *chiton*, the *chlamys*, the *himation*, and the *peplum* or *peplos*—the four garments most favoured by his patrons. In Sparta costume was scanty, and no great skill was demanded of those who fashioned it. In Ionia, the home of the Ionic column, Oriental influence made people incline to rich and delicate stuffs and fine stitchery.

THE HIMATION

The *chiton* was worn next the skin, and was very simple in design, consisting of two squares of wool, linen, or silk, sewn up the sides, openings being left for the head and arms. This garment formed the first item in the clothing of both men and women, though stern philosophers sometimes rejected it, and wore the long cloak called the *himation* over their bare skins. Women wore the *chiton* very long, and looped it up over a narrow girdle; over this, when they went abroad or when they took part in solemn ceremonies, they draped a shawl-like wrap called a *peplum*, which could be pulled up over the head so as to form a hood. Tiny metal weights were sewn to the corners of the *peplum*, so that it should hang in graceful folds, and not flap about.

Gods and heroes when travelling, and simple country folk, preferred a short cloak called a *chlamys* to the long *himation*.

The Tailor and the Hatter

This is the cloak worn by the Apollo Belvedere; and the god Hermes, so constantly 'on the road,' also appears in art wearing it.

In the meantime, what had people been wearing on their heads? It is curious to have to answer, "Well, very often nothing at all!" Primitive man had usually such a dense thatch of hair on his scalp that he would not find it necessary to invent any sort of hat or cap. In Egypt, as we have seen, hats seem to have been unknown, though wigs were frequently worn by the official classes, and the Pharaoh sported a magnificent double diadem, probably much less heavy than it looked. Egyptian ladies of high degree sometimes wore a sort of veil, held in place by a circlet of gold. The

GREEK GIRL WEARING CHITON AND PEPLUM

Sumerians and Babylonians seem to have favoured close-fitting caps, perhaps of wool, but we must remind ourselves that when we are looking at ancient pictures or carvings we may mistake helmets for caps, and give to the cap-maker credit really due to the armourer. At a very early date there seems to have been some connexion in men's minds between sacred or royal authority and the headgear worn by men wielding such authority: thence came the king's crown, the bishop's mitre, the judge's wig, the admiral's cocked hat. Babylonian kings are shown with fillets round their brows, holding their stiff, oily, black tresses in position, but these were probably made by the goldsmith, and so do not belong to this chapter. Cretan ladies wore bands of coloured wool round their dark locks, and Etruscan ladies draped veils of fine embroidered linen over their heads; but it is among the Greeks that we shall find the earliest traces of hats and caps well enough developed for us to feel they must have been produced by

The Book of Craftsmen

professional hatters and cappers. Travellers, shepherds, and others whose pursuits exposed them much to the weather wore a flat, shallow, broad-brimmed hat, the *petasus*, tied under the chin with strings, and slung back over the shoulders when not needed; seafarers affected a conical, brimless cap, less likely to be swept away by sudden gusts of wind. In Bœotia ladies wore hide hats, with crowns rising to such a sharp peak that it seems a marvel how they kept them on, even with the aid of strings.

GREEK HORSEMAN WEARING THE PETASUS AND CHLAMYS

Perhaps the most famous of all the varieties of headgear known in the antique world was the Phrygian cap, a red woollen cap with a peak towards the front. It became a highly symbolic object, for when a slave of ancient Rome received his liberty the Phrygian cap was solemnly placed upon his head, and for this reason the leaders of the French Revolution adopted the 'cap of liberty' as a sort of 'outward and visible sign' of their Republican principles.

The earliest craftsman to fashion head-coverings was probably one who worked in wool, and made simple, close-fitting caps. Then would come the worker in straw or other fibre, weaving and plaiting his brittle material into something we can call a hat. The art of making felt out of wool, fur, and hair, soaked and squeezed together, came next, and we know that the Greeks and the Romans used this fabric pretty extensively. It is mentioned by Pliny and by Xenophon.

In the matter of costume, as in many others, the Romans closely followed the Greeks, but they seem to have borrowed their most characteristic garment, the *toga*, from the Etruscans. This is said at one time, in the earlier and simpler days of Rome, to have been

The Tailor and the Hatter

worn by people of both sexes and all classes; but as one writer upon the subject suggests the women abandoned it "because they loved novelty," and the working folk because the long folds hampered them in their work. Even at a much later date the *toga prætexta*, the toga with the purple hem, was worn by both boys and girls, though only by those of free birth.

THE TOGA

It is interesting to realize that the only grown-up people who had the right to wear this garment were the priests and the magistrates chosen to offer sacrifices to the gods on behalf of the State. From this it is clear that the *toga prætexta* had a religious significance, and that it was given to children not only because they served as *camilli* (acolytes) before the shrines of the household gods, but also as a symbol of unsullied holiness and innocence.

How important this purple-edged toga was as a sign of free birth may be seen from an anecdote which a famous teacher of law told his students. . . . A company of slave-merchants were landing a boatload of slaves at Brundusium. Among the slaves was an unusually beautiful and intelligent boy, for whom the slavers hoped to get a very large sum of money. But they were a little nervous lest the customs-house officers should seize him. So before they took the boy ashore they hung a golden amulet round his neck and wrapped him in the *toga prætexta* of the free-born child. When afterwards they brought him to Rome to be sold it was declared that by giving him these recognized tokens of freedom they had made him free, and had therefore no further rights over him according to the laws of Rome.[1]

The toga was always made of wool. At first this was its own natural colour, a tawny white, though later it might be bleached a pure white, or dyed in various hues. Knights wore a striped purple-and-white toga, the *trabea*, and victorious commanders making a state entry into Rome wore a toga entirely of purple.

In shape this garment closely resembled the Greek *himation*.

[1] D. M. Stuart, *The Boy through the Ages*, pp. 78–79 (Harrap).

The Book of Craftsmen

It was more or less semicircular, the straight edge being some six yards long, while the width in the centre was about two yards. One end was usually flung over the left shoulder with the straight edge close to the middle of the wearer's body and the point nearly trailing on the ground. The rounded extremity would just cover the left hand. The rest of the *toga* was then drawn behind the back, either over or under the right arm, and then again over the left shoulder, so that the peak hung low behind.

Though, strictly speaking, the tailor had little or nothing to do with the making of women's clothes among the ancient Greeks and Romans, we must not in this chapter neglect the wives and daughters of those long-dead worthies. Here again Roman taste was influenced by Greek, for in Rome ladies wore a long tunic called a *stola*, and over it a mantle, the *palla*, not unlike the Greek *peplum*.

The centuries rolled on, the barbarians overthrew the pride and might of Rome, and the fashion of men's habits gradually altered in the West and in the Near East. In the East and the Far East such fashions have altered hardly at all with the passing of time. The tailor of Baghdad in the days of Haroun-al-Raschid made just the same kind of baggy breeches, sleeveless waistcoats, and long, close-fitting coats as the tailor of Baghdad made in the days of Shah-Nazr-ed-Din, at the end of the nineteenth century. In our own time the barriers created by old-fashioned national costumes are tending to disappear, and Turks and Chinamen, Arabs and Persians, Hindus and Japanese, are abandoning their often beautiful and becoming traditional dress in favour of the lounge suit and the bowler hat!

In the West, on the other hand, fashions have always changed at more or less regular intervals, and though it may seem at first

ROMAN MATRON
WEARING THE
STOLA AND PALLA

The Tailor and the Hatter

glance as if men's clothes had ceased to do so, it is only necessary to turn up some old volumes of *Punch* or the *Illustrated London News* to see that the cut of coats, waistcoats, and trousers, and the shape of 'toppers,' bowlers, and soft hats, *has* varied, even if only a little and by slow degrees. In the olden days men's fashions were quite as violently variable as women's—and sometimes even more so.

THE VICTORIAN 'TOPPER'
Punch cartoon by John Leech.

Let us turn back to the Dark Ages for a moment, and think what the tailor had to do among the Scandinavian and Teutonic tribes then harrying Christendom. Among the Norsemen the fashioning of the men's garments was probably done by the women. Tailoring is not mentioned among the 'nine accomplishments' which the Norse warrior had to master! But when the sea-kings were absent on their long voyages, far from their womenkind, they must have done the 'running repairs' to their warm woollen tunics,

The Book of Craftsmen

their short cloaks, and their long woollen trousers. Sailors are proverbially handy with their fingers, and after a successful raid on a Christian monastery the amateur tailors in the dragon-prowed ships would be quite capable of adapting embroidered copes and clerical mantles as garments for themselves and their companions. On occasions of ceremony, such as the giving of a name to an infant, the Norsemen wore cloaks lined with fur, and the seams of their highly coloured tunics were sewn with glinting threads of gold. Hats and caps, black, grey, or white, made of wool, were pulled over the Norseman's long (and often carefully combed) locks when he went out of doors.

As was the case with many other crafts, that of the tailor became specialized as people tended more and more to live in large villages and then in towns. The old, simple days, when a man's clothes—and his wife's too—were woven, spun, shaped, and sewn by members of his own household, passed by, and though this state of affairs lingered on in remote country districts life in general became more complicated, and men split up into various groups and carried on various trades, and so from the crafts of the home came the crafts of the workshop and the workroom, and from these (though this hardly concerns us here) came the vast industries now housed in huge, humming factories.

Early in the medieval period we find the craft of the tailor so well established in England that already its practisers are alluded to as such in Latin documents. In 1296 there is mention of a man whose name was Richard Masham, but who was called 'the Taylur,' and a year later it is clear that in most towns of any importance there was a special street almost entirely tenanted by 'taylurs.'

Tailors in these old times were men of many accomplishments. They made not only outer garments, but what we should now call 'underwear' and even 'lingerie'—as those items of attire were then understood. They made the tents and pavilions used at tournaments; they made the padded and quilted suits often worn by knights under their armour, and for this reason were sometimes

The Tailor and the Hatter

called 'linen-armourers'; and they made the long, trouser-like 'hosen' worn by most classes, except the clergy, all through the Middle Ages.

It was towards the end of the thirteenth century that the tailor of Western Europe found himself compelled to do more careful and skilful 'cutting' than ever before. For you must have noticed that throughout the earlier ages of the world's history men draped themselves in flowing garments, which, though very graceful, required little or no shaping, and were not intended either to follow or to reveal the natural lines of the body. About the time when the great English cathedrals were being built, and when the two great English Universities of Oxford and Cambridge were coming into existence, a change swept over fashions in costume, a change which had far-reaching effects on the craft of the tailor. This change, seeming slight and unimportant enough at first (as important changes often do), led to the substitution of the tunic moulded closely to the figure for the longer and looser garment in favour till then. Slowly the tunics grew tighter and shorter, to the alarm of seniors, old-fashioned people, who thought that these new-fangled ideas were most frivolous and wild. The sleeves, however, grew wider and longer, and were often ornamented with scalloped or indented edges called 'daggings.' Here again the tailor had to acquire new skill. He had to learn to 'dag' in the manner approved by the dandies of the Court. Presently he had to learn how to attach short pleated skirts to the tunics, and how to pad the tunics over the chest so as to give the wearer the appearance of a pouter-pigeon. He had to learn to sew on tiny buttons in neat rows!

Meanwhile it happened quite often that the tailor's wife made garments for the wives of his noble patrons. If she and his daughters were deft embroidresses the family calling was probably a profitable one for them all.

Let us turn now to the maker of caps and hats. He too had been striking out for himself and developing his craft. During the earlier part of the Middle Ages the wearing of hats was practically confined to the working classes, who wore them *over* their

The Book of Craftsmen

chaperons or *chapelaines*—woollen hoods with a peak behind and a hole in front, to let the face peep out, and deep collars covering the neck and part of the shoulders. The upper classes also wore hoods, but chiefly caps of many forms and colours. Pilgrims, especially palmers, sometimes wore hats, in which they stuck cockle-shells, or palm-leaves, or badges of brass or pewter showing what famous shrines they had visited. Night-caps were worn by all—it would have been considered very dangerous to go to sleep bareheaded, though to judge from many old carvings and illuminations gentlemen often went hunting, or walking in their gardens, or rode abroad, without any covering at all on their heads. The caps they *did* wear looked often like close-fitting bonnets!

KNIGHT WITH DAGGED SLEEVES

By the time we reach the fifteenth century, however, the great ones of the earth are beginning to adopt hats, usually of two colours, the brim being folded up in front to show the lining. Blue lined with white or red lined with blue seem to have been favourite schemes. Caps grew very lofty, had turned-up edges fitting closely round the foreheads of the wearers, and were often ornamented with very beautiful buckles, brooches, or clasps. And then came a quaint-looking type of hat not unlike the modern bowler, but tilted up at the back, the brim being pulled down over the eyes in front. This was often black in colour, with a clasp or a little tuft of gold.

TYPES OF HATS

(1) A fourteenth-century ploughman. (2) A fourteenth-century gentleman. (3) The fifteenth-century 'bowler.' (4) An Elizabethan dandy. (5) Early seventeenth century. (6) A Puritan hat. (7) An eighteenth-century Frenchman. (8) A nineteenth-century 'stovepipe.'

The Book of Craftsmen

The old English name for a maker of hats and caps was a 'hurrer,' that is to say, a 'hairer,' the hair of certain animals being used, as we have seen, to make felt. In London the men of this craft belonged to the Fraternity of St Catherine, and received a charter from Henry VI; later, in the time of Henry VIII, they joined forces with the haberdashers, the dealers in ribbons, buttons, pins, and all sorts of odds and ends imported from foreign lands. Nowadays we think of a 'milliner' as a person who makes or sells ladies' hats, but in earlier days the word meant very much the same thing as 'haberdasher,' and it came—as many of their wares came—from Milan. Thus, a 'milliner' was originally a 'Milaner,' and had not any particular connexion with hats.

St Clement was the patron saint of the felt-makers, and they boldly ascribed the invention of felt to him, though, as already mentioned, this substance was well known in the antique world. According to the medieval legend, the Saint, tramping along in his sandals over pebbly roads, had the happy thought of slipping some rabbits' fur between the sole of the foot and the sandal. At the end of a long walk he had trodden it into felt!

In these days, when everybody calls everybody else a 'gentleman,' we should not be very much impressed by the following story, but it is quaint enough to deserve re-telling, and the fact remains that journeymen-hatters are still described as 'gentlemen' in their own trade. Tradition says that they owe this privilege to Queen Elizabeth, who, visiting her good city of London on one occasion, was welcomed in Holborn by "a great congregation of well-dressed men wearing polished beaver hats." They were the hatters of Southwark and Blackfriars, and the Queen, pleasantly struck by their jaunty looks, asked "who these gentlemen were." When told that they were journeymen-hatters she remarked, "Such journeymen must be gentlemen."

A 'journeyman,' by the way, is a man who, having served an apprenticeship, is fully qualified to 'ply his craft,' but works *by the day* (French, *journée*) for a master. Probably the earliest 'apprentice' was a son learning from his father some art or craft which that

The Tailor and the Hatter

father, in turn, had learned from *his* father, but the system of apprenticeship is itself very ancient, and in England we meet it in the Rolls of Parliament of the thirteenth century, as well as in craft-charters and statutes. Seven years was the usual term served by the 'prentice-lad, though in some crafts, and some cities, the term varied between two and ten years. Charitable people left money in their wills to pay for poor boys and girls to be ' bound apprentice,' and during the time of their training the novices were boarded and lodged in the house of their master. The contract between the master and the lad or girl was called an ' indenture,' because it was written in duplicate on a sheet of parchment or vellum, which was then cut asunder with an irregular movement of the scissors—*indented*. If any dispute arose the two halves could be fitted together to demonstrate that here was the original document. This custom still survives!

Many of the guilds were very critical and exacting about candidates for apprenticeship. Thus, the London Clothworkers' Guild would have none who was not " clean of limbs and body, and well formed." At one time the Vintners' was the only company whose apprentices were allowed to wear badges in their caps. In return for lodging and instruction the 'prentice-lad was bound to serve his master faithfully, keep his secrets, regard his interests, and abstain from brawling, tippling, and low company. It sometimes happened that a boy became famous for his skill, and an unscrupulous master might try to tempt him away from the craftsman to whom he had been indentured. This was strictly against guild rules, and anyone detected in such a trick was severely punished.

The Merchant Taylors' Company, one of the most ancient and powerful in the City of London, began as a thirteenth-century guild of ' taylors ' and ' linen-armourers,' whose patron saint was John the Baptist. Edward I, law-giver, crusader, and warrior, formally recognized this guild. Its first recorded Master, Henry de Ryall, and all his successors for nearly a hundred years, bore the title of ' pilgrim,' part of the Master's duties being to go on a

The Book of Craftsmen

pilgrimage on behalf of the whole fraternity. The first charter of the guild was granted by Edward III, who, with his love of pageantry, was a lavish patron not only of the ' linen-armourers ' in their character of makers of raiment but also in their other character as makers of tents and pavilions. It was this king's own pavilion-maker, John of Yakeslee, who in 1331 bought the house which afterwards became the headquarters of the Company.

ARMS OF THE MERCHANT TAYLORS' COMPANY

Richard II, another splendour-loving prince, confirmed his grandfather's grants, but it was Edward IV who gave the Taylors their first coat-of-arms, and Henry VII, the first Tudor monarch, who gave them the title of '*Merchant* Taylors.' The second grant of arms (1586), surmounted by John the Baptist's lamb, shows two mantles and one pavilion or tent, thereby suggesting the twofold occupation of the original brethren. The lion hints at royal patronage, the supporting camels at transactions in distant lands, and the motto, *Concordia parvæ res crescunt*—From peace small things grow (great)—is a wise one, worthy of prudent citizens.

Henry VII elevated the Taylors into Merchant Taylors " in consideration of their having immemorially exercised merchandise in all parts of the globe." They retain the title he gave them, and

THE MERCHANT TAYLORS' HALL
By courtesy of the Merchant Taylors' Company

AN ELIZABETHAN ELEGANT
After a miniature of Sir Philip Sidney by Isaac Oliver.

The Tailor and the Hatter

their great Hall in Threadneedle Street stands on the site of John of Yakeslee's house; the crypt dates back to the fourteenth century, and the lofty kitchen to the fifteenth. The ancient iron spits in this kitchen are still used when feasts are held in the Hall; but the Company no longer makes practical use of the silver yard-stick, bearing its arms, which was once brought forth to measure cloth in any case where a dispute came before it for settlement.

These London tailors were a turbulent crowd in the olden days. In 1226 they had a street-fight with the goldsmiths, in the course of which there was quite a lot of bloodshed. In 1415 it was charged against them that they had " often assembled in great numbers ... and wounded, beaten, and maltreated many lieges of our lord the King."

Even more warlike were the tailors of Exeter, to whom Edward IV, another sovereign who loved fine raiment, gave a charter in 1466. Apparently it was their custom to walk abroad " in the manner of armed warriors, with swords, bucklers, doublets of defence, and wooden staves." Thus armed, they would go and attack any unpopular fellow-citizen *in domo*—in his own house! The City Fathers became alarmed, and sent a deputation to London praying the King to abolish this unruly guild, which his Majesty consented to do. It is recorded that the Mayor of Exeter, the King's two Commissioners, and twenty-four citizens were so much pleased with the result of this appeal that " they joyfully drank wine in the house of Matthew Tubbe, at the expense of the town, to the amount of 8*d*." Eightpence-worth of wine among twenty-seven people does not sound a very generous allowance, especially if they were feeling thirsty, but wine was cheaper in those days and money went further.

The rejoicings in the house of Matthew Tubbe took place a little too soon, for the guild proved too powerful to be abolished. In the end an agreement was reached, and it was allowed to continue its good, though not its evil, deeds. Among the good deeds done by this guild, and many others, were those actions by which the customer was protected from loss through the ignorance or

The Book of Craftsmen

dishonesty of a craftsman. For example, on one occasion an Exeter tailor called John Carter was accused of stealing some cloth. On examination it was decided that he had not stolen any, but that a quarter of the stuff had been wasted " through lack of skill." He was condemned to pay for the cloth—and to take back the gown!

A TAILOR OF THE SIXTEENTH CENTURY

According to an ancient but distorted proverb, " it takes nine tailors to make a man." The origin of this saying is curious, and has nothing whatever to do with the tailoring craft. Nine *tellers*, or strokes of the bell, denoted that the bells were being tolled for a man; three strokes were given to a child, and six to a woman. According to an old tradition, a deputation of eighteen tailors once appeared before Queen Elizabeth, who wittily saluted them with the words, " Good morrow, gentlemen *both*! " There is also a legend that three tailors of Tooley Street, in Southwark, once presented a petition to Parliament beginning, " We, the People of England! "

The Tailor and the Hatter

As the sixteenth century moved on its gorgeous way tailors found themselves confronted with more and more difficult tasks. Daggings had been complicated enough, but now came puffed, and slashed, and padded doublets and breeches. In the slashed doublets the silken or linen shirt was allowed to show through the 'slashings,' and as these shirts also were made by the tailors the craft was kept busy. The stuffed breeches had a quaint appearance, and at the time when they were worn at their largest it is said that seating arrangements in Parliament had to be readjusted so that each member should have sufficient room to sit down! The second Tudor and the last were lavish patrons of the tailors, and if you look at a portrait of either Henry VIII or Elizabeth you will be struck by the extraordinary elaboration of cutting, shaping, and stitching which their garments required. The big, drum-like frames on which women's skirts were distended at the end of the sixteenth and the beginning of the seventeenth century were called 'farthingales,' and special broad-seated chairs were made to accommodate them!

In the delightful picture by Moroni you see a tailor of this period at work, just going to cut into a length of rich, dark-coloured cloth. If you look very closely at the original you will see a faint, pale chalk-mark, made to guide those big scissors of his. Considerable skill must have been needed to keep all the slashings regular. Notice this tailor's own doublet, with its numerous neat little punctures, and the deep slashes in his trunk-hose.

Englishmen of this period followed French fashions in dress as faithfully as Frenchmen now follow English. But they followed Italian and German fashions as well, and jumbled them altogether, so that we hear Shakespeare's Portia saying of her English suitor, "I think he bought his doublet in Italy, his round hose in France, his bonnet in Germany, and his behaviour everywhere."

One London tailor of Tudor times who gained for himself a little niche in history was John Stow, but it was not by the excellence of his tailoring. This good man, described by one of his friends as "tall of stature, lean of body and face, his eyes small

The Book of Craftsmen

and crystalline, of a pleasant and cheerful countenance," was an ardent antiquary, who loved nothing so much as to wander through the ancient highways and byways of the city, musing on her former glories, and keeping a sharp look-out with his "small, crystalline eyes" for any fragments of Roman brickwork or medieval masonry. It is to be feared that he neglected his craft when he was preparing his great *Survey of London*, but he remained a member of the Merchant Taylors' Company, which in his old age allowed him a pension of £6 a year—a more generous sum then than it would be now. If you should happen to pass the church of St Andrew Undershaft, in Leadenhall Street, London, go in and have a peep at good old John Stow's monument, a life-sized effigy of the learned tailor sitting in a chair, with a book on a table before him. Look closely at his right hand and you will see that it clasps a real quill-pen. This quill is solemnly renewed every year on the anniversary of his death—April 6.

There is a famous scene in Shakespeare's comedy, *The Taming of the Shrew*,[1] where Petruchio, determined to break the proud and stubborn temper of his young bride Katherine, says to her:

> We will return unto thy father's house
> And revel it as bravely as the best,
> With silken coats and caps and golden rings,
> With ruffs and cuffs and farthingales and things;
> With scarfs and fans and double change of bravery,
> With amber bracelets, beads and all this knavery.
> What, hast thou dined? The tailor stays thy leisure
> To deck thy body with this ruffling treasure.

A tailor and a haberdasher enter with their wares, and the wily Petruchio proceeds to abuse everything they offer, while Katherine protests that the cap and gown please her very well. Of the cap her husband says:

> Why, this was moulded on a porringer;
> A velvet dish....
> Why, 'tis a cockle or a walnut-shell,
> A knack, a toy, a trick, a baby's cap.

[1] Act IV, Scene iii.

The Tailor and the Hatter

Of the gown he says:

> O mercy, God! what masquing stuff is here?
> What's this? A sleeve? 'Tis like a demi-cannon.
> What, up and down, carved like an apple-tart?
> Here's snip and nip and cut and slish and slash,
> Like to a censer in a barber's shop:
> Why, what, i' devil's name, tailor, call'st thou this?

The bewildered tailor answers,

> You bid me make it orderly and well,
> According to the fashion and the time.

But Petruchio will have none of it, and the poor man is dismissed with many hard words, though as he departs Petruchio's friend Hortensio whispers a few reassuring phrases in his ear.

In Shakespeare's time it seems that the scissors were no longer the distinctive mark of the tailor; he was more readily recognized by his yard-stick, and already his heavy iron was known as a 'goose.' The porter in *Macbeth*, who amuses himself by pretending that he is the gate-keeper of the nether-world, and makes rather clumsy puns, tells an imaginary English tailor, sent to eternal punishment for "stealing out of a French hose," that "here he may roast his 'goose.'" In *The Comedy of Errors*, when one of the two brothers is mistaken for his unknown twin, he says in a puzzled tone:

> There's not a man I meet but doth salute me
> As if I were some well-acquainted friend:
>
> . . . . .
>
> Some offer me commodities to buy;
> Even now a tailor call'd me in his shop
> And showed me silks that he had bought for me,
> And therewithal took measure of my body.[1]

The tailor who in *A Midsummer Night's Dream* is given the part of Thisbe's mother in the play performed by the artisans of Athens bears the suggestive name of Robert Starveling. Nobody

---

[1] Act IV, Scene iii.

The Book of Craftsmen

knows what was the origin of the ancient jest that tailors were feeble and weakly fellows, but Shakespeare alludes to it more than once, and actually gives the name 'Feeble' to the Gloucestershire tailor (2 *Henry IV*, III, ii) whom Sir John Falstaff calls to the colours in the King's name. There are various other tailors in the plays of Shakespeare, but one more example will suffice—from *King John*, where Hubert de Burgh is describing how rumours of a French invasion spread among the artisans and craftsmen of Northampton.

> I saw a smith stand with his hammer, thus,
> The whilst his iron did on the anvil cool,
> With open mouth swallowing a tailor's news,
> Who, with his shears and measure in his hand,
> Standing on slippers, which his nimble haste
> Had falsely thrust upon contrary feet,
> Told of a many thousand warlike French
> That were embattailed and ranked in Kent [1]

Like the tailor, the hatter was very much patronized in Europe during the sixteenth, seventeenth, and eighteenth centuries. Crowns got higher and higher under the first Stuarts and the Commonwealth, though the dashing Cavalier hat was of a different type from the exaggerated headgear with a steeple-crown affected by the Puritans. One observer of the period declared that hats sometimes perked up "like the sphere or shaft of a steeple, standing a quarter of a yard above the crown of their heads," but at a later date half a yard was nearer the height.

The English Government, always anxious to protect the wool trade and the crafts associated with it, became alarmed towards the middle of the sixteenth century by the increasing vogue of the velvet or taffeta hat, and in 1571 an edict was passed to the effect that every one over six years of age, except those of high degree, should upon all Sundays and holidays wear caps of wool manufactured in England. Of course, this edict, however welcome to the cappers and haberdashers, proved unworkable, and had finally

[1] Act IV, Scene ii.

THE TAILOR
After the painting by Moroni in the National Gallery.

QUEEN ELIZABETH
Showing the drum-shaped farthingale of the period.
From a print in the British Museum

The Tailor and the Hatter

to be repealed. English people have always resented dictation and interference with their personal and private affairs, and those of the lower ranks used in the old days to be rather fond of 'aping their betters.' Thus a severe satirist called Stubbes, a contemporary of Shakespeare, declared indignantly that "every poor cottager's daughter" had a taffeta hat. Embroidered hats, worn by both men and women, were garnished with huge tufts of plumes, usually ostrich, heron, or peacock. The hatters were kept busy producing headgear to suit the taste of various ranks and classes of society, and adapting their wares to the changeable whims of fashion, which sometimes declared for high crowns and sometimes for low, sometimes for broad brims and sometimes for narrow.

The tailors were encouraged by ladies quite as much as by gentlemen of high rank, for a tailor was a complete outfitter, and supplied padded petticoats and quilted stays as well as dresses. Of the gentlewomen of Elizabeth's day Mr Stubbes wrote:

> Their gowns be no less famous also . . . for some are of scarlet, some of fine cloth, of ten, twenty, or forty shillings a yard . . . Then have they petticoats of the best cloth that can be bought . . . And sometimes they are not of cloth, for that is thought too base, but of taffeta, silk, and such-like.

The great William Cecil, Lord Burleigh, wrote on behalf of his royal mistress, Queen Elizabeth, to Henry Norris, English Ambassador in Paris:

> The Queen's Majesty would fain have a tailor that had some skill to make her apparrell both after the French and the Italian manner: and she thinketh that you might use some means to obtain someone that serveth the French Queen without mentioning any manner of request in our Queen's Majesty's name.

You will remember that after the death of Queen Elizabeth more than a thousand gorgeous dresses were found dispersed among the various palaces where she had made her home.

"The apparell," says Shakespeare's Polonius, "oft proclaims the

The Book of Craftsmen

man," and this was never more true than during the early Stuart period, when you could tell at the first glance whether a stranger were a Cavalier or a Roundhead, a Royalist or a Puritan. The tailors of England between 1625 and 1660 had two totally different types of raiment to make—and so had the hatters two totally different types of hat. The Puritan demanded a plain doublet of

A CAVALIER
Plumes and silk.

A PURITAN
Buff and steel.

dark-coloured stuff, full breeches, rather like plus-fours, an austere linen collar, or linen bands, and a steeple-crowned hat with a wide, straight brim. The Cavalier made himself look gallant and gay in a doublet of satin or velvet, often slashed so as to show the lace-trimmed shirt beneath, close-fitting knee-breeches, usually ending with knots of ribbon or even frills of lace at the knee, a collar of rich lace, and a broad-brimmed hat, garnished with plumes and cocked defiantly on one side of his head. After the Restoration the contrast between the two styles of dress became less violent, though the shopkeeping class, true to their Puritan tradition, tended to darker colours and more severe forms.

A tailor who worked chiefly for Royalist clients had to be skilful

The Tailor and the Hatter

in slashings and purflings and embroidery in gold or silver thread: he had to know how to handle fine and costly fabrics to the best effect, and how to make knots of silk ribbon and laces of golden braid. He whose patrons were Parliament men had less need of nimble scissors and a deft needle, but the dark stuffs favoured by those patrons must have been trying to the eyes, and their heavy garments wearying to the hand.

The tailors of Restoration England must have blessed his Merry Majesty King Charles II when he was seized with a whim to introduce a totally new type of coat and waistcoat, "after the Persian fashion," both long, straight, and close-fitting. Every one with any desire to be smart and up-to-date hastened to his tailor with instructions to make him a suit, or perhaps several suits, of the kind now worn at Court, with the result that there was a regular epidemic of 'Persian' garments. And then the tailors had reason to bless King Louis XIV of France, who, hearing of the craze, and wishing to poke fun at his good brother of England, proceeded to dress all his lackeys in similar array. Then, of course, the English Court dropped the idea as violently as it had taken it up, and once again the tailors were busy.

CHARLES II'S COAT "AFTER THE PERSIAN FASHION"

If you come to think of it this craft has always been likely to be encouraged and enriched by the changes of fashion, though in our own days these changes—as regards men's clothes—are very slight, and people are less anxious not to be old-fashioned. Formerly fashion varied so wildly, and men as well as women paid so much heed to its decrees, that the tailor's craft used to be among the most flourishing in the land. And other forces combined to make it flourish. For example, the introduction of naval and military uniforms, which led to the development of a new technique in cutting out trim, well-fitting tunics of navy blue, or royal scarlet,

The Book of Craftsmen

or deep green, and making them magnificent with buttons and braid and gold lace. Then, when clerics ceased to wear cassocks or long gowns, and took to knee-breeches and waistcoats and coats, the clerical tailor came into being and specialized in sober raiment "of formal cut." Later still tailors had to tackle another new task—though to the ancient Gauls and Scythians it would have seemed less unfamiliar than it did to the craftsmen of the eighteenth century. This was when trousers came into fashion. At first the conservative people who preferred to wear knee-breeches looked with alarm and contempt at these new-fangled and almost revolutionary garments. But the new fashion persisted. And the adaptable tailors soon learned to cut elegant nether-garments descending to the ankle and strapped tightly under the foot. Meanwhile the hatters, by way of the three-cornered hat and the cocked hat, had reached a form of headgear which, like trousers, seemed at first to be inspired by destructive and alarming ideas. Elderly men who had always worn three-cornered hats looked with consternation at young men sporting that type of hat then called a beaver, but now usually described as a 'topper.' Like the many-caped, high-waisted overcoat, the 'topper' came from France. And as it came just about the same time as the terrible news of the French Revolution, and as it was favoured by the most prominent Revolutionaries, it was naturally considered to be a sign of revolt against the settled order of things.

AN OFFICER OF THE THIRD DRAGOON GUARDS
Late eighteenth century

Hatters and tailors profited, however. And presently the fluffy-looking top-hat, such as you see in the Johnnie Walker advertisements and the pictures of Sydney Carton in *A Tale of Two Cities*, with the rather broad-topped crown and the curled-up brim, gave place to the modern topper, glossy as a well-polished piece of

The Tailor and the Hatter

ebony when it is black, or smooth as a piece of velvet when it is grey. And certainly, whether black or grey, it does not suggest any thoughts of revolution or unrest. There is no more dignified and decorous form of headgear, though it is now seldom seen unless at weddings, funerals, and royal garden-parties.

One more influence used, in the olden days, to bring prosperity to the tailoring brotherhood. This was the custom among rich people of bequeathing sums of money to provide so many poor folk with hoods and gowns. Later, when there was less anxiety to do good deeds for the sake of one's soul, and more anxiety to make a fine show in the eyes of the world, wealthy families, upon the death of any member, would put their whole household into deep mourning. Then, as the slang of the day had it, the tailors 'drew their swords'—that is to say, made ready their needles, expecting large orders.

THE HEIGHT OF FASHION IN THE EARLY VICTORIAN PERIOD

> The tailors cross-legged on their boards,
> Needle-armed, hand-extended, prepared
> To stab the black cloth with their swords
> The instant that death was declared.

Against all these favouring influences we must set the various edicts, known as 'Sumptuary laws,' in which princes and parliaments have at different times endeavoured to prevent certain classes of people from wearing certain fabrics, ornaments, or articles of apparel. We came across an example of such an edict when we were talking about velvet and taffeta hats just now. The

The Book of Craftsmen

Tudors were particularly fond of dictating to their subjects upon such matters, though the Plantagenets also tried to regulate fashions in dress. It remained for a member of the much-abused Stuart dynasty—James I and VI—to repeal all these oppressive laws at one swoop, and so, incidentally, to deserve the goodwill of the tailors and hatters of Great Britain.

CHAPTER VII
THE PAINTER

THE earliest painter, like the earliest potter and the earliest workers in metal and clay, was a creator but hardly a craftsman. Where he lived we cannot tell, nor precisely when, nor do we know what it was which gave him the idea of smearing colours upon uncoloured surfaces, or upon surfaces of a different colour. But we are pretty safe in saying that at some very dim and far-off epoch in the history of the human race some people, a little more intelligent than most of the other people then alive, found that by dabbing streaks of certain substances upon the sides of their pottery or the walls of their caves they could produce certain rather pleasing effects. They were amused; they persevered; they tried out different methods. They took to decorating the clay beads of their necklaces with spots or stripes of red, yellow, and black. They began to try to imitate, in groups of rough lines and patches, the things and the creatures they saw around them. Gradually the art spread—not, I think, from one primitive tribe to another, but in that mysterious way in which most human arts have spread—almost as if some mighty Power had scattered seeds of thought far and wide. And so, not suddenly or quickly, but by gradual and irregular stages, man learned how to paint.

In some of the ancient cave-dwellings to be found in France and Spain there are marvellously vivid and vigorous paintings of animals, wild horses galloping, reindeer grazing, mammoths staring, boars charging, bison halting, head down and tail in air, or standing brooding in meditative pose.

If the painter chanced to have a small son his troughs of newly ground colours must have been a strong temptation to small fingers. Sometimes a boy may have been allowed to help in grinding the

The Book of Craftsmen

oxides of iron and manganese ore from which the yellow, black, and red were obtained; he could also scoop out a hollow bone, and stop it up at one end to hold the bright-hued powder. When the artist worked deep in the cave somebody must have held the flaring stone lamp for him. That was the sort of thing a boy would love to do, not only because it would make him feel important, but also because he could then watch the painted beasts growing on the cave wall under the artist's hand.[1]

Curiously enough, among all these lifelike representations of living creatures there is always one creature 'conspicuous by his absence'—*man*. We find no human figures, no human faces, among the bison and the boars upon the walls of these mysterious caves. This seems a pity. It would have been most interesting to see the cave-men as they saw each other, and if they had been as skilful in painting people as they were in painting wild animals we should not now be obliged to take measurements of fragments of bone in order to imagine what these remote forefathers of ours looked like. As we remarked in the chapter on the sculptor's craft, rough, crude images of semi-human beings *are* found carved in stone or ivory, or drawn on cave-walls, at an early date, but they probably had some religious significance, and they were quite evidently not *intended* to resemble real men and women. It was probably some religious idea which prevented the cave-painters from trying to depict their friends or themselves. Primitive people often believe that if the image of a man—or even his reflection in water, or his shadow on the ground—is injured he himself will suffer, and such superstitions as these are closely inwoven with the earliest religious beliefs of mankind.

MEN AS SEEN BY PRIMITIVE MAN
From the wall of a cave.

[1] D. M. Stuart, *The Boy through the Ages*, pp. 16-17 (Harrap).

THE CAVE-DWELLER AS AN ARTIST

PAINTED WALL IN THE THRONE-ROOM AT KNOSSOS
Photo Boissonnas, Geneva

The Painter

Many long centuries had to pass before the painter emerged from the community as a distinct craftsman, and many more centuries still before certain members of his craft climbed high above the heads of their fellows and became famous. The earlier painters were often potters, or carpenters, or masons into the bargain, and used paint only to beautify the objects in clay, wood, or stone which formed their chief output.

The ancient Egyptians—those very remarkable people—were, after their own fashion, very skilful painters. As we have already

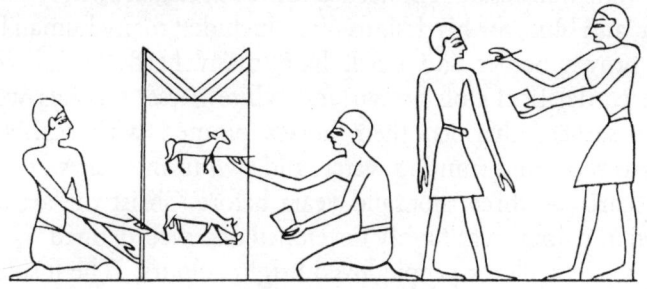

EGYPTIAN ARTISTS AT WORK
The one on the right is colouring a life-sized statue.

seen, one of the very earliest examples of painted pottery known to us is a prehistoric Egyptian jar showing a boat and a woman with two children. The dwellers by the Nile before history began apparently painted their faces as well as their pottery, for jars to hold cosmetics have been discovered in some of their hut-shaped tombs! Later—much later, as Egyptian history goes, though a long, long time ago—the painter became a craftsman much in demand, who adorned the interiors of houses, palaces, and tombs with gaily coloured pictures of national everyday life. He also decorated the heavy chests of tamarisk-wood which his fellow-craftsman the carpenter fashioned, and tinted the images, whether vast limestone statues or small statuettes, made by another of his fellow-craftsmen, the sculptor. Another task was to colour the outer coffins in which the mummified bodies of rich folk were enclosed.

The Book of Craftsmen

Thanks to the care and perseverance with which learned men have examined the teeming relics of Egyptian civilization we can gain a very fair idea as to how the painter of ancient Egypt went to work. He usually had a palette, made of wood or slate, with hollows to hold his colours. Scribes as well as artists used palettes, but these had seldom more than two hollows, and the colours were confined to black and red. Sometimes the painter would use a shell as a paint-pot, sometimes he had quite lovely little pots of blue glazed-ware. His paints were ground upon slabs of some hard stone like basalt. He needed lots of black, brown, white, red, green, and blue, for his designs often included many human beings with brown bodies and black hair, many herds of brown and white cattle, flocks of brown and white geese, officials wearing scarlet sashes, chariots, their horses plumed with scarlet, and papyrus-reeds and running water, and swimming fishes.

As early as three thousand years before Christ the art of the Egyptian painter was highly developed and well defined.

This lively, clever people loved bright colours. The insides and the outsides of their houses were painted, and the insides of their rock-hewn tombs. This custom gave constant employment to the painters, and helped them to perfect their art. Within certain limits their art *did* become well-nigh perfect, but to modern eyes these limits seem strangely narrow. It is true that Western painters did not master the art of perspective—by which distance and proportion are correctly shown—until the fifteenth century, but at least they did not, before that period, represent people in profile with their eyes flat against the sides of their heads, like the eyes of birds, and both their feet exactly in line. The Greeks and Romans, too, *did* understand something of the rules—they are quite exact rules—governing perspective,[1] and it seems odd that such an intelligent race as the Egyptians should have failed altogether in this important branch of the art of drawing and painting.

The Egyptian painter had anything but a monotonous life. He had to draw all sorts of people, animals, plants, objects, and scenes.

[1] Dorothy Furness, *Drawing for Beginners*, pp. 114–140 (Harrap).

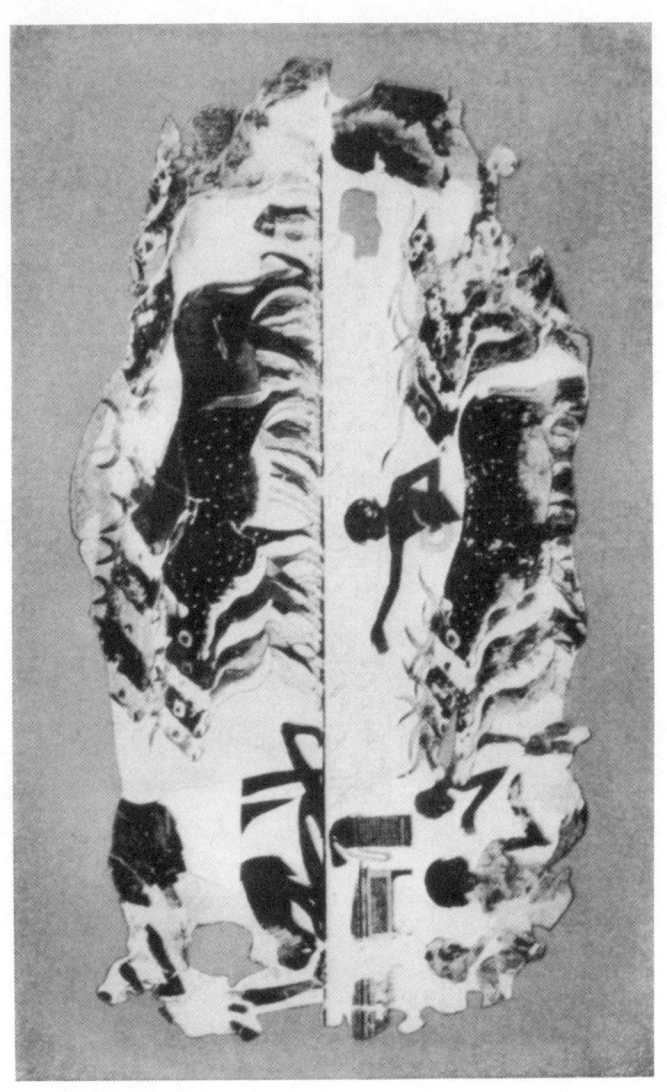

WALL-PAINTING ON A TOMB AT THEBES

The scene represents the driving of a large herd of cattle on an Egyptian farm.

Reproduced by permission from "Wall Decorations of Egyptian Tombs," published by the Trustees of the British Museum

The Painter

Sometimes it might be a battle that he had to trace, sometimes a fishing or fowling expedition among the high papyrus-reeds, sometimes a great ship, with sails and oars, setting forth on a long voyage, sometimes the mummy of a powerful priest or prince being borne to its limestone vault for burial. Scenes in the fields, with men and oxen at work, were very popular.

Just as a modern artist will make rough sketches on odd pieces of paper the artist by the Nile would dab outlines into flakes of limestone, correcting them when necessary, and often using—as some modern draughtsmen still use—a mesh of intersecting lines by which to regulate his design. There must have been regular schools of art in the valley of the Nile, for explorers discover 'dumps' of such flakes, on which the pupil has sketched, for example, a man's head and shoulders in black, and the master has indicated his mistakes in red.

Among the ancient Greeks and Cretans painters had plenty to do, for houses and temples, tombs and images, were adorned with many and gorgeous colours. The inside walls of the palace at Knossos were gay with frescoes—a 'fresco' means literally something painted in the open air, though it has come to mean anything painted on a wall. In what is supposed to have been the throne-room of the palace there is a startling picture of a creature like a griffin with a mane of peacock's feathers reclining very peacefully in a bed of tall, slender lilies.

The Greek painter, in addition to applying colour to the handiwork of his fellow-craftsman the sculptor, and painting stone or plaster surfaces either indoors or out, practised a method of producing pictures on wooden panels with coloured and melted wax. The Ionians and the Rhodians were especially skilful in this craft, but, the materials being so perishable, hardly any examples of their work have survived. Looking at the grim ruins of ancient temples, stained and scarred by the tempests of many centuries, it is difficult to imagine them blazing and glittering with colour. The Parthenon at Athens, for example, must have been gay to behold, with all its sculptured gods and men, horsemen and horses,

The Book of Craftsmen

painted in natural hues against a background as blue as the sea in summer.

The Romans, not naturally an artistic people, borrowed from the Greeks these ideas about the decoration of sacred and other buildings. The Roman painter-craftsman had to practise various little tricks such as some of his present-day descendants in many countries still employ—painting plain stone or blank plaster to

THE CUPID SHOP
A Pompeian fresco.

make it resemble costly marble, porphyry, or granite, and applying stencils to wall-surfaces so as to obtain uniform and regular borders, friezes, and dados.

Roman villas were often adorned with really delightful frescoes. That of the Empress Livia at Torre de Prima Porta was made gay with roses and anemones, poplars, olives, and pomegranates.

At Pompeii we find whimsical and charming as well as grotesque and impressive subjects. It is amusing to see hundreds of little winged cupids occupied in all sorts of unexpected tasks. Some you will see mounted on ladders gathering grapes; others heaping the fruit into baskets; others wheeling it in barrows; others treading it in the wine-press. One joyous little fellow is shown enjoying a ride on the back of a gigantic, fierce-whiskered shrimp!

MOONLIGHT AND MIST
By Hiroshige.

BANNERS OF THE KNIGHTS OF THE GARTER IN ST GEORGE'S CHAPEL
AT WINDSOR
Fox photo

The Painter

Among the quaintest of these Pompeian wall-paintings is one showing an imaginary shop where these cupids could be bought. Two ladies are buying one from an old shopwoman, and it appears that the 'stock' was kept in cages, just as puppies and kittens are at a modern livestock store. Another rich inhabitant of what has been called 'the Brighton of the ancient Romans' preferred to contemplate the sacrifice of Iphigenia—a rather depressing subject, one would have thought! And all round the walls, cornices, ceilings, door- and window-frames, and so forth, of the Pompeian houses, the busy painter had to weave wreaths of laurel, or stretch long strips of Greek-key or other conventional designs.

During the Dark Ages the craft of the painter, like so many other crafts, sank to a low ebb. People cared little then about the graces of life, and it did not seem to matter much whether one's surroundings were beautiful or not. Only in Byzantium frescoes still made the walls of churches and palaces gorgeous—stiff, brilliant frescoes, glittering with purple pigment and gold leaf. But we should always remember that at the very time when the West was plunged in barbarism the Far East was at a high pitch of civilization. The Japanese were painting lovely designs on silk and on rice-paper, and so were the Chinese; and in Central Asia the monks of the Buddhist monasteries were tracing religious scenes upon strips of silk. Some years ago a great dump of such pictures was discovered concealed in a cave in Mongolia—a place since known as the 'Cave of the Thousand Buddhas.'

As we saw when speaking of Chinese and Japanese pottery the art of these two great Eastern peoples is quite unlike anything that Western man has developed. It is a queer mixture of quaint, conventional ideas and startling realism. For example, in Japanese pictures the men and women look like fantastic images cut out of paper, their faces resemble masks, their fingers and toes seem unnaturally long and curly, their attitudes are exaggerated and ungainly—to Western eyes. But the Japanese painter could, at the same time, depict a spray of wistaria, or a monkey crunching a pomegranate, or a sprig of green bamboo, or a flight of ashen-grey

The Book of Craftsmen

cranes, so faithfully that they all seem on the point of waking into life.

To return to Western Europe at the end of the Dark Ages. Even though the poor people, harassed by barbarian invaders, had little time or energy to cultivate the gentler arts they did not lose their instinctive craving for colour. And when better days came this craving reappeared, and the tailor, the glass-worker, and the painter were among the craftsmen who helped to satisfy it.

In medieval England the handles of hoes and the shafts of carts, the spokes of wheels and the stocks of whips, were coloured gay blue and green. The walls of the churches flamed with pictures of hell-fire or glittered with visions of the golden towers of heaven. Angels and saints, stately though startled-looking, adorned the pillars; and trails of vine-leaves and grape-clusters wreathed themselves over the arches. Presently the spread of luxurious habits led rich folk to encase the rough stone and cement of their inner walls with wainscot painted to imitate woven hangings. Later came the painted cloth, imitating tapestry of Arras.

Let us think of some of the multifarious tasks which a medieval painter-stainer, as he was called, might have to undertake. You will find many of them mentioned in the following song, supposed to be sung by one of these clever fellows in praise of his own craft:

> The weaver wearieth of his loom,
>   The potter of his clay,
> The cook likewise of cauldron-fume,
>   The minstrel of his lay;
>   But never weary I
>   Of the rainbow craft I ply,
> And I would the day were longer, for I work best by day.
>
>   Mine is a valiant craft, I swear,
>   For many a shield is dight
>   By me with goodly *gules* and *vair*,
>   And *or* and *argent*[1] bright;
>   In tourney and in tilt
>   The shields my hand hath gilt
> Ward off the shattering lances from the casque of many a knight.

[1] *Gules, vair, or, argent*—heraldic terms meaning red, blue-and-white, gold, and silver.

The Painter

This craft of mine may merry be
  As morris-bells rung o'er;
My handiwork men smile to see
  Above the tavern-door;
    With green and purple scale
    I deck the 'Mermaid's' tail,
To the 'Crown' I give great rubies, and long tusks to the 'Boar.'

Mine is a craft of brave emprise,
  Of journeys strange and far;
The ships that fare where sunset dies
  Are painted, sail and spar;
    The high embattled bows
    Are gay with gold and rose,
And on the great square mainsail I set a flaming star.

And oft is mine a pious task,
  As clerks and friars can tell;
For oft I make the awesome mask
  And the grim scarlet hell,
    When on the creaking stage
    Sir Sathanas doth rage;
And I paint the azure turrets wherein the Blessèd dwell.[1]

If you think for a moment you will realize that in several of these activities the painter-stainer was working almost hand-in-hand with the craftsman whose raw material was wood. The kinght's shield, which he carried "in tourney and in tilt," was made of wood; and so was the sign swinging outside the tavern-door; and so were the beams and spars of the ships; and so were the turrets used in the miracle plays to represent Paradise.

It was not only outside taverns that gaily painted signs used to creak and sway. Before people knew how to read they had to depend a great deal upon pictures, just as savages do to this day, and a man who could not spell out the name of a merchant over his shop-front might remember that 'At the Sign of the Porcupine' or 'At the Sign of the Three Unicorns' Alderman Blank sold spices, or silk stuffs, or harness for horses. So arose the craft of the sign-painter, and it has not died out yet.

[1] D. M. Stuart, *Historical Songs and Ballads* (Harrap).

The Book of Craftsmen

The designs of these trade-pictures were of immense variety. In feudal times the coat-of-arms of the lord of the manor often influenced the ideas of the village inn-keeper, and the dolphin, lion, white hart, golden cross, or silver bell over his door was usually traceable to some heraldic device. Merchants in big towns tended to choose objects suggestive of their wares. To this day you see a large gilt pestle and mortar outside the chemist's shop in practically every Scottish town and village! Caxton set up his printing-press 'At the Sign of the Red Pale'; Chaucer's pilgrims assembled 'At the Sign of the Tabard'; merry Prince Hal, afterwards Henry V, revelled 'At the Sign of the Boar's Head' in Eastcheap. The Crusades made the Saracen's Head a popular image, and after Edward IV's Sun-in-Splendour had become old-fashioned the establishment of the Tudors on the throne brought in the Rose and Crown. Bankers, and at a later date pawnbrokers, adopted the three golden balls which were originally the family device of the Medici of Florence. A Dutch perfumer in London sold his fragrant wares 'At the Sign of the Lily.' After King Charles "enjoyed his own again" a fine crop of 'Royal Oaks' sprang up on the signboards of his loyal subjects. And even now you not infrequently catch sight of a striped pole outside a barber's shop, reminding passers-by that once upon a time the barbers were barber-surgeons and could 'bleed' you as well as cut your hair or shave your chin—the stripes representing bandages.

A TAVERN SIGN

The idea of such sign-pictures goes back into the remote past, for Egyptians, Greeks, and Romans had it, though they did not

The Painter

commonly use sign-*boards*. A Gaulish apple-merchant of the Roman period had a carved slab outside his shop with the figure of a man, presumably himself, with a basket of fruit slung round his neck, one hand upraised in an arresting pose, and the inscription: *Mala, mulieres meæ!*—Apples, my ladies!

The streets of any medieval city were forests of waving signs, and regulations had to be made to ensure that the signboards did not hang so low as to touch the crown of a horseman's head. In 1764 an Act of Parliament was passed attempting to abolish these signs in London, as they had become a danger to pedestrians.

Besides painting signs the medieval 'stainer,' as we have seen, painted the ornamental woodwork of ships, and also their big square sails. This task gave him opportunities for using gorgeous colours and introducing picturesque or pious designs. The "flaming star" of Dorothy Margaret Stuart's poem was a usual device, but there were many others, a favourite being a representation of the Virgin and Child larger than life-size.

The painting of rough scenery and fearsome masks for the miracle-plays would be quite an important branch of this craft up to the Reformation, and even after that. Shakespeare's remark, through the lips of Lady Macbeth, that the "eye of childhood fears a painted devil" has been accepted as evidence that when he was a small boy he was taken to see the mystery plays still acted at Coventry at that time. But on the wall of the Guild Hall at Stratford-on-Avon there was a most terrifying fresco of the Mouth of Hell which young William probably saw, and, if he saw, must have shuddered to see.

Like most of the craftsmen of medieval Europe the painter-stainers had their own guild or company. Indeed, there was a time when they had two guilds—one for the Painters, who exercised their art upon "timber, stone, iron, and such-like," and one for the Stainers, who worked on "cloth, silk, and such-like." The 'cloth' would be canvas, not woollen cloth, and it would be hung from walls, not stretched upon frames. St Luke, himself said by tradition to have been a painter, was the patron of the craft, of

The Book of Craftsmen

which the two branches amalgamated early in the sixteenth century, when it was laid down that they should possess in common " one Hall, one Box, one Barge, and one Light." The ' box ' was, of course, the money-chest; the ' barge ' was a necessity when the Lord Mayor's procession went by water; and the ' light ' was a lamp or large candle burning before the altar of St Luke.

HELL-MOUTH
From a wall-painting formerly at Stratford-on-Avon.

Besides painting the shields used in battle and in the lists the painter-stainers adorned with gay or proud devices the high saddle-bows and cantles of the wooden saddles made by the joiners. One result of these activities was a fierce squabble, ending in blows and bloodshed, between the Painters, the Joiners, and the Saddlers. These last, who were responsible for the actual saddles, of which the wooden portions were made by the joiners and painted by the painters, complained that the timber used was bad and the workmanship no better. Rivalries and criticisms finally led to a sort of general battle among representatives of the three ancient and

The Painter

honourable crafts. It does not appear which of the three emerged triumphant!

The Painter-stainers in their turn carried on quite a bitter feud against the plasterers who, in their opinion, were invading their own special domain when they used paint or coloured plaster on walls and ceilings.

Like all the other craft-guilds of London the Painter-stainers not only liked good fare themselves, but saw to it that their guests were well and richly fed. In the eighteenth century the menu for one of their banquets included fowls, oysters, bacon, sausages, and force-meat balls, mince-pies, tongues, pepper tarts, roast geese with sauce, bread, beer, and cheese. The lady-guests dined separately, and evidently it was considered that their appetites would be less hearty, for they were regaled only with " fish, mince-pies, tarts, and partridges."

As wheeled vehicles came into fashion another branch of the painters' art developed—painting coats-of-arms and other devices on the panels of coaches and carriages. Sedan-chairs, too, were often elaborately decorated, sometimes with heraldic devices, sometimes with garlands of flowers, flights of doves, or groups of cupids. Then, when anybody of importance died, large wooden panels called 'hatchments,' painted with their coats-of-arms, used to be fixed on the outsides of their houses, and sometimes on the walls of the churches where their tombs stood, and many of them may still be seen there. The painting of these demanded a special technique. Perhaps you may have noticed in some old churches that, either over the main door inside or near the font, a big painting with the Royal Arms has been set up. Such paintings often have the initials ' C. R.'—*Carolus Rex*—showing that they were executed during the wave of loyal enthusiasm which followed the Restoration. The craftsmen who produced them must have grown very skilful in depicting lions and unicorns, though their lions do not resemble any real lion that ever roamed through any jungle or roared in any zoo. As nobody has seen a real unicorn we cannot tell whether the painted unicorns are lifelike or not!

The Book of Craftsmen

Let us go back now for a little while to the Middle Ages, before the time of wheeled coaches and the reign of *Carolus Rex*. Let us go back to the days of the Plantagenets, when, in the great monasteries up and down the country, monkish illuminators were doing

ANGLO-SAXON SAINTS
From the Benedictional of St Ethelwold.

exquisite work upon leaves of parchment or vellum. During the Dark Ages the monasteries had been the last refuge of art and of culture. If the patient monks had not persevered in making copies of the Scriptures and of various works of devotion and philosophy the loss to later ages would have been immense—though, of course, we should not know how much we had lost. At a very early date these scribes began to adorn their manuscripts with drawings and

The Painter

paintings, naturally on a small scale. The capital letters with which chapters began gave them an opportunity to introduce curly garlands and even curlier dragons, or perhaps a little seraph—or even a little demon. The Anglo-Saxons of the ninth and tenth centuries excelled in representing slender saints draped in graceful robes. They also enlivened their more serious work with gay and lifelike

ST DUNSTAN WORKING AS AN ILLUMINATOR

little scenes from country life—people ploughing, sowing, and reaping, cutting wood, and winnowing corn. These scenes reappear again and again in the manuscripts of illuminators, English, French, and German, and thanks to them we know a great deal about the daily lives of long-ago men and women of humble degree.

St Dunstan, Archbishop of Canterbury, is said to have been a skilful illuminator as well as an expert goldsmith, and to judge from this ancient picture of him he used to work wearing his mitre and his gorgeous episcopal robes. Notice the ink-horn—or perhaps it is a paint-pot—knotted into a fold of the tablecloth, the huge

The Book of Craftsmen

quill, and the curved blade with which the Saint keeps the lines of lettering straight and even.

Parchment, made of sheepskins, and vellum, made of calfskins, were the materials of which these wonderful illuminated books were made. Some very gorgeous early examples are of purple-tinted parchment with silver lettering, and gold-leaf was freely employed. The preparation of the parchment or vellum was quite an elaborate and lengthy business, and a rather costly one, so that books were expensive luxuries enough even before a scribe set to work upon them! Paper was not absolutely unknown in Christendom—it had, of course, been used for generations in the Far East—but for a long time it was very poor and perishable stuff. In 1221 the Emperor Frederick II issued a decree that all documents, charters, etc., inscribed upon paper were, within the space of two years, to be copied on to parchment, otherwise they would be cancelled!

In addition to the fragile and precious gold-leaf the scribe used blue, called ultramarine, and made from powdered lapis lazuli, and a very rich scarlet. The finest scarlet colour of all came from China, and was difficult to obtain, as for many centuries it was supposed to be available only for Imperial decrees. He would smooth his parchment or vellum leaves with ' pounce '—powdered pumice-stone—sharpen his quills with a keen knife, and carefully rule the lines upon which he was going to inscribe in black, red, or gold, psalms and prayers, legends and poems, and the offices of the Church.

The place where the monkish scribe worked was called a *scriptorium*. In winter it must have been bitterly cold, for though he was allowed to heap straw round his feet there was no fire at which he could warm his hands. He had to remain constantly watchful and alert, for if he nodded over his task he was apt to make foolish blunders, and such blunders might have serious results.

In the ninth century it was laid down by an ecclesiastical authority that " if the gospels, the psalter, or the missal are to be

The Painter

copied, only careful, middle-aged men are to be employed: verbal errors may otherwise be introduced into the faith."

By degrees rich people who could afford to pay for beautiful books written by hand and adorned with little pictures in gold and colours began to demand other things besides psalters (psalm-books) or missals (mass-books). They wanted tales of chivalry, histories and chronicles, fables and legends, poems and songs. And

A MONKISH SCRIBE OF THE FIFTEENTH CENTURY

so grew up a great multitude of scribes and illuminators who were not monks or churchmen. Kings and princes employed these men, gave them posts in their households, and rewarded them for their skill. They were often commanded to paint little pictures of scenes in the lives of their royal or noble patrons, and some of these give us a vivid glimpse into a vanished world. The borders of the pages are often of wonderful beauty, closely speckled with roses and strawberries, birds and butterflies—even beetles and caterpillars! Women were sometimes employed, as may be seen from the picture overleaf of a lady painting her own portrait with the aid of a mirror.

The painting of banners to be hung in the chapels of knightly orders was another task which gave the medieval painter frequent

The Book of Craftsmen

employment. These banners were made of oiled silk, and looked very gay. I ought not to use the past tense, because you may see modern examples in St George's Chapel, Windsor, and Henry VII's Chapel, Westminster, where the banners of living Knights of the Garter and Knights of the Bath hang stiff and gorgeous in

A LADY PAINTING HER OWN PORTRAIT
Fifteenth century.

a double row. The banner of the Sovereign is not painted, however; it is richly embroidered in gold thread and coloured silks.

The painters of bygone days, perhaps more than the men of any other craft, were encouraged and enriched by the whims of wealthy patrons. And their handiwork was influenced by many of the great ideas of the Middle Ages, religion and chivalry among them. Peaceful pageants gave them work, and so did weddings and wars, funerals and tournaments, and all events or occasions which called for heraldic pomp or stately colour. The Reformation

CORNER CUPBOARD FROM DAVID GARRICK'S BEDROOM
Showing Chinese influence on the designers of English painted furniture.
Victoria and Albert Museum

The Painter

did not affect them so seriously as it did the sculptors of alabaster and the makers of stained glass, because when men ceased to have painted images of saints and angels in their churches they began to hang painted images of classical and Biblical characters on the walls of their rooms.

At many points, as we have seen, the daily round of the painter brought him into contact with members of other fraternities, masons, joiners, metal-workers, plasterers, saddlers, and others; but there was one amusing department of his trade which made him collaborate with the cook! This was in the preparing of magnificent or fantastic table-decorations for royal or other banquets. Such decorations, made of wood, straw, plaster, and other fragile materials, were often exceedingly elaborate, and consisted usually of clever models of buildings, beasts, birds, and men. At the wedding-banquet of Henry V and Catherine of France one of the decorations was a model of a tiger looking into a mirror! Mermaids were great favourites, and so were dragons. Tiny windmills with sails that would really turn, lions whose tails would really wag, and warriors whose swords would really flash and swoop often figured in these miniature pageants, which must have made the long dining-tables look like so many toyshops.

PAINTED 'SHIELD OF PARADE'
It shows figures of a knight and a lady.
British Museum

As time passed the changes of fashion led to changes in the painter's craft, though even to this day there are many branches of that craft which have altered very little in three or even in five hundred years. Certainly the painter does not now paint saddles for cavalry commanders, or barges for Lord Mayors, or sedan chairs for ladies; but he paints the panels of motor-cars and the

The Book of Craftsmen

wings of aeroplanes. If you look round you, you will soon realize that the painter, apart from the painter of pictures, has a great deal to do in the modern world, which would be a much duller and greyer place without him. Indeed, people seem to want to surround themselves with ever gayer and gayer schemes! And so you see a revival, among other things, of the painted furniture, imitating Chinese and Japanese lacquer-work, for which there was a craze in the England of Queen Anne, George I, and George II. Some of this furniture was—and is—very amusing, for all the flat surfaces, panels, doors, table-tops, and so forth are sprinkled with quaint Oriental figures, mandarins and warriors and ladies, dragons and birds and fishes, varied with tufts of willow and pine, and flimsy-looking, angular bridges, while up and down the legs of the chairs trail sprigs of prickly foliage. David Garrick, the famous eighteenth-century actor, had a marvellous set of bedroom furniture in his villa at Hampton-on-Thames. You can see it for yourself without going back a hundred and fifty years and without travelling to Hampton-on-Thames, for it is now preserved in the Victoria and Albert Museum. Some London painter of George II's reign must have had very good sport, as well as exercising very great skill, when he decorated with such fantastic Chinese designs the chest-of-drawers and wash-stand, towel-rail and dressing-table and chair of the celebrated Mr Garrick, whom all London flocked to applaud when he acted at Drury Lane in the days of powdered wigs and buckled shoes.

CHAPTER VIII
THE BAKER AND THE COOK

WISE men sometimes debate solemnly as to what was the exact point at which the far-off dweller in the cave began to fumble his way towards the arts leading to civilized life. Surely one of his longest and earliest forward strides was marked by the discovery, probably the chance discovery, that raw meat laid in red ashes turned a rich brown colour, and at the same time became a thousand times nicer to eat. Thus, no doubt, was roasting invented before either baking or boiling! Baking probably came next, and it must have come early in the history of mankind, otherwise we should not find such primitive people growing corn to make bread. They may, of course, have used barley or oats to make a kind of porridge before they thought of grinding up the grains of wheat into a coarse sort of flour and putting them to cook on hot stones; but it is known that very far back in the mists of time our ancestors were bread-eating animals.

As we have already learned was the case with other crafts, the art of the cook, the 'culinary art,' began as what we may call a 'home industry.' The cave-father killed the bison or the wild ox, the flesh of which the cave-mother grilled over the cave-fire, so he was the first butcher and she was the first cook. And ever since that time mothers of families in all lands have prepared food with the aid of fire in order that their husbands and children might have toothsome things to eat. Like the art of the tailor this art of cooking passed very gradually in its more elaborate branches from women to men, and at the present time, though there are plenty of skilful women-cooks, the upper ranks of the profession are reserved for *men*-cooks, or 'chefs' as they are called. And this word 'chef' shows what importance we attach to the idea, for it means a 'head.'

The Book of Craftsmen

All through the dim and wild early chapters of human development each group of people, each subdivision of the tribe or clan, each separate family, would do their own cooking. It was not until quite an advanced stage of luxury and refinement was reached that the professional man-cook began to take his place among the craftsmen. And this happened in Egypt, where people enjoyed comfort and elegance at a period in history when in many other parts of the globe there was nothing but bleak and squalid simplicity.

Thanks to the annual rise and fall of the Nile, which made the soil marvellously fertile, the fortunate Egyptians had abundance and variety of fruits and vegetables, and the richness of their cornfields was proverbial in the antique world. The river teemed with fish, and its tall, green, blue-flowering reeds with wildfowl of all sorts. They had also flocks of geese and herds of kine. When the children of Israel were delivered by Moses they looked back wistfully to the good fare they had enjoyed in Egypt. "We remember," they said, "the fish, . . . the cucumbers, and the melons, and the leeks, and the onions, and the garlic."

One of the vegetables which flourished in Egypt was the homely onion. You may perhaps have heard of a variety of onion, still known and used, called a 'shallot.' Well, the Crusaders brought it home with them from Ascalon—hence its name, slightly altered from the Latin *Allium Ascalonicum*, onion of Ascalon. This shows that a bulb of that family still grew particularly well in that part of the world many centuries after the Greek historian Herodotus had noted that it did. The workmen who built the pyramids are said to have lived chiefly on onions, lentils, and garlic. The poor folk in this land of plenty depended much on such vegetarian foods, but the rich folk also appreciated them. Only priests were forbidden to eat onions, though they offered them, with other "kindly fruits of the earth," upon the altars of the gods.

When an Egyptian of high rank was feasting his friends his kitchen was a scene of tremendous activity. You may imagine what it looked like if you examine these figures from the tomb of

The Baker and the Cook

Rameses III, who began to reign about 1230 B.C. You see a large cauldron boiling on a small fire. One man pokes the fire while the other stirs or skims the contents of the vessel. Next is an energetic person pounding up some ingredients. Baking had reached the level of a high art, and after the dough had been kneaded with the feet—you can see two people doing it—it was taken in slabs to the pastry-cook, who rolled it out on a table-top and then cooked it in

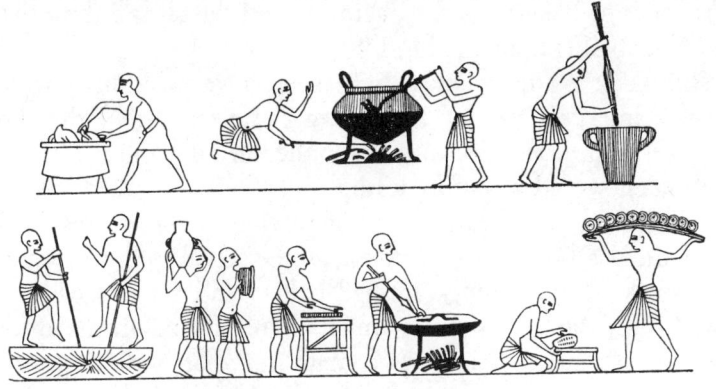

EGYPTIAN COOKS AND BAKERS AT WORK
From the tomb of Rameses III.

a flat metal pan over a fire. Loaves would be sprinkled with seeds sometimes, or marked, by way of ornament, with impressions of the baker's finger and thumb. Cakes were sometimes cleverly moulded into fanciful forms, crocodiles, oxen, triangles, and globes. Then they were stacked on a tray and borne on the baker's head to the oven. A picture from another tomb shows a cook putting a goose and a joint of meat in a stew-pan. Spices and herbs would be used to flavour the stews, and honey to sweeten the cakes. An Egyptian banquet was as long and as varied as the banquet of a modern Lord Mayor of London on the ninth of November.

Pharaoh's chief baker would be a very important officer of his household, responsible for a regular army of other bakers, cooks, turnspits, scullions, butchers, and people employed to pluck fowls, grind spices, tend the ovens, and watch the stew-pans. We are not told in the fortieth chapter of Genesis *why* Pharaoh was so

The Book of Craftsmen

angry with his chief baker that he cast him into prison, but the chief baker's dream, which he related to Joseph, his fellow-prisoner, reminds us of the Egyptian habit of carrying not only loaves and cakes but other eatables in baskets or trays on their heads.

"Behold," said the chief baker to Joseph, "I had three white baskets on my head. And in the uppermost basket there was of all manner of bakemeats for Pharaoh: and the birds did eat them out of the basket upon my head."

The baker's offence must have been a very serious one, for Joseph's interpretation of the dream came true—that the three baskets meant three days, and that on the third day the unfortunate chief baker would be put to death.

Owing to the Egyptian custom of placing food in tombs for the use of the dead man's *ka*, or double, some actual specimens of the handiwork of these long-vanished bakers and cooks have come down to us, though in a very much altered form. In the British Museum are terra-cotta bowls containing what once were dried fish, cakes, and loaves of bread. There is also a sort of stand, made of reeds, on which still lie, shrivelled and darkened beyond recognition, two ducks and a wheaten cake.

Pharaoh's chief baker must have prepared many sorts of food besides bread, but it is bread of which one naturally thinks in connexion with the verb 'to bake.' Far back in the Stone Age the Swiss lake-dwellers were cooking lumps of coarsely ground barley and wheat upon the hot stones of their hearths. It has been suggested that the earliest 'bread' ever made by man was made not of any variety of grain but of acorns and beechnuts!

In the ancient world two kinds of bread were eaten, leavened and unleavened. 'Leaven' was fermenting dough which, used with fresh dough, made the bread 'rise.' No people excelled more in the making of bread than the Egyptians, among whom white bread, very similar to a modern muffin, was considered a great delicacy. By that time and in that country baking was no longer a home-industry, but had developed into a highly skilled craft. The

The Baker and the Cook

story of Joseph in the Bible shows that bread was the recognized food, lacking which men might not live. Bread, especially unleavened bread, was, and still is, an important part of certain Jewish ceremonies, and it had to be baked by Israelites, not by " a stranger's hand." The second chapter of the book of Leviticus gives elaborate instructions upon this point—it must be remembered that ' meat ' here means *something to eat*, not necessarily the flesh of any animal.

> And when any will offer a meat offering unto the Lord, his offering shall be of fine flour; and he shall pour oil upon it, and put frankincense thereon : . . . And if thou bring an oblation of a meat offering baken in an oven, it shall be unleavened cakes of fine flour mingled with oil, or unleavened wafers anointed with oil.
> And if thy oblation be a meat offering baken in a pan, it shall be of fine flour unleavened, mingled with oil. . . . And if thy oblation be a meat offering baken in the fryingpan, it shall be made of fine flour with oil. . . . No meat offering, which ye shall bring unto the Lord, shall be made with leaven.[1]

The bread used at the feast of the Passover (Exodus xii) was also to be unleavened, and the lamb was not to be eaten " raw, or sodden at all with water," but " roast with fire," and with it bitter herbs were to be eaten. According to some authorities, the " bitter herbs " would be a sort of wild lettuce. During the Passover the children of Israel were forbidden to have any leaven in their houses. On the other hand, certain offerings of first-fruits were to be loaves of fine flour " baken with leaven " (Leviticus xxiii).

We thus see that even among a primitive people, not yet living in walled cities, cookery was advancing beyond its first rough stages. In addition to mutton goats' flesh was much in favour, sometimes ' seethed ' or stewed in milk, and cheeses made of goats' milk added variety to the Biblical bill of fare.

When people *did* settle in towns and cities bakers and cooks multiplied, and bakehouses and cookshops became a common feature of everyday life.

[1] Leviticus, ii, 1–11.

The Book of Craftsmen

The ancient Greeks, despite their wonderful intellectual gifts, did not cultivate the more gracious arts of living, and cared little for what are called 'the pleasures of the table.' They liked salads, and grew onions, parsley, radishes, and cress in the gardens behind their pink brick houses. They indulged in a queer sort of broth made of pulse flavoured with honey, and, like the people of Egypt and Babylonia, they had goats' milk cheese. The philosopher Socrates on one occasion recommended cabbage as an *hors-d'œuvre*, a dish eaten before the actual meal begins, and another Greek of the same period declared that the onion not only improved the taste of wine but inspired courage in the day of battle! It is from Socrates too that we learn that the Athenians of his day liked pancakes!

LOAF OF BREAD FOUND IN A BAKER'S SHOP IN POMPEII

Homeric banquets were probably prepared by the women of the household, but when conquerors like Alexander the Great gave gorgeous banquets to celebrate their victories the services of professional cooks must have been needed. These professionals make their appearance in Greek history towards the fourth century B.C. Alcibiades employed what would now be called a 'chef,' and the principal cook of Demetrius of Phalerum earned enough in two years to buy three blocks of house-property. The Greeks were very fond of sea-creatures which might, to our eyes, have a most unappetizing appearance; all sorts of squids, and cuttlefish, and other odd-looking things formed part of the menu. They liked salted fish, quails, and young pigs. Athenian pastrycooks baked special cakes for religious festivals, and as offerings for the gods, and Crete and Samos were celebrated for their delicate sweetmeats and preserved fruits.

In Rome, from the first century B.C. onward, there were public bakehouses, where much of the more arduous labour, such as grinding the grain in a hand-mill, was performed by slaves and criminals. Mills were also turned sometimes by long-suffering

The Baker and the Cook

horses and donkeys. Ovens had been introduced under Tarquinius Superbus in the fifth century B.C. In Pompeii the baker's name had to be stamped on the loaves, to ensure that they were of full weight and proper quality. His wares often resembled hot cross buns in shape. As by degrees the early severe and simple habits of the Romans gave way to luxury the professional cooks had to prepare the most complicated and amazing meals, and to provide banquets to consume which occupied the feasters for several hours. The 'chef' of some greedy and luxurious Emperor, like Heliogabalus in the later days of Roman splendour, found himself confronted with such curious tasks as preparing a dish of nightingales' tongues. Great skill must have been needed in the preparation of fantastic

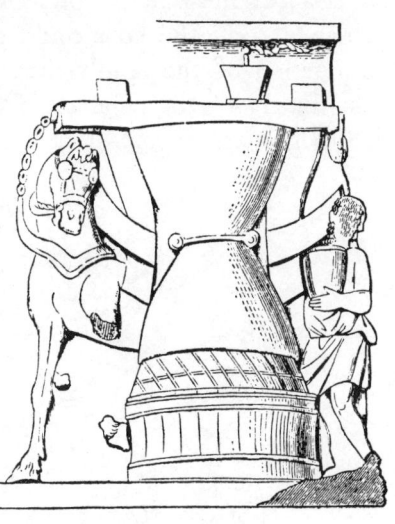

A ROMAN HORSE-MILL

ROMAN BAKERS KNEADING DOUGH

foods, richly spiced and wildly decorated, intended to appear at the banquets of gluttonous and critical hosts and guests.

The Book of Craftsmen

The Emperor Trajan showed especial favour to the bakers of Rome, thinking thereby to prevent the danger of famine. Bread, whether of the fine sort preferred by the rich or the coarse kind which was all the poor could get, was there, as elsewhere, the foundation of the family diet. "Give us bread and circuses!" was the cry of the populace when the decay of the vast Empire had begun at the core—that is to say, in Rome itself. The Latin

ANGLO-SAXONS AT DINNER

word *panis*, like the French *pain*, meaning bread, comes from an immemorially ancient verb *pa*, to feed. So the cry of the Roman mob might be rendered, "Give us food and fun!"

During the darkest part of the Dark Ages men had little leisure to cultivate the elegant arts of the table, but when a certain measure of comfort and security began to return to Europe the baker and the cook began to flourish once more. In the dialogues written by the Anglo-Saxon Abbot Ælfric one of the speakers is a baker's apprentice and another a cook's. The first says that no man could live either very well or very long without *him*, that the bread he makes strengthens the heart, and that little children cannot bear to pass him by. The second points out that lacking *his* craft meat would be eaten raw, and there would be no good sauces to go with it.

The Baker and the Cook

The Anglo-Saxons were remarkable for their healthy, not to say hearty, appetites, and their cooks would not find it necessary to invent anything very delicate or complicated in the way of new dishes. Roast pork was prime favourite, boiled fish, and chickens cooked on the spit. All roasting was done in front of a huge open fire, the meat, flesh or fowl, being transfixed by a long iron rod, or 'spit,' attached at one end to a wheel and pulled and kept revolving by a person called, on that account, a 'turnspit.' Honey was the chief sweetening medium; sugar began to be imported in small quantities in the Middle Ages, but its high price put it beyond the reach of any but the wealthiest purchasers. Salt, pepper, and spices were in constant and anxious demand, and one of the results of this demand was the development of trade with the East and the opening up of trading centres and trading routes in distant parts of the then only half-known world.

A MEDIEVAL BAKER

THIRTEENTH-CENTURY BAKERS AND COOKS

Why did the cooks of medieval Europe, and their patrons and employers also, clamour for pepper and other strong condiments? Was it because people enjoyed hot and powerful seasoning with their food? Well, perhaps it was partly on account of that. But there was another reason. Before the introduction of root-crops, turnips, mangold-wurzels, and so forth, there was so little fodder for the cattle in winter, and such poor pasture, that great numbers of animals had to be slaughtered

The Book of Craftsmen

every autumn, and their flesh pickled for use during the cold months.

If you look at the two pictures on the preceding page, taken from ancient stained-glass windows, you will see how little the craft of the baker and the cook had altered during the centuries which divide the Egyptians of the reign of Rameses III from the subjects of King Philip the Fair of France. The spit is of the most primitive design, without any wheel or pulley, and the same

A FOURTEENTH-CENTURY KITCHEN
From the Luttrell Psalter.

fire that roasts what appears to be a small sheep or pig is serving to boil something in a large cauldron. One man holds the hook from which the cauldron swings, another stirs the broth or soup, or whatever it is, bubbling within, and yet another carries off a plate with something like a dumpling on it. This last man carries a sort of wand, and is probably a major-domo, the medieval 'opposite number' of the modern butler.

The chief cook's duties were arduous and his responsibilities were heavy. He had to work in a vast, vaulted kitchen, with only the primitive utensils, and with spits and ovens heated usually by smoky wood fires. His water supply was uncertain, and frequently failed altogether. Also he had to be able to handle enormous quantities of eatables, such quantities as would nowadays be required only for a huge state banquet or a civic feast. Princes of the Church vied with kings, nobles, and knights in the splendour—and the number—of the dishes they offered to their guests on occasions of rejoicing. For example, in the fifteenth century, when

The Baker and the Cook

Richard Nevill, Chancellor of England, became Archbishop of York he entertained his friends and kinsfolk to a repast at which he and they devoured one hundred and four oxen, six wild bulls, one thousand sheep, three hundred calves, two thousand pigs, four hundred swans, a hundred dozen quails, eight hundred bream, six hundred pike, twelve porpoises and seals, a hundred and four peacocks, and two hundred pheasants. A modern cook might be painfully surprised if he were called upon to cope with peacocks and porpoises, seals and swans, and no modern cookery-book would be likely to give him any help. Birds such as pheasants and, of course, peacocks, which had gay and brilliant plumage, were sent to table with their feathers on, and made a gorgeous show. Bustards, herons, and cranes were also much appreciated, and were served with a variety of highly spiced sauces. But there were as yet no potatoes and no turnips, no foreign fruits to make the end of the meal more interesting, and no coffee to follow! Almonds and rice were not unknown, but in general people cared more for meat, game, and fish than they did for vegetables, and the cooks directed their activities accordingly.

CHAUCER'S COOK

Among the pilgrims described by Chaucer who met at the Tabard Inn, Southwark, before setting out to Canterbury, there was a cook. We are not told why he was going to the shrine of St Thomas Becket, but it may have been in order to ask " the holy, blissful martyr " to cure him of a sore place which he had on his shin. What we *are* told is something about his accomplishments. He could roast and seethe, and boil and fry; he could boil chickens and marrow-bones; he could make dishes with such odd-sounding names as ' powder-marchant tart,' ' mortreux,' ' galyngale,' and ' blankmanger.' This last sounds rather like the familiar ' blancmange,' but when you hear the recipe

The Book of Craftsmen

you will realize that the result would not in the least resemble what *we* mean by 'blancmange.' By a lucky chance we are able to find out quite a lot about these quaint productions. That 'chance' is the survival of a treatise on cookery, containing numerous recipes, written by the master-cook of that gorgeous and rather tragic sovereign Richard II. Let us suppose that Richard of

'DISHING UP'
From the Luttrell Psalter.

Bordeaux had expressed a wish to have the dish called 'mortreux' for his royal dinner. These are the instructions which his cooks would have to follow:

> Take hens and pork and boil them together. Take the flesh, and hew it small, and grind it all to dust. Take grated bread, and mix it with the broth, and add to it yolks of eggs. Boil it, and put therein powder of ginger, sugar, saffron, and salt; and look that it be stiff!

Sugar *and* salt—it does not sound at all attractive. And it would be rather a risky business to try to concoct 'mortreux' from the above recipe, for no instructions are given as to the *quantity* of the ingredients, nor as to the *time* necessary to bring them to perfection. Perhaps the two cooks in the picture from the Luttrell Psalter on page 210 are making 'mortreux.' The fierce-looking fellow on the left may be mixing the grated bread with the broth, while the milder person on the right is hewing the hens and pork small, preparatory to grinding them to dust! In the 'dishing up' scene the master-cook seems to be chopping a small pig in two.

'Powder-marchant' was a spiced powder used for flavouring—

The Baker and the Cook

the 'tart' in Chaucer's phrase is an adjective, not a noun—and some of it may be contained in the little pots on the table. 'Galyngale' was the root of a West Indian plant, much prized in sauces. Among the spices which in the fourteenth century were imported from the East, mostly by way of Venice or Genoa, were cinnamon, ginger, pepper, and a sort of cardamom-seed picturesquely known as 'grains of Paradise.'

Then what of 'blankmanger'? This was made of rice boiled in milk of almonds till it was quite soft, to which had been added chickens' livers " ground small " and cooked in white grease. When served at table blanched almonds and saffron would be sprinkled on the top, producing a pretty white-and-yellow effect.

The master-cook, as we have already seen, sometimes collaborated with the painter-stainer to produce fantastic table-decorations. On one occasion, when Philip the Good, Duke of Burgundy, was giving a banquet, his master-cook had to bake a perfectly enormous pie, large enough to hold a small orchestra of pipers and fiddlers, who began to play when the crust was cut. Perhaps the " four-and-twenty blackbirds baked in a pie," who began to sing when the pie was opened before the king, were really only a quaint item of this kind. A queen who had a similar surprise prepared for her by the royal cooks was Henrietta Maria, whose pet dwarf, Jeffrey Hudson, was, if not precisely 'baked' in a pie, at least sent to table concealed in one.

Great demands were made by the city guilds and companies upon the bakers and cooks of London when the time came round for the annual banquet of each fraternity, to be held in its own particular hall. The Salters' Company, for example, had a special Christmas recipe of its own for a pie, which contained, among other ingredients, pheasant, hare, capon, partridge, pigeon, the hearts, livers, and kidneys of sheep, spices, mushrooms, and—naturally—salt.

But if the merchants and aldermen of London were liberal patrons of the crafts to which some of them themselves belonged they were also watchful critics of bad workmanship or short

The Book of Craftsmen

measure. A baker whose loaves weighed less than they ought to have done, or were not of good bread, was severely punished if detected in his crime. Such a culprit would probably be drawn through the streets on a hurdle, with one of his loaves hanging

A SELLER OF BAD BREAD PUNISHED

round his neck, to the pillory, where he was to spend a certain number of uncomfortable hours with his head and his hands projecting through three holes in a perpendicular plank.

A GERMAN COOK AND BUTLER OF THE FIFTEENTH CENTURY

What the cook and the butler of a German noble looked like in the fifteenth century you may see from this picture. Notice the cook's apron tucked up in many folds, his case of knives swinging on his right side, handy for use, and the ladle in his left fist. The butler has two bunches of keys on his belt, and a pouch apparently containing two small flasks. Perhaps the sword he holds has just been handed to him by one of his master's guests, as in modern times such a guest would hand him his umbrella.

The London bakers and the London cooks had two separate companies to watch over their interests in this world and the next.

The Baker and the Cook

As early as 1155, when the first of the Angevin kings was on the throne, a Brotherhood of Bakers was paying dues into the Royal Exchequer. At one time this important Brotherhood had two branches, the bakers of white and the bakers of brown bread. The general public, which after the habit of home-baking declined depended upon the professional bakers, kept a sharp eye upon them. If a member of the craft were detected three times in baking bad bread, or loaves under weight, his oven would be demolished, and he himself forced to " forswear the trade of Baker in the City for ever."

The association between monarch and baker, going back to Biblical times, continued in England throughout the Middle Ages, and in 1252 Henry III, the " King with the heart of wax," issued a royal mandate forbidding bakers to stamp sacred names or emblems upon their loaves. It is said to have been his grandson, that splendour-loving, foolish, and ill-starred sovereign Edward II, who gave to the White Bread Bakers their first formal royal charter.

You have probably heard of ' a baker's dozen,' and you probably know that it is thirteen of anything. The origin of the saying, and of the meaning, lies in the anxiety of bakers in olden days to avoid the severe penalties imposed for giving short weight. With every twelve loaves the master-baker gave one over and above, called the ' vantage loaf,' thus showing what a powerful effect the penalties had. After several ups and downs the company settled down to a prosperous and useful career, continuing to the present day, though an Act of Parliament passed in 1822 transferred some of their rights and responsibilities to the Government and the civic authorities. They still hold their annual banquet, though neither dwarfs, fiddlers, nor blackbirds are baked in their pies, and their ' grace before meat ' is the motto on their arms, *Praise God for All*. A quaint toast always drunk on these occasions is " To the Merry Maids, the Good Wives, and the Buxom Widows of the Bakers' Company! "

The original name of the Cooks' Company gave them the title

The Book of Craftsmen

of 'Pastelers,' or pie-makers. They combined the various branches of activity now divided into cooking, catering, restaurant-keeping, and so forth. Their members might be the experts hired to prepare stately banquets or the humble hawkers who made and sold small pies, or boiled ribs of beef, and cried them in the streets; they might be the proprietors of eating-houses, called in Elizabethan times 'ordinaries,' or of little shops, not much larger than the modern coffee-stall, where poor travellers by land or sea might refresh themselves. Almost every wharf or riverside street had one or more of such unpretentious establishments, where all sorts of picturesque people, honest and otherwise, rubbed elbows.

An edict of 1379 forbade cooks to sell refreshments before ten o'clock in the morning—we cannot imagine why. They were also forbidden to make rabbit-pie, to use the giblets of poultry, and to serve roast goose to their patrons. If a cook offered for sale meat or fish which had become 'high' before being cooked he was liable to be placed in the pillory!

In the matter of the rabbit-pie it may be that a certain number of the king's subjects had been made seriously ill by partaking of such a pie, in the crust of which no holes had been left open by the cook.

A very responsible task was entrusted to the cooks who made—and still make—the turtle-soup for the Lord Mayor's yearly banquet in the Guildhall. This delicacy was introduced only after the returning explorers from the South Seas brought home all manner of queer things, including turtles; but before long it became a prime favourite with the City Fathers and their guests, and has now almost become a proverb.

Strictly speaking, I suppose neither a grocer nor a fishmonger could be called a 'craftsman,' as neither the one nor the other made, fashioned, or produced anything; but their fellow-citizens, the bakers and the cooks, depended upon them for many of the raw materials, without which their crafts would have languished. The butchers, too, had an important part to play, and *their* particular craft is mentioned in the City records as early as 1299.

The Baker and the Cook

Grocers were at first known as 'pepperers,' and the main part of their trade concerned those spices which, as we have seen, were exceedingly important in a state of society wherein fresh meat was unknown during the winter months. In the fourteenth century they changed their name to 'grocers,' because they sold many commodities *en gros*, or wholesale. In France, however, they are still called *épiciers*, or 'spicers.'

The Fishmongers' Guild was one of the most ancient in London, and one of the most wealthy. Every one, rich and poor, ate fish at least once a week all the year round and every day during Lent, so the demand for their wares was brisk. They had their own wharf on Thames-side, at the place once called Belinns' Gate and now called Billingsgate, which is still the centre of the fish-trade. In 1340 a dispute broke out between them and the Skinners, which led to a pitched battle in Cheapside, resulting in many broken heads and bleeding noses.

We learn something, though not, perhaps, as much as we should like to learn, about the ways of Elizabethan cooks in the plays of Shakespeare. In the second part of *Henry IV*, when the fat knight, Sir John Falstaff, arrives at the Gloucestershire manor-house of his old acquaintance Justice Shallow, his host orders "William, Cook," to prepare a pleasant little meal, "some pigeons, a couple of short-legged hens, a joint of mutton, and any pretty little tiny kickshaws." No fish, you will notice, and no sweets or vegetables, unless the "little tiny kickshaws" included these. In the eating-houses of Elizabethan London eggs and butter, stewed prunes, and roasted capons were favourite dishes. The seafarers of that restless time were bringing new and wonderful dainties to charm the palates of their stay-at-home brethren, potatoes and pineapples among them.

During the eighteenth and early nineteenth centuries it was much the custom in London and the larger towns for poor folk to buy a joint of meat, or a goose, or even to make a pie, and then take it to be cooked in a cookshop. This was particularly the case on a Sunday, the only day in the week when the very poor enjoyed anything substantial in the way of good things to eat. You will

The Book of Craftsmen

remember in Dickens's *Christmas Carol* how on Christmas Day " there emerged from scores of by-streets, lanes and nameless turnings innumerable people carrying their dinners to the bakers' shops," and how the small son and daughter of the Cratchit family thought they could smell their very own goose as they passed the baker's.

Like every other human invention, but perhaps to a greater degree than some of the others, the craft of the cook is affected by time and place. People have always—and everywhere—liked good things to eat, but their ideas as to what is good depend upon the land and the period in which they live. The Chinese cook, who prepares pickled fir-cones, soused sharks' fins, and eggs many years old, would find difficulty in giving satisfaction to a Persian master who wanted legs of mutton cooked with rice and raisins, or a Spanish mistress who ordered the dish known as *arroz valenciano*, consisting of rice, olive oil, red pepper in the pod, and beef, rabbit, or mutton.

Different nations obviously have different tastes, not only because the national temperament varies, but also because in each country the vegetables, fishes, and fruits vary too. The Italian cook, like the Spaniard, lives in a land where olives grow, and uses lots of olive oil. The Scot lives in a land where many acres are sown with oats, so oatmeal, not only in the proverbial form of porridge, plays quite a large part in Scottish dishes. Poultry is found in almost every country, except those in the extreme Arctic and torrid regions, but it is noteworthy that hens are not mentioned in the Old Testament at all, though they appear in the New. Gourd-like vegetables, such as marrows, pumpkins, and cucumbers, abounded in Bible lands, and so did the so-called ' bitter ' herbs used as flavourings for sauces. Eggs were probably eaten by prehistoric people, who raided birds' nests long before the jungle fowl of India were domesticated and became the ancestors of all the strutting cocks and clucking hens in Europe. We get a glimpse of a man, probably a Babylonian or Assyrian Jew, employed in this traditional manner in the tenth chapter of Isaiah:

THE CHEF OF THE HOTEL CHATHAM, PARIS
Sir William Orpen.
Diploma Gallery, Royal Academy of Arts

The Baker and the Cook

> And my hand hath found as a nest the riches of the people : and as one gathereth eggs that are left, have I gathered all the earth; and there was none that moved the wing, or opened the mouth, or peeped.

The prophet Jeremiah alludes to the " partridge that sitteth on eggs and hatcheth them not," and Job to the lack of maternal feeling on the part of the ostrich, who lays her eggs in the sand and leaves them to be crushed by any passing foot. Ostrich-eggs are said to be quite good to eat, and, instead of crushing them with his foot, the wayfarer through the Chaldæan desert probably picked them up sometimes and took them home with him.

The Romans liked game-birds, and the Roman cook had often to prepare pheasants, partridges, guinea-fowl, peacocks, and quails. Even less familiar birds, such as flamingos, found a place in the poultry-yard of a rich Roman's country house, and, as we have seen, some of the more foolish and fantastic emperors used to eat nightingales' tongues, perhaps in the hope that by so doing they might make their own voices sweeter. The Roman cook did not depend upon home produce for his raw materials. His kitchen was furnished, and his master's banquets were adorned, with bacon from Spain, oysters from Britain, cockles from Africa, lentils from Egypt, prunes from Damascus, saffron from Cilicia, white wine from the island of Cos, honey from Attica, pickles from Byzantium. With these he was able to produce wonderful meals, and so greatly did the Romans appreciate good things to eat that a really skilful cook was quite an important person, and if he was born a slave he was often able to save up enough money to purchase his freedom long before he grew too old to enjoy it.

Here is the menu of a modest Roman dinner, prepared by the cook of the poet Martial: mallows, mint, lettuce, leeks, elecampane, slices of egg topped with anchovies, by way of *hors-d'œuvre*; a young kid, served with green beans and sprouts of cabbage, chicken and ham, formed what we should call the *entrées*, and ripe fruits provided the dessert. Wild mushrooms were prized above the cultivated sort, and long-shaped eggs more than the rounder kind. Beans cooked in red earthenware pots were

The Book of Craftsmen

considered a delicacy, and soda was put in the water with green vegetables to preserve their clear colour.

The cook figures in many proverbial sayings. "Too many cooks spoil the broth" is an easy one to understand, though neither the ancient Egyptians nor the medieval English seem to have thought it unwise to have their meals prepared by a regular regiment of culinary craftsmen. "God sends the meat and the devil sends the cooks" is more complimentary to the butcher than to the cook. Other less well-known sayings are: "It is a bad cook that will not lick his own fingers," and "Every cook praises his own sauce."

How little things have changed in England—or, for the matter of that, anywhere—since Anglo-Saxon times we realize when we look back at the youths taking part in the colloquies of Ælfric. It is still true that without cooks we should have to eat our meat raw, and we should have no sauce with it; and it is still true that without the baker we could live neither very well nor very long—the baker in whose alluring window children still find an irresistible charm!

CHAPTER IX
THE WORKER IN LEATHER

WE shall find him in a cave when we come to the end of our quest for the first worker in leather: we shall see him stooping over the carcase of some wild beast slain with his flint-tipped arrows or his flint-headed axe, stripping off its skin, and scraping it industriously with yet another tool made of the ever-helpful flint. In the very beginning of things he would merely take the hide, dry it either in the sun or by the cave hearth, and wrap it round himself. Slowly—but this part of the story belongs to the tailor—he would learn to hack the hide into the shape of a rough tunic, and then he or his wife would sew up the two sides with needles made of thorn or bone and threads made of animal fibre. At first the hide would be left all shaggy and hairy, and, for lack of the processes of curing or tanning, which came later, would be very liable to harden and crack.

Then, no one knows how far back in the distant past it may have been, men took to rubbing the newly stripped hide with the natural fat of the beast to which it belonged, and then, when it was well saturated, drying it and smoothing it, and so fashioning from it something much more serviceable, and also decidedly nicer to look at, than the old uncouth pelts.

The introduction of bronze led to many improvements in the conditions under which our predecessors lived their hard and perilous lives. And as the centuries passed new uses were found for the more tough and supple leather which they had learned how to produce. The lake-dwellers of the late Stone Age stretched skins over hollow pieces of wood, and over earthenware rings, in order to make drums. One of the earliest forms of the small boat of which we have any knowledge, after the raft made from tree-

The Book of Craftsmen

trunks lashed together, and the dug-out scooped out of a tree, is the coracle, made of leather stretched over a framework of wicker. Big ships are another matter, and even *they*, after they came into being, sometimes had leather sails!

It seems that one of the first animals to be tamed by man was the horse. Therefore one of the earliest uses to which leather was put must have been the same as one of the most frequent uses to which it is put to-day—the making of harness. The small, fleet, thick-necked horses which drew the chariots of the prehistoric chieftains were controlled by reins made of hide, attached to the chariot by traces made of hide, and probably stimulated to activity by whips made of hide. The people who harnessed, drove, and rode them wore not only garments but footgear of the same material. Already the harness-maker and the sandal-maker were emerging from the stage of home-workers and specializing in their several crafts.

The ancient Egyptians—we can never go very far without finding ourselves face to face with them—understood the method of curing leather with the aid of animal fat and either natural or artificial heat

EGYPTIAN LEATHER-WORKERS
The man at the top is cutting thongs; the two men below are twisting them; the man at the bottom is piercing the sole of a sandal to receive one of the thongs which you can see to the right of his head.

at a very remote period. They also knew how to remove the hair from a hide by steeping it in water and then treating it with lime,

The Worker in Leather

and they could dye it in beautiful colours, and emboss it with beautiful designs.

So many things were made of leather in the land of the Pharaohs —sandals, seats for chairs, bow-cases, harness, shields, water-bottles, straps for fastening mummy-wrappings and for many other purposes, girdles, and thongs—that the worker in leather was an important member of the community, and in the great royal city

EGYPTIAN SANDAL-MAKERS AT WORK
Notice the man on the right tightening a thong with his teeth.

of Thebes a whole quarter was occupied wholly by practisers of this craft. Outside the shop, or the workshop, of the leather-cutter hung a complete hide, showing the original form of the animal, with four legs and a tail, but without a head. Inside you would see coils of straps and dangling rows of sandals, with busy workmen cutting leather, or smoothing it, or shaping it into the soles of sandals, piercing it with awls, polishing it with stones, or stitching it over a wooden form.

The simplest kind of Egyptian sandal consisted of plaited papyrus-reeds attached with leather thongs; but a people who loved beautiful things, and who knew how to fashion them, was not likely to be satisfied with anything so rough. Elegant sandals and gorgeous slippers adorned the slim, tawny feet of the princes and priests, merchants and scribes and rich ladies, dwelling on the banks of the Nile four or five thousand years ago. The leather was stained with many rich colours, the thongs were clasped with

The Book of Craftsmen

buckles of gold. Sometimes the women's shoes were dangling with golden tabs that tinkled as they walked—to the strong disapproval of the prophet Isaiah when he heard them in the streets of Zion!

Shoes figure largely in the Bible. It was the Jewish custom in the olden times, just as it is still the Mohammedan custom in the East, to slip off the shoes—more properly speaking, sandals—when entering a holy place. When the captain of the angelic host came, sword in hand, to Joshua at Gilgal " he said unto Joshua, Loose thy shoe from off thy foot, for the place whereon thou standest is holy "; and you will remember that when God spoke out of the bush that burned with fire and was not consumed Moses also was bidden to " put off his shoes from off his feet." A curious custom mentioned in the Old Testament is that of a man plucking off his shoe and giving it to his neighbour as a pledge or testimony confirming an act of purchase or exchange. You find this custom in the story of Ruth. Even if, as some modern scholars hold, it was a glove and not a shoe which is meant by the original Hebrew word, this custom brings us near to the leather-worker, for the glove also would be fashioned from some sort of hide. In the Psalms the phrase " over Edom will I cast out my shoe " suggests a symbolic ceremony in which a conqueror flings his sandal over the head of a captive. To put—or to have—one's shoes upon one's feet was a recognized sign that one was going forth to war, or setting forth upon a journey. The pious child of Israel was bidden to eat unleavened bread at the Passover with his staff in his hand and his shoes upon his feet. On the other hand, to remove the shoes from the feet was a sign of mourning as well as of reverence. The 'shoes' in question would be plaited-reed sandals with leather thongs of the simplest kind, and that they were of very small value may be gathered from the sixth verse of the second chapter of the Prophet Amos, where Israel is reproached for having " sold the righteous for silver, and the poor for a pair of shoes." This verse may have been the origin of the old nursery rhyme beginning,

The Worker in Leather

*Nebuchadnezzar, King of the Jews,
Sold his wife for a pair of shoes.*

There was, of course, a further symbol connected in the Oriental mind with the shoe or sandal—the unfastening or unloosening of the strap of one person's shoe by another as an act of homage or respect. You will remember that John the Baptist declared: " There cometh one mightier than I after me, whose shoes I am not worthy to stoop down and unloose."

Among the more civilized peoples of the antique world the rough sandal gave place to the elegant and beautiful slipper, the coloured leather shoe with the peaked and upturned toe, and even to something not unlike the top-boot of eighteenth- and nineteenth-century Europe. The Assyrians wore high boots of leather laced up the front and also curious slippers with stiff soles and leather heel-coverings which left the instep and the toes bare. That warlike people, the Hittites, of whom we hear a great deal in the Old Testament, wore stout leather boots with curled-up toes and very thick soles.

From all these facts it is clear that the cobbler, the shoemaker, the skinner, the currier, and every other craftsman who worked in leather, were kept busy during those long pre-Christian centuries, when the centre of civilization lay to the south and east of the eastern hemisphere, and when those countries which afterwards led the world in science, industry, and invention were as yet wild, misty, almost unimagined places beyond a wide and perilous sea.

The beautiful and spirited horses which drew the light, highly polished chariots of the Egyptians were, like the queer little nags of prehistoric men, harnessed with thongs, traces, reins, and headstalls of leather, often made gay with plumes, with studs of coloured enamel, and with bits of burnished bronze. The seats of the painted or inlaid chairs used in the houses of well-to-do people were often made of interlacing thongs of hide, dyed blue, or crimson, or purple. The bottles in which water was carried were—as they still are in many Eastern lands—bottles not of glass or of

The Book of Craftsmen

pottery but of leather. This is the kind of bottle into which you are warned against putting new wine in the second chapter of St Mark.[1] For smaller and more elegant bottles other materials were used—glass, probably introduced by the Phœnicians, alabaster, ivory, and gold.

Owing to its comparatively perishable nature, leather has not been able to endure the destructive influence of time as successfully as many other materials have done, and examples of very ancient leatherwork are not numerous. None the less there *are* sandals, shoes, thongs, and fragments of cured hide here and there in museums, examples which give us quite a good idea of how people were shod, and horses were harnessed, and shields were covered, and chairs were seated in the vanished pre-Christian world.

In the epics of Homer we hear much about the shields of " well-tanned bulls' hides " used in battle by the bronze-helmeted warriors, both " the horse-taming Trojans " and " the long-haired Achaians " who came to besiege them in the little walled town of Troy. Their helmets were held on by chin-straps of embroidered leather; their swords were sheathed in well-wrought leather scabbards. We actually learn the name of the leather-worker who made the shield of Ajax—" Tychios, far best of curriers, who made him his shining shield of sevenfold hides of strong bulls, overlaid with bronze." And we are told, too, that this skilful craftsman " had his home in Hyle." Perhaps it was he also who made the hero's " belt, bright with purple." The custom of dyeing ox-hides and sheepskin this royal colour seems to have prevailed throughout Homeric Greece. In the palace of Odysseus and Penelope on the island of Ithaca there was a bed fashioned of the wood of a living fig-tree and laced with thongs of purple leather. The ivory cheek-pieces of horses' harness might be steeped in the same hue. Owing to the constant use of chariots by Greeks, Macedonians, and Ionians, the harness-maker can seldom have been long idle in their lands.

Like the Egyptians, the Greeks wore chiefly sandals, and these

[1] Also the fifth chapter of St Luke.

The Worker in Leather

items of attire play as important a part in Greek myth and story as they do in Biblical history. Thus you have the story of a beautiful lady called Rhodope, who left her pretty little sandals on the edge of the river while she was bathing. An eagle snatched up one of them and carried it off, and dropped it at the feet of Psammetichus, King of Egypt. The astonished monarch decided that the owner of such a dainty sandal probably had a dainty foot, and was seized with a great wish to find and behold her. So, after the manner of the Prince in the fairy-tale of Cinderella, he sent messengers far and wide to discover the lady. And when she was discovered he married her—again like Cinderella's Prince. And you will remember how Jason, on his way to Iolcus, lost one sandal, and so alarmed the usurper Pelias, the stealer of his rightful kingdom, who had been warned by an oracle to beware of a youth who should enter the city with one foot shod and the other bare.

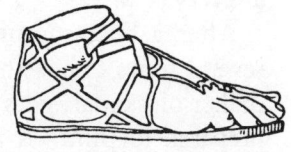

A GREEK SANDAL
The foot of Hermes of Olympia.

In ancient Athens, at the time when the " violet-crowned city " was at the summit of her glory, the tanners, shoemakers, and cobblers formed well-defined groups of craftsmen, all very flourishing. The philosopher Socrates must have been unpopular with all these groups, since it was his habit to stride about unshod in every sort of weather!

With the aid of various Greek authors and dramatists it is possible to reconstruct the daily life of one of these Athenian sandal-makers. No sooner does the cock crow than the industrious fellow springs out of bed and, carrying his pet bird in its cage, hurries round to his workshop. Presently a lady comes in and asks for a pair of slippers; a sportsman clamours for a pair of stout buskins for hunting; a young girl in a scarlet cloak asks for a pair of cork soles. Other ladies want new latchets, and are anxious to see the latest 'parrot-coloured' shoes. Presently a perfumed dandy with a flower behind each ear enters, and requests that he may be shown the fashionable shoes called after the famous fop Alcibiades.

The Book of Craftsmen

Visitors from Arcadia demand sandals decorated with moons, and the quaintest request of all comes from a flute-player, who wants a special kind of sandal with a very thick sole, having in the toe-part a small metal gadget which makes a tuneful tinkling sound at every step.

After a busy morning, in the course of which he is obliged several times to box the ears of his idle or clumsy apprentices, the maker of sandals goes home to the dinner his wife has meanwhile prepared for him. It is a frugal meal, consisting only of a mess of wheat and kidney beans, but probably the unfortunate apprentices have even harder fare, and not so much of it. On a half-holiday, when business has been brisk, he takes his wife to the great open-air theatre, whither all Athens throngs to enjoy and to criticize the wonderful tragedies and the gay, audacious comedies written by the Greek dramatists of the Golden Age. If the play happens to be *The Knights* of Aristophanes our sandal-maker will enjoy seeing a tanner, in the person of the mob-leader, Cleon, made to look ridiculous. It seems that tanners and shoemakers used to find it very difficult to appreciate each other's good qualities! In any case, a leather-worker, whether a tanner, or a cobbler, or a fashioner of delicate sandals, would take a professional interest in the buskins, or high-heeled half-boots, worn by the actors. Another name for this type of theatrical footgear was 'cothurnus.' The thickness of the sole and the height of the heel added between two and four inches to the natural stature of the wearer.

You have probably heard the saying, 'Let the cobbler stick to his last,' but perhaps you may not have heard its supposed origin. Once when the famous Greek painter Apelles—whom we met in an earlier chapter—was painting a picture of Venus a cobbler ventured to criticize the goddess's sandal. The painter, far from being too proud to take a hint, promptly made the alterations indicated; but when the cobbler, waxing more bold, began next day to carp at the outline of the foot and ankle in the picture Apelles exclaimed indignantly, "Let the cobbler stick to his last!"

The Worker in Leather

That energetic people, the Romans, wore both boots and sandals, stout boots, good for marching over rough country in uncouth lands, and elegant sandals, suitable for donning in the privacy of the house, where the floor would be of polished and tessellated marble. The gay ladies of Pompeii loved slippers of white or scarlet leather, or of leather steeped in gold paint. The senators of Rome sometimes sported black buskins ornamented with the numeral ' C ' in gold, as a proud reminder of

A ROMAN BOOT
Guildhall Museum

the fact that they belonged to a body of men whose original number was fixed by Romulus at exactly one hundred. The spiked military boot of the legionaries was called ' caliga,' and it was because that very queer person the Emperor Caius used to wear miniature military boots as a child that the soldiers gave him the nickname of Caius Caligula.

The shoemakers of Rome were among the most important of the craft-guilds. They had their own special quarter in the city, near that of the booksellers, and their shops were painted in bright colours to attract the attention and please the eyes of their customers. The Greek shoemaker's habit of keeping a pet bird in his shop descended—like so many other Greek habits—to his Roman counterpart. Usually these

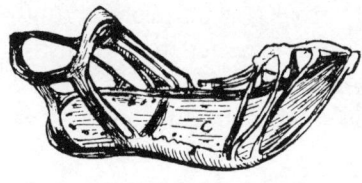

A ROMAN SANDAL
Guildhall Museum

birds were of a breed that could be taught to talk—and thereby hangs a rather delightful tale.

In the year 30 B.C. there was some uncertainty among the people of Rome as to the probable outcome of the struggle between Octavius Cæsar, nephew of Julius Cæsar and afterwards the Emperor Augustus, and Marcus Antonius. A certain shoemaker who regarded Octavius Cæsar as the likelier man taught his tame

The Book of Craftsmen

crow to say, "Hail, conquering Cæsar!" Another and more cautious member of the same craft taught *his* pet to say, "Hail, conquering Antony!" *as well as* "Hail, conquering Cæsar!" When Cæsar, having defeated Antony at the battle of Actium, returned in triumph to Rome his victorious procession traversed the *Vicus Sandaliarum*, the sandal-makers' street, on its way to the temple of Jupiter Capitolinus. You can imagine how quickly the sandal-makers flung their tools aside and swarmed out into the street to see the conqueror pass! First came a band of musicians trumpeting loudly; then led oxen, destined to be sacrificed as a thank-offering; then carts laden with the spoils of victory; then captives clanking in chains; and finally Octavius Cæsar himself, crowned with golden leaves, and drawn in a magnificent golden chariot.

At the right moment his humble supporter dashed out of the crowd, carrying his pet crow in a wicker cage. And—also at the right moment—the clever bird cried clearly, "Hail, conquering Cæsar!" "Conquering Cæsar" was so much amused that he decided to buy the crow for twenty thousand sesterces.

Next day the cautious shoemaker went to the palace with his crow in its cage, hoping that he too might win a rich reward. But the stubborn creature would only croak, "Hail, conquering Antony!" and its dismayed master quite expected that punishment, instead of reward, would be *his* portion. Octavius Cæsar was, however, in a benign mood, and to this shoemaker also he gave a generous 'tip.'

Then a *third* member of the craft thought that it might not be too late for his talking crow to come on the scene. So he began to try to teach it the precious greeting. For some time his efforts were in vain, and he exclaimed more than once, in angry tones, "There is all my labour wasted!" Finally, however, his slow pupil learned its lesson, and he carried the crow hopefully to the palace. When Octavius Cæsar heard that yet *another* shoemaker had arrived bearing a bird in a cage he said, "Take it away! I am sick of talking crows!" Whereupon a gruff voice spoke from

The Worker in Leather

the wicker cage. "There," it remarked, "is all my labour wasted!" Greatly amused, the Emperor decided to buy the bird and to pay for it an even larger sum than the other two had cost him.

More than one sandal-maker rose to wealth and power under the later Cæsars. There was, for example, Alfenus, a cobbler of Cremona, who forsook his last and his awl and tramped to Rome, no doubt in a pair of stout marching-boots made by himself. He became a lawyer, and attained the rank of consul; yet for this he would not be remembered, nor for anything else, unless he had happened—as he did—to enjoy the friendship of two famous Roman poets, Horace and Catullus. It is true that some authorities say that he was a barber, not a cobbler, a cutter of hair rather than of hides,

A GAULISH COBBLER

but Horace's allusion to "the humble tools of his trade" suggest the awl rather than the razor! Another Roman cobbler who prospered was the one mentioned by the poet Martial—a cobbler who became so rich that he was able to sit crowned with roses, drinking rare wine out of a costly bowl.

The leather-worker had many things to do besides making sandals, buskins, marching-boots, and slippers. Another branch of his craft was concerned with the preparation of vellum and parchment for the scribe, the chronicler, and the illuminator. And in Egypt, Greece, and Rome yet another branch was concerned with the fashioning of gloves. A rough sort of glove was worn by cultivators in Homeric Greece " to protect their hands from the thorns "; and a beautifully made pair of gloves was found in the tomb of King Tut-ankh-Amen. Xenophon, the Greek historian, sneers at the Persians for wearing gloves, and according to Virgil the Trojans wore gauntlets of bulls' hide, weighted with knots of iron.

The Book of Craftsmen

Most of the gloves here mentioned would be like babies' gloves, with no separate divisions for the fingers, and only a little pouch for the thumb. Gloves with such divisions came into use among the more luxurious of the Romans under the earlier Cæsars, and were regarded as being somewhat unmanly. When, however, Roman officers and magistrates found themselves stationed in cold and dreary outposts of the Empire they were only too glad to protect their numbed fingers with warm and strong gloves.

Among the ancient Britons the craft of the leather-worker must sometimes have overlapped with that of the tailor; yet there, again, we find the harness-maker, the sandal-maker, and the maker of thongs, straps, belts, and girdles already well established.

During the Dark Ages many of the poorer folk had to be content with leather raiment. Footgear was so crude in form, consisting usually of a shapeless sort of boot, something like a Red Indian's moccasin, laced criss-cross up the leg with strips of hide or wool, that no very remarkable skill can have been needed to be a cobbler. Even in this comfortless period, however, we find traces of luxury. Prelates and princes wore gloves of deerskin, but monks and the inferior clergy were bidden to wear sheepskin only.

As the Dark Ages wane, and Christianity begins to spread over Europe, we find cobblers popping up here and there in pious legend and story. According to ancient tradition, the first Christian bishop of Alexandria, Anianus, was a cobbler, who, while fastening a new thong to St Mark's sandal, was converted by that apostle. Another cobbler-bishop was Alexander of Coana, who died a martyr's death in the third century. Very quaint is the tale of St Hugh—not St Hugh of Lincoln, a real person who lived in the twelfth century—but Hugh of Wales, a more misty and romantic figure.

Hugh was—as the hero of a fairy-story should be—a king's son, and—again like the hero of a fairy-story—he fell in love with a king's daughter. ('Kings' in Wales were only tribal chieftains.) Winifred, the fair daughter of the King of Flintshire, turned a deaf ear to the wooing of Hugh, the son of the King of Powys.

The Worker in Leather

She was a Christian, and her chief desire was to lead a solitary and meditative life in a lonely cottage beside a fountain. So Hugh went off on his travels, hoping that strange sights in distant lands might help him to forget her. They did not, and the poor young man returned to Britain. He then sought a cure for hopeless love by apprenticing himself to a shoemaker, from whom he learned the whole art and craft of the trade. Just about this time the

ST WINIFRED AND ST HUGH
As a seventeenth-century artist imagined them.

Emperor Diocletian issued severe edicts against the Christians in his dominions, and among the hapless victims of Imperial cruelty were both Hugh and Winifred! By a coincidence, which may either have comforted or appalled the prince, the princess whom he loved was executed at the same place, on the same day, at the same hour. His fellow-shoemakers gathered round to bid the royal 'prentice farewell, and, having nothing else to bequeath to them, he told them that he left them his bones. Of these bones the shoemakers later obtained possession, and from them they are said to have fashioned a set of tools, for which reason a cobbler's tools used, in the olden days, to be called 'St Hugh's bones'! But this is rather curious—modern cobblers *still* use a piece of bone—though not human bone—for rubbing the welt (the edge of the sole) and the under-surface of the sole itself.

The Book of Craftsmen

St Hugh, in spite of his picturesque associations with the cobbler's craft, is not the patron saint of shoemakers. That honour belongs to St Crispin, who sometimes has to divide it with his brother, St Crispianus. They were real people, two young Roman Christians who fled from Rome during the Diocletian persecutions and took refuge in the Gaulish city now called Soissons. There they earned their living by working as shoemakers, and distinguished themselves by the ardour with which they preached the faith of Christ. This ardour attracted the attention of the Roman officials in the district, and in the year 287 the brothers suffered martyrdom. Legend declares that they were thrown into a cauldron of boiling lead. Their feast-day is October 25, the day upon which the battle of Agincourt was fought, as the English King and his soldiers did not fail gratefully to remember at the time.

So many cripples adopted the profession of shoemaking that St Giles, the patron saint of cripples, is often found sharing with St Crispin and St Crispianus the honourable responsibility of befriending members of the craft.

As years passed the leather-workers split up into a number of different branches. There were skinners, tanners, leather-sellers, whittawers (or makers of light-coloured leather), loriners (or makers of bridles and bits), saddlers, glovers, girdlers, pouch-makers, and cordwainers. The difference between the tanner and the tawer, or whittawer, was this: the first dressed ox-, cow-, and calf-hides by steeping them in a preparation of oak-bark; the second dressed the skins of deer, sheep, lamb, or horse with the aid of alum and oil. It was commonly said that the tanner's craft made his *own* skin tough and brown, and this alleged fact was the source of various jokes at his expense in Tudor times.

ST CRISPIN

As imagined by a French wood-carver of the fifteenth century.

The Worker in Leather

The cordwainers were so called because they specialized in the very fine leather imported from Cordova in Spain. This leather was prepared by a method introduced into the Spanish peninsula by the Moorish invaders of the eighth century.

For quite a long time the various leather-workers of London-town were united in a single fraternity, and in the earliest known

FLORENTINE HARNESS OF THE FIFTEENTH CENTURY
The horseman is Lorenzo de' Medici, nicknamed 'The Magnificent.'

ordinance concerning them they are described as *alutarii*, that is to say, workers in leather dressed with alum—Latin *aluta*. In 1340 " twelve good and lawful men " were chosen to direct the activities of the craft, and in 1439 Henry VI granted a charter, under the name of 'cordwainers,' to one of the craft-groups.

The wardens of the Cordwainers' Company were entrusted with the task of ensuring that Spanish leather should not be mixed with ordinary sheepskin and then sold as if it were all Spanish. In 1345 one of these wardens charged a cordwainer called William Cokk

The Book of Craftsmen

with selling shoes of this kind. The case was tried before the Lord Mayor of London, and the culprit was fined forty pence—about ten times that amount in modern currency.

Strictly speaking, a cordwainer in medieval London was a craftsman who worked in *new* leather, while a cobbler was one who worked in *old*. There was a good deal of rivalry between the two, and in 1409 an ordinance was passed to regulate their constant disputes. The curriers, who broke away from the cordwainers late

THE LEATHER-SELLERS' 'CROWN'

in the reign of Henry III, were wont to bicker with the haberdashers, and the skinners with the tailors; from which it would appear that the workers in leather, the wielders of St Hugh's bones, were a somewhat quarrelsome breed!

The glovers and the pouch-makers were merged into the important guild of the leather-sellers early in the sixteenth century, and the combined fraternities used to go in procession on certain appointed days to the ancient chapel of St Thomas of Acon, near Cheapside, built on the site of the birthplace of St Thomas Becket, and founded by his sister. When a new master is elected he has still to don the curious embroidered head-band known as the leather-sellers' crown—for the leather-sellers form an important City company to this day, and, like many of the other great companies, they cling affectionately to their old traditions.

Edward III gave the skinners of London their charter, and his weak-willed, gorgeous grandson, Richard II, elevated them to the rank of a religious fraternity dedicated to the Body of Christ. Upon the feast of Corpus Christi the members of this brotherhood

The Worker in Leather

used to walk in procession through the City, wearing their livery, carrying "more than a hundred costly, garnished torches of wax," and followed by "more than two hundred" priests and clerks, chanting as they went.

In Edinburgh the cordwainers had their guild by the middle of the fifteenth century, and they were among the fourteen craft fraternities which, on all occasions of tumult or civic indignation, rallied to the famous Blue Blanket, the popular name for the azure-coloured banner which hung in St Giles's Church during the peaceful intervals between such occasions. All the principal towns of England and Scotland had their leather-workers' guilds, flourishing and active, in the time of the later Plantagenets and the earlier Stuarts. In Northampton, now a great centre of the trade, we find shoemakers mentioned as early as 1401.

Two Popes, Urban IV and John XXII, were the sons of shoemakers, and one famous poet, Hans Sachs of Nürnberg, was himself a cobbler. Wagner introduces this poetical shoemaker into his opera, *Die Meistersinger*, and one scene takes place in Sachs' shop. A handsome tribute to the handiwork of *his* shoemaker was paid by Thomas Coryat early in the seventeenth century. This enterprising West Country gentleman journeyed one thousand nine hundred and seventy-five miles on foot, through Paris, Lyons, Turin, Venice, Zürich, and Strassburg, and on his safe return to Somerset hung up his travel-worn shoes in Odcombe Church, of which, when he was a child, his old father had been the Rector.

Fashions in shoes varied violently in Plantagenet and Tudor times, and the cordwainers were kept busy satisfying the whims of their patrons. In the reign of Richard II a shoe with an exaggeratedly long peaked toe was introduced from Poland, and for that reason was dubbed a 'poulaine,' or else—from the city of Cracow in Poland—a 'cracowe.' Humorists of the period made very merry at the expense of the dandies who sported this fantastic footgear, and described gleefully

A 'POULAINE' OR 'CRACOWE'

The Book of Craftsmen

how they pricked each other's ankles when they stood herded together in church. The peaks grew and grew, until finally they had to be attached with cords or chains to the wearer's knees. In 1468 a papal decree limited the length of such peaks to two inches, but even the Pope could not prevail upon the dandies to give up their poulaines while the craze lasted.

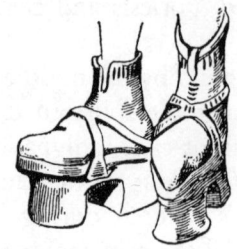

WOODEN CLOGS WITH LEATHER THONGS WORN BY FRENCH PEASANTS IN THE TWELFTH CENTURY

As medieval streets were in wet weather mere rivers of horrible mud, clogs, called 'pattens,' were worn to raise the foot above the danger-level. To make these the worker in wood and the worker in leather usually collaborated. The patten had to follow the form of the shoe, with the result that the late fourteenth- and many fifteenth-century examples are as fantastically narrow and pointed as the poulaines which they served to hoist clear of the mud.

On the Continent, especially in Venice, these clogs reached such a height that the wearer was elevated as if upon stilts, and some skill was needed to walk in them.

With the Tudor period a change came over the shape of the shoe, which broadened until the sole was almost square. According to one account, the fashion for excessively broad shoes was introduced by an Emperor who had had the misfortune to be born with six toes instead of the usual five!

BROCADE SHOE WITH PATTEN ATTACHED
London Museum

Before we go on to talk about the Elizabethan shoemaker let us pause for a moment to look at another worker in leather—the maker of wallets, pouches, purses, and scrips. Poor folk carried at their girdles pouches of rabbit-skin clasped with pewter or

The Worker in Leather

'latten' clasps. Knights and nobles had swinging purses of fine Cordova leather, coloured, embossed, or even embroidered, and fastened with fine metalwork in silver-gilt, bronze, or even gold. Pilgrims carried scrips of sheepskin, and workmen kept their tools in bags of the same homely hide. Lawyers used for their parchments a receptacle made of lambskin and known as a 'budget'—and that is the reason why, in this year of grace, the Chancellor of the Exchequer is said to 'open the Budget' when he produces the facts and figures determining taxation for the next financial year.

The hero of the delightful Elizabethan comedy called *The Shoemakers' Holiday* is a certain Sir Simon Eyre, who in the middle years of the fifteenth century endowed the city with a lead-roofed granary and market. This old play belongs to our study of the leather-worker because it gives a lively picture of the household of a London shoemaker at the period when it was written and acted—that is to say, in "the spacious days of great Elizabeth." We make the acquaintance of cheery, bustling Simon Eyre, his sharp-tongued wife, Margery, and his three apprentices, Hodge, Firk, and Ralph; we see him early astir, clamouring for the street to be swept outside his door, for his men to wash their faces, for breakfast to be got ready, and for 'St Hugh's bones' to be "set a-work"—all this before seven o'clock in the morning!

Simon Eyre is on excellent terms with his apprentices. "Am I not Simon Eyre?" he exclaims. "Are these not my brave men, brave shoemakers, all gentlemen of the gentle craft?" And he shouts for "a dozen cans of beer" for his journeymen—four cans apiece, which sounds a generous allowance. When he is elected sheriff, Margery, his wife, determined to live up to her new dignity, orders a French hood and a farthingale, and says to Hodge, the foreman-apprentice, "Thou knowst the length of my foot—prithee, let me have a pair of shoes made; cork, good Roger—wooden heel, too." When Simon is chosen Lord Mayor of London his men rejoice. "Oh, rare, my hearts," cries Firk, "let's march together for the honour of St Hugh to the great

The Book of Craftsmen

new hall . . . which our master, the new Lord Mayor, hath built! "

The new Lord Mayor entertains the King at dinner. Before the banquet begins he says to the throng of shoemakers who attend him, " all with napkins on their shoulders," " My meaning is that

A FRENCH SHOEMAKER'S SHOP OF THE SEVENTEENTH CENTURY

none but shoemakers, none but the livery of my company, shall in their satin hoods wait upon the trencher of my sovereign."

The King is evidently much impressed by the fine appearance of those who wait upon him, and asks Simon if they are all shoemakers. To this his merry host replies: " All shoemakers, my liege; all gentlemen of the gentle craft, true Trojans, courageous cordwainers. They all kneel to the shrine of holy St Hugh."

Though Queen Elizabeth loved gorgeous shoes her influence did not make the leather-workers more prosperous, as her favourite footwear seems to have been fashioned of silk brocade. The literature of her reign is, however, full of allusions to shoes; to high cork heels and silken rosettes; to slashed or ' razed ' uppers;

The Worker in Leather

to 'pumps,' which were worn by actors then as the buskin had been worn by the actors of ancient Greece; to slippers, then, as now, a sign of unceremonious ease; and to cobblers, shoemakers, and their productions.

In Shakespeare's *Julius Cæsar* we meet a saucy Roman cobbler who bandies words with the Tribune Marullus, and even makes puns under his stately nose.

> *Marullus.* What trade art thou? Answer me directly.
> *Second Commoner.* A trade, sir, that, I hope, I may use with a safe conscience; which is, indeed, sir, a mender of bad soles.
> *Marullus.* What trade, thou knave? Thou naughty knave, what trade?
> *Second Commoner.* Nay, I beseech you, sir, be not out[1] with me: yet, if you be out,[2] sir, I can mend you.
> *Marullus.* What meanest thou by that? mend me, thou saucy fellow!
> *Second Commoner.* Why, sir, cobble you.
> *Flavius.* Thou art a cobbler, art thou?
> *Second Commoner.* Truly, sir, all that I live by is with the awl. . . . I am, indeed, sir, a surgeon to old shoes; when they are in great danger, I recover them.[3]

It is to be hoped that this cobbler was more skilful with his awl, his cutting-knife, and his needle than he was with his tongue, for his jokes are both clumsy and feeble.

Leather-workers, apart from shoemakers and cobblers, were, in one way or another, associated with the arts of war. It was they who made the belts and the buckles to which swords and daggers were attached, and the scabbards in which they were sheathed; they who made the leather jerkins and buff coats worn by men-at-arms; they who made the holsters in which pistols were carried; they who made the saddles and bridles of the chargers, and the traces of the gun-teams. Again, it was they who made the gloves which figure so largely in romantic legends, both the perfumed and embroidered

---

[1] Out of temper.
[2] Out at heel, or with his feet coming through his shoes.
[3] Act I, Scene i.

The Book of Craftsmen

gloves given by ladies as love-tokens to their knights (and carried by those knights on their helmets), and the stouter type of gauntlet worn by gentlemen, and occasionally flung down by them by way of a challenge. The steel gauntlet forming part of a complete suit of armour, as well as the mitten-like chain-mail glove, would, of

A SEVENTEENTH-CENTURY SHOEMAKER FITTING A
DISTINGUISHED CUSTOMER

course, be the handiwork of a craftsman whose medium was not leather, but iron or steel.

Though leather has always had—and still has—these associations with the more violent and strenuous aspect of human activity, it is also intimately connected with the more contemplative side of life. Even in ancient Rome the shoemakers and the booksellers lived and worked in adjacent quarters, and this neighbourly attitude between the two crafts continued all through the Middle Ages. Paper gradually took the place of parchment and vellum as printed

The Worker in Leather

characters took the place of letters laboriously traced with quill pens, but many books were still encased in bindings of leather—as most fine books are to this day. In the antique world books were written on long strips of papyrus, parchment, or vellum, and rolled round two wooden cylinders. When the shape of the book underwent a drastic alteration and it ' put forth leaves ' the craft of the bookbinder came into being. Some of the earliest and most exquisite examples of this craft belong to the realms of the metal-worker and the ivory-carver, but for many centuries bookbindings of leather have been common wherever books are known. Such bindings can be veritable works of art, embossed with delicate designs, stained with rich colours, and enriched with gold.

A FINE EXAMPLE OF ENGLISH BOOK-BINDING, EXECUTED FOR CHARLES II
British Museum

Though the custom of using leather instead of tapestry as a hanging for walls never became so popular in England as it was in some Continental countries, furniture-makers have long exercised their skill in giving cushions or seats of leather to sofas and chairs. It is as useful an ingredient in the making of a pair of bellows as it is in the making of a big drum. Many workmen still carry the tools of their trade in leather bags, and not a few of them, such as the blacksmith, wear leather aprons, too.

We have seen how leather has been connected with the fierce arts of war and the quiet arts of peace. Among those arts is the art of music, for the bag of the bagpipes is made of leather. We are

The Book of Craftsmen

apt to think of the bagpipes as a distinctive Scottish or Irish instrument, but their piercing tones have been heard in many different lands from a very early period, and there was a time when Englishmen both heard and produced them frequently. Chaucer's pilgrims rode forth to that barbaric music, and Shakespeare speaks of the melancholy " drone of a Lincolnshire bagpipe."

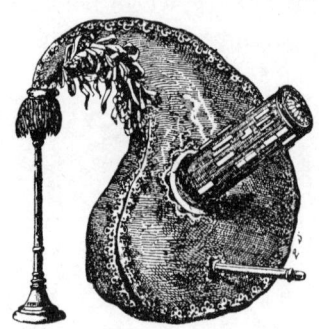

A FRENCH BAGPIPE
Seventeenth century.

Leather is also associated—in the form of bottles and stoups—with the more jovial and homely side of life. The Englishman of Tudor and Stuart times—and even of times nearer to our own—loved to quaff his nut-brown ale from a 'black jack.' Now a 'black jack' was a sort of stoup or flagon made of leather hardened by an external coating of tar, and astonished foreign visitors, noting these objects and also the use to which they were put, hastily concluded that Englishmen drank out of their boots! A particularly hard and tough form of leather called *cuir bouilli*, or boiled hide, was used for many purposes. It was often employed as a substitute for wood, or even for metal, could be embossed with handsome designs, and acquired a dusky, glossy surface as years passed.

As for the leather bottle, or the 'leather bottél' as you often see it spelled, it was a familiar and friendly sight, a favourite tavern-sign, and the subject of more than one cheery lay—for example, the lay of which these two stanzas are the last:

> Now, what do you say to these glasses fine?
> Oh, they shall have no praise of mine,
> For, if the bearer fall by the way,
> There on the ground your liquor doth lay:
>   But had it been in a leather bottél,
>   Although he had fallen, all had been well,
>   So I wish his soul in Heaven may dwell
>   That first found out the leather bottél!

The Worker in Leather

> And when the bottle in time grows old
> And will good liquor no longer hold,
> Then of the sides you may make a clout[1]
> To mend your shoes when they're worn out.
>   Or take and hang it up on a pin,
>   'Twill serve to hold hinges and odd things in;
> So I wish his soul in Heaven may dwell
> That first found out the leather bottél!

All gloves were not—and are not—made of leather, and thence it follows that all glovers were not—and are not—leather-workers. The 'fabric glove' of ancient times was a beautiful piece of needlecraft in linen or silk, meet to cover the hands of princes, prelates, and fair ladies. But the leather glove, as we have already mentioned, goes back a long way in history. The centre of that particular industry was in France at Grenoble, and in England at Worcester, Woodstock, and Ludlow. The glovers of medieval France were also sellers, though not distillers, of perfumes, and perfumed gloves were in vogue for many centuries on either side of the Channel. The glove trade in Grenoble rose into prominence late in the sixteenth century, when it was realized not only that the skins of the goats which abounded in the neighbouring hills afforded ample raw material, but also that the waters of the river Isère were particularly good for certain stages of the tawing and tanning processes. St Anne, the patron saint of glovers, was held in much honour in this city, and pageants and processions took place on her feast-day every year.

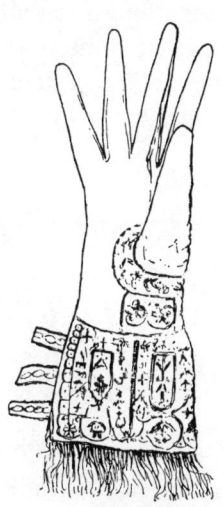

FRINGED AND EMBROIDERED LEATHER GLOVE WORN BY QUEEN ELIZABETH

London, though not, perhaps, to the same degree as the provincial towns mentioned above, was also a flourishing centre of the

---

[1] A patch.

The Book of Craftsmen

glove-maker's craft, and in 1638 Charles I granted the petition of his "loveing subjects" living in and about London and Westminster and "using the arte, trade, or mistery of Glovers" that steps should be taken to check the competition offered by unskilled or rival glovers crowding to the capital in "a disordered multitude," working in odd holes and corners, disregarding the edicts of the Glovers' Company, and making "naughtie and deceitful gloves."

The unhappy Charles, whose interest in the fortunes of his poorer subjects has already been noted in the section dealing with the potter, himself loved to wear beautiful gloves, with gauntlets richly embroidered or adorned with knots of many-coloured silken ribbons.

ENGLISH PEASANT WOMAN WEARING GLOVES
Fourteenth century.
From the Luttrell Psalter

CHAPTER X
THE FURNITURE-MAKER

IN all our previous chapters we have begun with the very first beginnings of human life and activity. We have journeyed back through the uncounted centuries to the smoky cave where our far-off ancestors began to chip flints, and mould pots, and bake bread, and twist wicker. But *this* time we shall not have to go back so far, for nothing seems more unlikely than that prehistoric man had chairs and tables! Indeed, many men of quite civilized ages had no dinner-tables, and preferred to dine recumbent on cushions or rugs.

The craft of the furniture-maker often merges into that of the worker in wood—often, but not always. Bronze, ivory, iron, marble, even gold, have been used, and still are used, though less frequently than wood, for the fashioning of chairs, beds, tables, and other necessary things coming within the furniture-maker's range. The lake-dwellers of the Stone Age probably had some sort of rough wooden contrivances to do duty for shelves, boxes, and beds, though instead of sitting on chairs they would squat on the floor, and they may have slept on the floor too. The ancient Egyptians were the real pioneers, for they had beautiful furniture of many different kinds, and their craftsmen were equally skilful in wood, bronze, and gold.

In speaking of the Egyptian worker in wood we have already remarked that his raw material was hard to come by, and that only the coarser kinds of timber could be obtained in his own country. He became skilful not only in staining the rough sycamore, tamarisk, and acacia to imitate cedar, ebony, and other rare woods, but also in the process called 'veneering.' In this process thin strips of fine wood are glued upon the poorer quality so as to give the

The Book of Craftsmen

appearance of being solid all through. In the illustration you can see Egyptian cabinet-makers at work—on the left of the picture one is applying a layer of veneer, and on the right another is dabbing glue on a flat board with a very modern-looking brush.

To show that the lighter-coloured wood is the less costly the artist has made a workman stick his adze carelessly in a block of that colour. The neat little inlaid box is his tool-box, and would contain

ANCIENT EGYPTIAN FURNITURE-MAKERS
The one on the left is veneering; the one on the right is applying glue with a brush.

his axe, adze, handsaw, chisel, mallet, drill, plane, ruler, right angle, hone, a hornful of oil, and a leather bag of nails. The tools would be of bronze, with handles of tamarisk- or acacia-wood.

The Roman writer Pliny ascribes to Dædalus, the mythical inventor to whom the first aeroplane may be traced, the invention of glue, as well as of the axe and the plumb-line. It was certainly a most useful invention!

The chairs made by the Egyptian craftsmen were often very similar to those which we see all about us in modern homes. They were sometimes upholstered, sometimes of plain wood, sometimes provided with arms, sometimes armless. The seats might be of leather, or of plaited leather thongs, or of a network of stout cords. The legs often ended in the form of the claws or the paws of some animal. Folding stools, similar to what we call camp-stools, were popular. Ebony inlaid with ivory was a favourite material, and the craftsmen reached a wonderful degree of skill in fashioning graceful and yet strong and serviceable pieces of furniture. Couches and beds were occasionally so lofty that a small set of wooden steps was needed in order to climb up on to them. They had ample cushions stuffed with feathers and covered with

The Furniture-maker

hide, linen, or embroidered tapestry, but for his head the sleeping Egyptian did not use a nice, soft pillow: he preferred a sort of neck-rest of polished and painted wood. All these objects may be seen depicted on the walls of the tomb of Rameses III at Thebes. Sometimes the legs of an Egyptian chair or table would be carved in the form of a cowering captive, one of the prisoners taken in the course of a victorious campaign. Tables were used, as in modern times, to dine at, to place various objects upon, and for ornamentation.

From a very distant period in history kings have been wont, on ceremonial occasions, not only to wear a special sort of headgear, but also to sit upon a special sort of chair. Thus it came about that the metal-worker learned to make crowns, and the maker of chairs to make thrones. In its earliest form the throne was often a mere block of stone, neither carved nor polished, like the ancient Stone of Destiny, brought from Scotland to England by Edward I, and now preserved in Westminster Abbey underneath the Coronation Chair. Various materials were used when the rough stone gave place to a throne, ivory and gold being among the chief, and by degrees the chair in which the sovereign sat became almost as much an emblem of his power as the royal diadem.

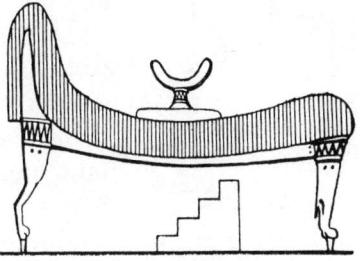

AN ANCIENT EGYPTIAN BED, WITH HEAD-REST AND STEPS

The Assyrians and Babylonians, like their neighbours and rivals, the Egyptians, adorned their houses with furniture of fine workmanship and beautiful design. Obviously they did not 'loll' in their chairs, for the backs are rigidly upright and do not suggest a restful pose. Amber, tortoiseshell, and mother-of-pearl were used for inlay, and figures of bearded men, lions, horses, and rams, and plant-forms resembling the lotus, the poppy, and the fir-cone, seem to have been admired.

That strenuous people, the ancient Greeks, went in very little for

The Book of Craftsmen

costly chairs and tables, though in the palace of Odysseus and Penelope in the rocky island of Ithaca there were " goodly carven chairs," and polished stands for spears, and tables which before meals were wiped over with " porous sponges " ! There was a bed of fig-tree wood with thongs of oxhide dyed purple, and there was a chest with " great store of iron and bronze," the battle-gear of a warrior-king. But in general a Greek house was rather sparsely furnished, and what furniture there was consisted largely of chests made to contain blankets, weapons, and objects of value.

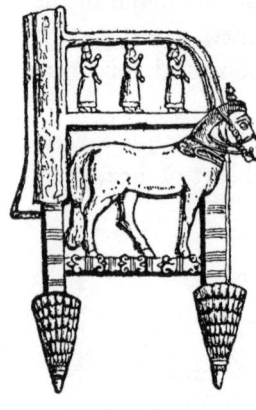

ASSYRIAN CHAIR

Though the Homeric heroes sat up to table in the modern manner, and the Greeks until the Macedonian period (fourth century B.C.) did the same, we must not imagine the Romans as following this custom—at least, not after the Punic wars of the third and second centuries before Christ. They preferred to lounge upon couches round a rather small table. For this purpose they had a group of three couches, called a *triclinium*, upon which the guests reclined during meals. Both the Greeks and the Romans borrowed this rather indolent habit from Oriental people, many of whom have retained it to this day. Beds and couches were marvels of beautiful craftsmanship in wood, metal, and other materials. Sometimes the legs were hidden by silk embroidered with scenes representing people hunting or feasting. The Roman poet Martial mentions a rich man who pretended to be ill and received his friends in his bedroom simply in order that they might see and admire the gorgeous new bedclothes he had just got from Alexandria! Chairs, however, were by no means unknown, and there were folding stools, with striped cushions, which could be carried from room to room.

In the days of the first Cæsars there was a great demand among beauty-loving patricians for table-tops made from the wood of a

The Furniture-maker

kind of cypress-tree which grew nowhere but in the Atlas Mountains. It was called Thuia-wood, and had to be cut from a section of the trunk near the root of the tree. When polished it revealed wonderful mottled markings, like the spots on a leopard's hide or the 'eyes' in a peacock's tail. The famous orator Cicero possessed a table of Thuia-wood for which he is said to have paid a million sesterces, the value of this coin being, in modern currency, about twopence.

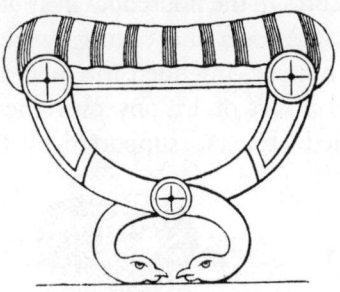

ROMAN FOLDING CHAIR

Meanwhile, what of the Far East? One of the most striking points of contrast between the Japanese and the Chinese is that the former have always tended to sit on the floor and the latter to sit on chairs. Chinese chairs can be—and often have been—things of exceeding beauty. This is particularly true of the marvellous red lacquer chairs used by emperors and mandarins and other mighty folk. The lacquer is intricately carved, with a delicacy that delights the eye: the colour is one of the richest and most satisfying shades of red ever produced by human ingenuity.

In the West the main needs of most families would be something to sit on, something to sleep on, and something to eat off; and these simple needs were met in a very simple way during the Dark Ages, though even during that rather grim period kings and bishops had thrones and other furniture of some beauty and value. When conditions improved the carpenter and the joiner came into their own, and they showed how strength, beauty, and utility can be combined in one object.

Beds, even among the Anglo-Saxons, were often elaborate and costly pieces of workmanship, with carved legs and posts and brilliantly coloured bedclothes. Sheets were unknown, but coverlets were sometimes lined with grey squirrel fur.

Owing to the medieval custom of the whole household taking their meals together at trestle-tables, the table was one of the last

The Book of Craftsmen

pieces of furniture to show any great advance in construction or design. Medieval beds and chairs were, however, important features in the household gear of well-to-do people. It was probably because roofs and ceilings were not always watertight that chairs of honour, intended for men and women of distinction, usually had a sort of canopy over the top. Beds had wooden ceilings, called 'testers,' supported by four posts—hence the term 'four-

AN ANGLO-SAXON KING IN BED

poster'—and curtains which could be drawn at night, forming a cosy, if stuffy, sort of tent. During the day these curtains were looped up, forming four bundles, one at each corner of the bedstead. Another kind of bed had a canopy only over the head.

The picture opposite, of the interior of a fifteenth-century bedroom, will give you an excellent idea of the sort of furniture which a craftsman of that period would be expected to make.

The bed, a canopied one, not a 'four-poster,' stands on an elaborately plaited rush mat. At the head is a high-backed chair, the lower part of which forms a box in which devotional books would be kept. Owing to the artist's lack of skill in perspective it is difficult to tell whether the small object by the casement has or has not a sloping top like a desk. The bench or settle on which

The Furniture-maker

the knight and the lady are seated is a solid-looking piece of woodwork, evidently drawn perilously near to the hearth, for you can see the broad ledge of the mantelshelf projecting above it. Perhaps, in spite of the fast-shut window, the season is really summer, and there is no log-fire crackling in the fireplace.

A FIFTEENTH-CENTURY FRENCH INTERIOR

Canopied chairs were richly carved in oak or chestnut, often painted and gilded, and sometimes provided with cushions covered with red Cordovan leather, or pillows of silken stuffs studded with clusters of pearls. Tables, even when not of the trestle variety, were long and narrow, the guests sitting at one side only. Movable tables were called 'boards' in England, and there must have been a fine clattering when they were folded up after meals. Stately buffets or sideboards, for the display of fine examples of

The Book of Craftsmen

goldsmiths' work, stood in the great halls, and sturdy wardrobes, with beautifully wrought hinges, locks, and handles were used for storing garments and tapestries and furs. Chests and coffers played an important part, as people not only kept valuables in them, but used them as seats. Italian furniture-makers of the fifteenth and sixteenth centuries specialized in a sort of painted and gilded coffer known as a *cassone*, and intended for the particular purpose of holding a bride's dowry.

A FRENCH CHEST OF THE FOURTEENTH CENTURY, DECORATED WITH CARVED BEASTS AND WARRIORS

The Parisian carpenters and makers of carved chests, chairs, and coffers were so famous for their skill that in lists or inventories of household gear the fact was never omitted that such and such an article was *ex operagio Parisiensi*—of Parisian manufacture. But the rather meagre amount of furniture required by even rich families in the Middle Ages meant that the demand was comparatively small, and that the craftsmen were not encouraged to try out new ideas. Only the master and mistress of a household and their most honoured guests enjoyed the privilege of a carved and canopied chair with soft cushions upholstered in stained hide or embroidered silk. Their sons and daughters perched upon small folding-chairs, or three-legged stools, or squatted on pillows on the floor.

The Renaissance, which brought so many new ideas into the

The Furniture-maker

world of the intellect, did not at first have a very marked effect on the daily life of men and women, except that, as we have seen already, classical—or what were supposed to be classical—designs appeared in metal-work, wood-work, and textiles. The shapes of chairs—and this too we have said before—were influenced by the padded breeches and hooped skirts which the tailors made for their patrons of both sexes; sideboards became larger and more ornate, and beds tended to blossom into masses of oaken fruit and foliage.

AN ENGLISH GENTLEMAN OF THE FOURTEENTH CENTURY SITTING IN A FOLDING CHAIR

One of the most famous beds ever made by English craftsmen is the Great Bed of Ware, now to be seen in the Victoria and Albert Museum. This bed, which takes its name from the Saracen's Head Inn at Ware, where it was a popular 'sight' for many years, enjoys the honour of having been mentioned by Shakespeare in *Twelfth Night*. It is elaborately carved and painted, and ornamented with grotesque figures of bearded men. Eight feet nine inches in height, ten feet eight and a half inches across, and eleven feet one inch long, it must have been a tight fit for the six London citizens and their wives who were once accommodated in it "for a frolic"!

Some idea of the sort of productions which would be expected at the hands of an Elizabethan cabinet-maker may be gathered from an inventory of the 'parler' in the house of a Cheshire alderman of the period. This 'parler' contained the following: a folding table; two benches covered with 'Turkey work'— probably coloured and patterned woollen stuff imported from the Levant; a little side-table; six 'joint-stools' covered with needlework; six stools without covers; one chair, covered with needlework; two little footstools; one long 'carpett of Turkey work' and one short one (these were not floor-coverings but

The Book of Craftsmen

table-cloths); six cushions of 'Turkey' and six of 'tapestree'; some velvet cushions with heraldic embroidery; and some framed maps. From these details we may conclude that the worthy alderman was a hospitable fellow, with a large circle of friends and kinsfolk, and, moreover, that he took an interest in the explorations and discoveries which his compatriots were then making. Of

A FLEMISH SIDEBOARD OF THE SIXTEENTH CENTURY

A FLEMISH BED OF THE SIXTEENTH CENTURY

carpenters, furniture-makers, and importers of Turkish fabrics he must have been a generous patron!

Queen Elizabeth characteristically had a fondness for gaudy and fanciful chairs and tables, and liked to recline on a sofa or 'day-bed' with a large imitation shell at the top, thereby suggesting to the admiring beholder the goddess Venus in her cradle-shell.

It was about this period that solid and handsome tables with carved legs began to take the place of the old thirty-inch-wide 'boards,' hinged so as to be easily folded up, and supported on trestles: but the word 'board' has survived in modern English, meaning not only a table at which people sit, for example, at a

The Furniture-maker

'board' meeting, but also the food which they may eat at the 'festive board,' or at a 'boarding'-house!

Another historic piece of furniture in the Victoria and Albert Museum is the chair upon which Charles I is believed to have sat during his quite illegal 'trial' in Westminster Hall. It is upholstered in velvet now so faded that the original colour can only be guessed at, studded with innumerable nails, shagged with fringe, and provided with an ample footstool to match.

Up to the period of the later Stuarts oak was the favourite wood of the English cabinet-makers: but then walnut began to push itself into favour, and very fine pieces of furniture were made from this beautifully dappled and mottled timber. Increasing contacts with the East led to the introduction of Oriental designs and of 'Japanning' or lacquering. Then French Protestant refugees who found a harbour in England after the Revocation of the Edict of Nantes in 1685 brought with them the French fashion of gilding chairs and tables so that they seemed to be wrought in pure gold. Commerce with Spain gave us seats and cushions of embossed leather, while from the Dutch our craftsmen learned to do 'marquetry,' a delicate form of inlay.

Inlaying, indeed, appealed to the taste of the English, who not only imported large quantities of genuine Dutch marquetry, in which dark-coloured woods such as walnut or mahogany are inlaid with foliage, seaweed, birds, and butterflies in box-wood, hollywood, or satin-wood, but developed a slightly different technique of their own, reaching a high degree of skill towards the end of the eighteenth century.

All over Europe, from a very early date, furniture-makers had been fashioning special chairs for small children—dumpy little chairs on which a child could sit by its mother's knee, and high chairs in which it could be hoisted up to the level of the dining-table. A picture of a French interior of the late sixteenth century shows a great many items of furniture and gives us an excellent idea of everyday life in that time and country. The room is a bedroom as well as a dining-room. There is a large, stately bed

The Book of Craftsmen

in one corner, and a little wash-hand bracket, with a roller-towel beside it, to the left of the sideboard. On a rather clumsy chair with a low, carved back sits a bearded gentleman, probably the father of this pious family, which is saying its grace before meat. One small child is sitting up to the table in its high chair; two others are planted by the open fire on stumpy little stools. In a metal bracket over the hearth burns one lonely candle, and four apples are roasting in a tray before the fire. The dog is looking up with a puzzled expression at his master, but the cat is characteristically enjoying herself while the 'humans' are occupied in prayer.

French furniture-makers of the seventeenth and eighteenth centuries loved gorgeous effects and rare woods; they loved gilt, enamel, porphyry, malachite, and even tortoiseshell. One of the most successful of these craftsmen was André Charles Buhl, Louis XIV's 'engraver and gilder.' Born in 1642, he invented a method of ornamenting furniture with a veneer of tortoiseshell adorned with patterns inlaid in thin and delicately cut brass. He also made free use of ormolu, an alloy of copper, zinc, and tin, covered with a film of gold or bronze, and easy to mould into scrolls, foliage, and other patterns. Buhl's four sons were his apprentices, though he had many other disciples as well, with the result that France and all the countries where French taste was followed were soon amply supplied with specimens of Buhl furniture.

An English gentleman of taste and fashion in the Georgian era would spend quite a lot of time and thought, as well as considerable sums of money, in planning and choosing pieces of furniture. These were often specially made for him by craftsmen who would submit to him designs for sideboards, cabinets, writing-tables, or armchairs, just as an architect would submit plans for a house, a church, or a mausoleum.

Thomas Chippendale, a Worcestershire man, who lived and worked in St Martin's Lane, London, towards the middle of the eighteenth century, published an album of designs entitled *The Gentleman and Cabinet-maker's Director*, and some thirty years later Thomas Sheraton was making similar collections of original

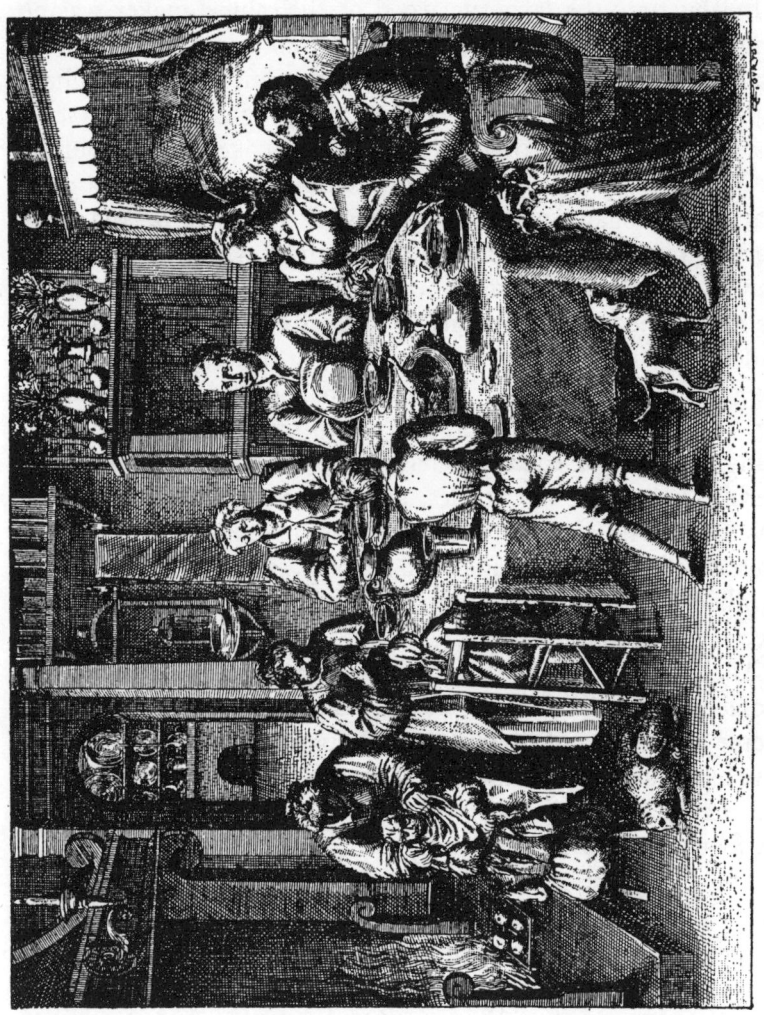

A FRENCH INTERIOR AT THE END OF THE SIXTEENTH CENTURY
Bedroom and dining-room furniture of the period is shown.

The Book of Craftsmen

drawings for the guidance of his fellow-craftsmen and their wealthy patrons.

By this time the favourite wood of the cabinet-maker was no longer oak or walnut: mahogany was more in vogue, a hard, beautifully veined wood, difficult to carve, but taking a brilliant high polish, and ranging in colour from a light orange-chestnut to a rich dark brown that in the shadow looked almost purple. Sir Robert Walpole, George I's great Prime Minister, used a great deal of mahogany in the furnishing and fittings of the huge Norfolk mansion which he built for himself with the money he won by speculating in South Sea stock, and thus helped to make the newfangled wood popular. William Kent, who combined the trades of painter, architect, landscape gardener, and furniture-designer, planned a large number of mahogany ' pieces,' and the big, stately houses erected by the Adam brothers soon contained many examples of equally stately broad-backed chairs, and shimmering, polished dinner-tables, and neat escritoires, and shining tea-caddies, and circular card-tables, and towering bookcases, and chubby little stools, all made of mahogany, either plain mahogany, or inlaid with pale yellow satin-wood and box-wood, or with dull green holly-wood.

All these things reflect the changing tastes and habits of the people whose wishes influenced the craftsman in his work. These people now demanded comfort and appreciated elegance. They gave big dinner-parties; they wrote innumerable letters; they drank tea; they played cards; they read books; they suffered from gout. (A footstool came in very handy to support a gouty foot!)

The title-page of Chippendale's *Gentleman and Cabinet-maker's Director* gives a list of the objects which the gentleman of the period was likely to request his cabinet-maker to supply, and these include " shaving-stands, basin-stands, and tea-kettle stands," as well as " stands for china jars " and cases for clocks. Chinese fashions, and the recent revival of enthusiasm for Gothic—or what was imagined to be Gothic—art, are reflected in many of Mr Chippendale's designs, and apparently some of his envious rivals

The Furniture-maker

suggested that the more fantastic of these designs could not possibly be executed " by any mechanic whatsoever." In the preface to his book the indignant designer thus vigorously—and pompously—expresses himself on the subject of these suggestions, which he attributes to " Malice, Ignorance, and Inability."

> I am confident I can convince all Noblemen, Gentlemen, and Others who will honour me with their Commands that every design in the book can be improved, both as to Beauty and Enrichment, in the execution of it by
>
> Their most obedient Servant,
> THOMAS CHIPPENDALE

Many ' Noblemen, Gentlemen, and Others ' showed their appreciation of Mr Chippendale's skill by honouring him with their

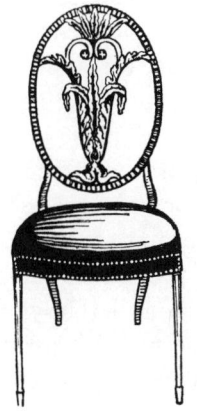

A HEPPLEWHITE CHAIR,
WHEATSHEAF DESIGN

A HEPPLEWHITE CHAIR,
PRINCE OF WALES'S FEATHERS
DESIGN

commands, with the result that most modern museums of decorative art and numerous private collections contain examples of his work. Another eighteenth-century craftsman whose name has endured was George Hepplewhite. He too published a book of designs, some of which had a political flavour, as he introduced the Prince of Wales's feathers into the backs of chairs intended to attract patrons who sympathized with that rebellious young

The Book of Craftsmen

prince, the future George IV. Another idea of Hepplewhite's, though it was not *his* idea only, was the cluster of wheat-ears in the carving of the chair-back.

During the Georgian period English cabinet-makers were recognized as masters of their craft, and rich planters in the West Indies used to barter cargoes of rum for suites of English furniture. When, as was most frequently the case, these suites were made of mahogany, either plain or inlaid with satin-wood, the actual raw material might well be returning to its original home!

There is a rather amusing, and probably quite true, story as to how mahogany came to be introduced into England. A certain Dr Gibbon, who lived in King Street, Covent Garden, had received from his brother, a West Indian captain, certain planks of very hard, pinkish-coloured timber, which he had put aside without paying much attention to them. It happened one day that Mrs Gibbon wanted a candle-box, and her thrifty-minded husband suggested that the joiner might make use of this West Indian wood. But when the man tried to saw and plane the mahogany—for mahogany it was—his tools were neither strong enough nor sharp enough for the task. The doctor, who seems to have been obstinate as well as thrifty, insisted that fresh tools should be made or found, and when this had been done the candle-box duly appeared, and was so uncommonly beautiful that the rest of the neglected planks were promptly made into a bureau. Every one who saw the bureau and the candle-box was enchanted by the beauty of the strange West Indian wood;[1] privileged friends and patients begged the doctor to give them any odd bits he might have left over; and so—if the tale be true—began the vogue upon which Sir Robert Walpole set the seal of his approval not long after.

In France so-called 'classical' ideas enjoyed a violent vogue during the Revolutionary and Napoleonic periods, but with the restoration of the Bourbon dynasty early in the nineteenth century a more heavy and pompous style of furniture came in. Our illustration of an interior dating from 1818 shows how the earlier and later

[1] A great deal of mahogany also came—and still comes—from South America.

A FRENCH FAMILY OF THE EARLY NINETEENTH CENTURY
This interior shows furniture both of the pre-Revolutionary and later Bourbon period.

The Book of Craftsmen

fashions in dress, decoration, and furnishing overlapped. One gentleman is wearing a tie-wig, and would probably wear a three-cornered hat out of doors: the other sports his own unpowdered locks, and has a 'topper' in his hand. Portraits of bewigged ancestors adorn the walls; the clock, the stiff gilt chairs, and the clustering candles suggest the days before the Revolution. But the ponderous panels on the walls, the glass dome over the clock, and the prim ornaments on the mantelshelf show that we are in the century of top-hats, not of tie-wigs!

CHAPTER XI
THE MAKER OF WEAPONS

Now for the last time in this book let us again pay a brief visit to our old friend the cave-dweller. We want to know what weapons he used in his fights with fierce beasts and almost equally fierce fellow-men. At the very beginning of that long struggle he would take a branch of a tree or a lump of rock—something to smite with, something to hurl. Later he would take chipped flints, roughly fastened to wooden hefts, and make of them axes, javelins, and spears. He was his own weapon-fashioner, just as he and his family were their own potters, hide-curers, and flint-polishers. At first there would not be a very great difference between weapons and tools. Both were simple, and both were used for very similar purposes. For example, a flint axe might kill a big brown bison one day and chop up his bones the next; and the same flint knife that was brandished in single combat with a quarrelsome neighbour at dawn might serve at dusk to scrape the flesh off the bison's shaggy hide.

By degrees, however, tools and weapons evolved along different lines and fell into separate groups, the first peaceful, the second warlike. When the separation was complete a man would have one spear for hunting and another for fighting; one axe for felling trees and another for wielding in battle.

It is mainly of the weapons used in single combat and in war that we shall be thinking in this chapter. For, alas, the human race has a fierce and violent history, and its more civilized subdivisions have never been the most tranquil and peace-loving!

The ancient Egyptians, at the height of their splendour, were an aggressive people, constantly engaged in warfare with their

The Book of Craftsmen

various neighbours. Their weapon-makers must have been kept in regular employment producing spears and swords, bows and arrows, especially as, according to the law of the land, a son was compelled to follow the same occupation as his father. This meant that the military profession, like those of the scribes, priests, and craftsmen, was being automatically increased in numbers all the time. The army was divided into regiments of bowmen, spearmen, swordsmen, club-wielders, and slingers, and each battalion had its distinctive standard, borne on a tall pole, and its trumpeters and drummers to inspire it with warlike music.

The Egyptian bow was from five to five and a half feet in length, and the bow-string was of hide, catgut, or string: the arrows were from twenty-two to thirty-four inches in length, made of wood or of reed, and tipped with bronze, flint, agate, or sharp stone. The skill of the bowmen of Egypt was as famous in the antique world as was the skill of the English archers of the Plantagenet period. The Egyptian shield, like the shields of the Greeks,

AN ASSYRIAN STANDARD
Note the bearded warrior drawing his bow.

EGYPTIAN SOLDIERS, ARMED WITH BATTLE-AXES, SHIELDS, AND SPEARS

was usually of bull's hide, stiffened with bands of metal. Spears were of wood, with metal tips, the shaft being between five and six feet in length. Javelins, or throwing-spears, were lighter and

The Maker of Weapons

shorter, terminating at one end with a diamond-shaped or leaf-shaped bronze head and at the other with a knob skilfully weighted to balance the head, so that when thrown the weapon would describe an accurate parabola. This skill in adjusting the respective weights of knob and tip must have been acquired by long practice, and it enabled the Egyptian armourer to provide the Egyptian soldier with a weapon of a remarkably deadly character.

Now we come to what is probably the most famous and romantic of all these tools of war—the sword. It evolved from a primitive form of dagger, and most of the earliest types are obviously in-

SUMERIAN DAGGER OF GOLD, WITH LAPIS LAZULI HANDLE

tended rather for thrusting than for cutting. The beautiful leaf-shaped swords of the Bronze Age can never have had sharp edges. Among the ancient Egyptians and their neighbours, however, a two-edged blade was in common use—a blade of bronze, from two and a half to three feet in length, tapering sharply to a point, and used either for stabbing or slashing.

The art of tempering the metal and fashioning the keen blade was a delicate one, and through the ages swordsmiths in many lands devoted all their cunning to making it perfect. Great princes and their captains had swords and daggers with curiously wrought hilts, and among the treasures of the royal graves at Ur was a marvellous poignard of gold, with a handle of deep blue lapis.

Making slings was a sort of subdivision of the craft of our old friend the leather-worker, though it is quite possible that a clever youth could make a very useful sling for himself with the aid of a looped leather strip and a well-chosen pebble or two. Goliath would need the services of a Philistine armourer to fashion his helmet of brass, his coat of mail, his greaves, his shield, and his mighty spear-head weighing " six hundred shekels of iron "; and some Jewish armourer must have made Saul's helmet, sword,

The Book of Craftsmen

and body-armour, which the youthful David rejected in favour of a sling and " five smooth stones out of the brook." Goliath had a sword as well as a spear, and it must have had a cutting edge as well as a thrusting point, for with it the young shepherd cut off the giant's head.

Maces—clubs made of metal instead of being made of wood—were used by the warlike peoples of the antique world, as well as battle-axes. Indeed, the armourers were both inventive and resourceful in supplying the needs of the warriors! The Egyptians, though they wore coats of mail sheathed in metal plates, seem to have favoured padded or quilted caps rather than the helmets of brass sported both by Goliath and Saul. (' Brass,' as we have already noted, meant bronze.)

The weapons of which we read in the Old Testament are for the most part very similar to those we see in the wall-paintings of the Egyptians—sword, spear, javelin, sling, and bow.

Saul, when the evil spirit was upon him, hurled a javelin at David (1 *Samuel* xviii), and David removed from beside Saul's " bolster " the spear which the King had placed there before he lay down to sleep (1 *Samuel* xxvi). The famous lament of David over Jonathan is commonly called " The Song of the Bow," and in it he declares that the " bow of Jonathan turned not back, and the sword of Saul returned not empty." It was by arrows that Saul was " sore wounded " in his last fight against the Philistines at Gilboa, and the skill of the men of Philistia as archers was probably one of the causes of David's anxiety that Judah should learn " the use of the bow." In battle each chariot would carry in addition to a charioteer an expert archer, and in some cases a duel would take place between two archers in chariots, such a single combat as that in which Jehu " drew a bow with his full strength " and smote Jehoram (2 *Kings* ix).

The arts of peace are certainly gentler, fairer, and more diverse than the arts of war, but man's fighting instinct has given inspiration and employment to generations of craftsmen, who have evolved things beautiful in themselves as well as terrible in their purposes.

The Maker of Weapons

While the weapons of the Greeks were similar to those of the Egyptians in character, they differed from them in certain details. The Greek sword was a thrusting weapon, rather than a slashing one, though we read in Homer of a blade having two edges. Greek helmets—we are speaking of Homeric as well as later times—were of polished bronze, with plumes of horsehair, and the bow, the spear, the javelin, and the shield formed part of the warrior's equipment. A corslet or a coat of mail might afford additional protection to the body of the warrior. In the *Iliad* we read of a hero called Alexandros who made ready for battle by donning his " beauteous armour."

Upon his legs he set his brazen greaves clasped with silver at the ankles; upon his breast he buckled the shining corslet . . . across his shoulders he slung a bronze sword studded with silver; upon his arm he took a large and stout shield; " and on his mighty head he set a well-wrought helmet with terribly nodding horsehair plume "; while

GREEK SOLDIER PUTTING ON HIS GREAVES

he bore a strong spear, " fitted to his grasp." The shaft of the spear would be of the wood of the ash-tree, and the tip of polished bronze.

The long-drawn-out struggle between the Greeks and the Trojans must have kept the armourers, the coppersmiths, the bowyers, and the fletchers very busy replacing the battle gear and the weapons broken or seized in the course of the war. A bowyer was, of course, a maker of bows: the fletcher's name comes from the French *flèche*, an arrow. But gods as well as men patronized the armourer's craft, and had their own smith, Vulcan, who forged the thunderbolts with which Zeus shook the clouds. The red glow from Mount Etna was believed by the ancients to be caused by the

The Book of Craftsmen

fire of Vulcan's smithy! During the Trojan war the sea-goddess, Thetis, prevailed upon Vulcan to make a new set of armour for her son, Achilles. She found him " busy with his bellows," welding chains, and as he was grimy from his work he wiped his face with a sponge before coming forth to speak with her. When Thetis " of the silver feet " told the divine smith how her son had lost his armour through lending it to his friend, the ill-starred Patroklos, Vulcan agreed to make a fresh set of weapons, and set himself at once to the bellows and the hammer, the anvil and the tongs. The shield which he made for Achilles was a marvel of elaborate design, and when he had wrought it " he wrought him a corslet brighter than fire, and a massive graven helmet for his brows, crested with gold, and therewithal greaves of pliant tin." The hero must have looked most impressive when he was armed in Vulcan's handiwork, for we are told that the brightness from his shield " shot up to the sky," and that when he set the helmet on his head " round it waved the golden plumes that Vulcan had made."

The bow of Odysseus plays an important part in the romantic story of that far-wandering warrior's return to his island kingdom of Ithaca. You will remember that in the chapter on the weaver we spoke of his faithful queen, Penelope, beset with wooers in his absence. When he returned, but before he had revealed himself, Penelope, inspired by the goddess Athena, declared that she would wed whichever of her wooers should be able to draw the great bow of Odysseus and shoot an arrow through twelve iron axes standing upright in line. (Exactly how this could be done nobody knows, but probably there was at the back of each blade a crescent of metal through which an arrow might pass.) Then, one by one, the assembled chieftains strove in vain to bend that mighty bow, and at last the stranger threw off his disguise, bent the great weapon which none might bend but himself, and sent the keen shaft flying to its mark before the astonished crowd.

A bow, too, figures in one of the legends associated with the founder of Buddhism—the bow which young Prince Siddartha, afterwards called Buddha, or the Enlightened One, bent and

The Maker of Weapons

drew to prove that he had come to man's estate. Where the arrow fell it was said that a river gushed forth which had the power of cleansing a man from all his sins.

The size of the Greek sword was doubled, and its form slightly altered, in the fifth century B.C. by an Athenian general called Iphicrates, an innovator whose ideas on the subject of weapons had a strong influence on the work of the Greek armourer. He was the son of a shoemaker, and seems to have been sensitive about his

ROMAN GLADIATORS, SHOWING THEIR QUAINT HELMETS

humble origin, for when some one taunted him with it he replied grimly, " I may be the first of my family, but you shall be the last of yours."

Warlike peoples such as the Romans encouraged swordsmiths and armourers and kept them constantly employed. In the quarter occupied by these craftsmen there must have been great bustle and activity when one of the more enterprising Cæsars was making ready for a campaign in some far country. Each Roman legionary was armed with a long javelin and a short sword; he wore a bronze helmet and defensive body-armour covered with overlapping plates of iron or bronze. As much of his time was spent in digging trenches and making roads his equipment included a stout trenching-tool. His shield might be either oval or square.

It was not only for soldiers that the armourers of Rome had to

The Book of Craftsmen

make helmets, shields, and blades. The gladiators demanded a great variety of fighting gear, and the smith who had toiled at his grimy and smoky anvil hammering and welding gladiatorial weapons must often have seen these weapons used with deadly effect in the sanded arena of the circus. Gladiators' helmets were of a special design, often with cheek- and chin-pieces, and sometimes with a sort of mask over the face. They wore leg-guards not unlike modern cricket-pads, and their arms ranged from swords and sickles to tridents and nets!

Bronze and iron were the metals mainly used by European armourers in classical times and in the Dark Ages, though, as we have seen,[1] the Greeks were not wholly ignorant of the process by which iron can be turned into steel, and the Chinese had practically mastered it as early as the fifth century B.C. It was the Arabs, however, who brought this complicated process first to perfection, and whose lances and scimitars, keen, supple, and bright, showed such a long advance beyond the duller and heavier productions of other swordsmiths. The Persians also were far ahead of their Western fellows.

From the Arabs the craftsmen of Toledo learned the secret of tempering hot steel in very cold running water: that is why Shakespeare makes Othello say that he has " a sword of Spain, the ice-brook's temper." But the most skilful weapon-makers of the early Islamic period—and later, too—were they of Damascus. Their skill was proved long before the Arab conquest of the city in the year 635, for the Roman Emperor Diocletian took them under his protection; but it was during the heyday of the Arab rule that they brought to its finest pitch the art of ' damascening ' steel. The method was to undercut an elaborate design upon the surface of the steel and then press fine threads of gold, silver, or copper wire into the tiny furrows, thus giving to the finished product the appearance of delicately woven brocade.

The swordsmiths of Damascus continued to flourish within the walls of their ancient city until the year 1401, when Tamerlane, the

---

[1] Chapter II, p. 58.

The Maker of Weapons

fierce Mongol conquerer, captured it, and bore them all away as captives in his triumphal train.

From the very dawn of craftsmanship men seem to have desired instinctively to make beautiful as well as serviceable things. That is why the Sumerians gave lapis hilts to the royal daggers and the Arabs inlaid their bright blades with a fine tracery of golden wire; and that is why the Scandinavian sea-kings studded the hilts of their bronze swords with deep red garnets.

THIRTEENTH-CENTURY WARRIORS WEARING TWO TYPES OF CHAIN-MAIL

As steel became more generally known in Western Europe the craft of the armourer and the smith became more complicated. Chain-mail, such as Duke William's Normans wore, gradually gave way to plate-armour, and the long rivalry between the maker of offensive and of defensive weapons went merrily on. That rivalry began when the shield was invented to protect the fighter from the assaults of arrows, swords, or javelins: it continues in our own day, when every advance in attack is speedily met by some new invention for defence.

Just as the Roman armourers had to provide for the needs both of active fighting-men and of gladiators their medieval successors had to satisfy both warriors riding forth to war and warriors running courses in the lists. Knights of the Plantagenet period wielded with equal energy sword and lance, battle-axe and mace. Simple men-at-arms, other than the archers, to whom we shall turn in a minute, used rough weapons not unlike agricultural tools. Edward I made a law in 1285 that " every man should have in his house harness wherewith to keep the peace," each according to the value of his goods and lands. A man, for example, who held land worth £15 and goods worth forty marks had to have at hand a hauberk of iron, a sword, and a dagger, while a poor fellow

The Book of Craftsmen

whose total worldly belongings were worth only forty marks must have bows, arrows, knives, and *guisarmes*, these last being broad blades fixed to long wooden shafts.

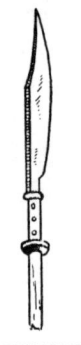

A GUISARME SUCH AS EDWARD I WISHED HIS POORER SUBJECTS TO KEEP AT HAND

The upper classes used the bow only for hunting, but among the stout yeomen who fought in France under Edward III and Henry V archery was a fine art. The type of bow they used was the long bow, six feet or so in length, taking arrows each measuring about a yard. The arrows were feathered with goose-quills, and the fletcher (whom we have met already) took the utmost care to keep the shafts straight, as a crooked shaft might put the archer 'out' in his aim, with serious results. The tough and yet flexible wood of the yew-tree supplied the bowyer with material for the bow. Have you ever noticed how often a very large and ancient yew-tree is to be seen flourishing in the churchyard of some quaint old village church in England? It is said that both the bowyers and the archers for whom they worked were happier if the wood of the bow were taken from a tree growing on consecrated ground. But a great deal of timber was imported by England from Italy to make bows. The cross-bow, in the use of which the Italians excelled, was a more complicated affair. It needed less strength and less dexterity than the long bow. On the other hand, its aim was less accurate, and the string had to be rewound with the aid of a little winch between each 'shot.'

"Now thrive the armourers," says Shakespeare, describing the preparations made by Henry V before the campaign which ended in the victory of Agincourt; but the plain fact is that the craftsmen of Spain, Italy, and Germany were at that period much more skilful than their English

ENGLISH ARCHER

The Maker of Weapons

brethren, and every warrior who could afford to do so purchased armour and weapons fashioned overseas. They who throve most in England would be the bowyers and fletchers, and the smiths who made the rough weapons used by the men-at-arms.

These Continental armourers attained a high degree of perfection in their work, and either borrowed, bought, or guessed some of the secrets of the Arab smiths. They made 'harness' for both men and horses, and they contrived to make it beautiful as well as strong. When the plate-armour period was at its height they were wont to provide complete suits of steel, jointed like the shell of a lobster, and made slightly thicker on the right side, where the wearer was most likely to receive hard knocks.

A FINE SET OF FIFTEENTH-CENTURY PLATE-ARMOUR FOR MAN AND HORSE
Note that very little chain-mail now remains.

Spurs and the steel peaks of the foot-pieces would hamper a warrior who was unhorsed in battle, so both were so designed as to be easily detachable. After the 'Battle of the Spurs' fought at Courtrai in 1302 fourteen hundred spurs were found upon the field.

The spurrier, or spur-maker, was another craftsman whose work might be needed either by peaceful or by warlike people. Women as well as men wore spurs when hunting or when travelling on

The Book of Craftsmen

horseback, and the gilded or ' golden ' spurs buckled on the heels of the newly dubbed knight were the ' outward and visible sign ' of his knighthood. The prick-spur is the earlier and more cruel type, but from the middle of the fourteenth century onward the more decorative and humane rowel-spur, provided with a little spiked wheel (*ruelle*), was most in favour.

That rather unwarlike monarch Henry VI granted to the armourers of London their first charter. Like many other crafts they had numerous subdivisions, the Heaumers, or helmet-makers, and the Bladesmiths among them. Makers of body-armour were forbidden by law to sell breastplates, etc., with silken or velvet coverings, since such coverings were often used to hide faulty workmanship. Henry VIII, jealous for the fame and prosperity of the London armourers, requested his fellow-sovereign Maximilian, Emperor of the Holy Roman Empire, to send some of the most skilful of his craftsmen to England, to " practice their mystery " here, and incidentally to instruct our less experienced workmen in their craft. Maximilian complied, and the strangers were admitted to membership of the Worshipful Company of Armourers. There is in the Tower of London a magnificent suit of equestrian armour given by this Emperor to the second Tudor King.

The English armourers seem to have been a quarrelsome set of men, perhaps as the result of their interest in the harness and the tools of war. One of them was fined for pulling a fellow-armourer's beard during a meeting of the company, and another for calling the Master and Wardens " knaves and cheats."

The spurriers of London were apparently revellers, for a city edict forbade them to work after the curfew had been rung in St Sepulchre's Church, Newgate. It had come to the notice of the City Fathers that these gay spurriers were wont to frolic and tipple all day, and then start working at their forges after dark, when, owing to their drowsy—and perhaps tipsy—condition, they were a danger to their neighbours, as they plied their bellows with excessive zeal! Giltspur Street, near St Sepulchre's Church, was their headquarters, as its name still reminds us.

The Maker of Weapons

The Fletchers had a guild of their own, and so had the Bowyers, though until 1370 they formed one fraternity. There was a third guild known as the Long Bow Stringers. Before the middle of the fifteenth century three separate classes of workmen were engaged in the making of swords and daggers: they who fashioned the blades, they who fashioned the hilts, and they who fashioned the sheaths.

Henry VIII's red-haired nephew, King James IV of Scotland, also desired to encourage native industries, and, with that

A BOMBARD: USED FOR THROWING STONE BALLS PROPELLED BY GUNPOWDER

end in view, invited skilful strangers to come and ply their craft in his domains. Artillery, as well as swords and daggers, interested him, and in his reign was founded the great, cumbersome cannon nicknamed 'Mons Meg,' which, after a period of exile in England, now stands on the Castle Rock at Edinburgh. 'Meg' weighs nearly four tons and could once fire a stone ball of 300 lb.

The introduction of gunpowder into Western Europe had a decisive influence upon the armourer's craft, though it took some time to make itself felt. The Arabs, who probably learned the secret from the Chinese, were using a rough sort of cannon, throwing stone balls, in the thirteenth century, and by the middle of the fourteenth century guns were generally used, not only in siege warfare, but also upon warships. Small cannon were used in the battle of Crécy (1346), and large, lumbering ones at the siege of Orleans (1428). It has been said with some truth that the

The Book of Craftsmen

English conquered France with the long bow and were driven out by gunpowder.

Huge 'engines of war' came into existence as the fifteenth and sixteenth centuries moved on their stormy way. One of these, the mangonel, resembled the Roman *ballista*, which flung large missiles with the aid of tightly twisted ropes and cleverly handled levers. Bombards, mortars, and petards required gunpowder to propel their balls of stone or metal, and Shakespeare speaks of an

A MANGONEL: A GIGANTIC SLING EMPLOYED CHIEFLY IN SIEGE WARFARE

engineer being "hoist(ed) on his own petard." This, he unkindly says, is "the sport"! The earliest type of cannon was of wrought iron, a tube of rough metal made by a smith who had 'moved with the times' and adopted the new craft, though without specializing in it. So awkward and unwieldy were these 'engines' they could each be fired off only once in the course of a battle! But man's desire to find even deadlier methods of mowing down his fellow-men led to the development of the gunsmith's art, the establishment of gun-foundries, and the gradual introduction of explosives far more powerful than gunpowder.

Portable guns, muskets, arquebuses, and pistols were the next invention, heavy and uncouth at first, and often a hindrance rather than a help to the man who had to drag them about and fire them. Yet the ingenuity of the craftsman kept pace with the demands of the soldier. It seems that for some time the loud report of a musket

The Maker of Weapons

frightened the enemy more than its bullets hurt him; but here, again, skill and perseverance produced a constant succession of more and more complicated firearms.

Though Shakespeare was quite right in saying that Henry V used cannon—'ordnance,' as he calls them—at the siege of Harfleur, the type of artillery he describes is more of the Tudor than the Plantagenet period.

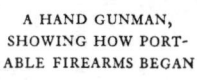

A HAND GUNMAN, SHOWING HOW PORTABLE FIREARMS BEGAN

> Behold the ordnance on their carriages,
> With fatal mouths gaping on girded Harfleur.
> ... and the nimble gunner
> With linstock now the devilish cannon touches,
> And down goes all before them.[1]

The "linstock" was the long staff used for holding the lighted match with which the cannon was discharged, and as the explosion not infrequently blew the whole thing to pieces the gunner's nimbleness would be useful to him in helping him to get quickly out of the way! King James II of Scotland was not quite nimble enough at the siege of Roxburgh Castle, where he was killed by the bursting of a cannon.

Until the Great War of 1914-18 brought forth its crop of trench helmets, otherwise 'tin hats,' it used to be said that the introduction of gunpowder had made every form of body-armour obsolete. The breastplate and the cuirass, the leg-pieces and the arm-pieces, lingered on until the early eighteenth century, but, roughly speaking, armour vanished between the time of Marlborough and the time of Wellington. The sword was much slower in yielding to the march of modern ideas, and long after the gunsmith had taken possession of the battlefield swords of various designs continued to be used as personal weapons of attack or defence, and in those private duels which replaced the public combat in the lists.

The craftsmen of Germany, Italy, and Spain excelled in the production of every sort of weapon, and one of the most famous

[1] *Henry V*, Act III, Prologue.

The Book of Craftsmen

of all swordsmiths, a man whose name has come to mean a certain type of blade, was working at Belluno, in Northern Italy, towards the end of the sixteenth century. His name was Andrea Ferrara, but whether the second half of it indicated that he was a native of Ferrara or a worker in iron (Italian, *ferrajo*) we do not know. He had two brothers, Cosimo and Gianantonio, who worked with him, but it is his name which rings down through history like the clang of one of his own incomparable swords. Some of his productions are marked with his name, others bear, as a sort of trademark, the head of a beast which looks like a fox but was more probably a wolf. The Elizabethans decided that it was a fox, and so closely were the two ideas connected in their minds that they fell into the habit of calling *any* sword a ' fox.' That is why the comic braggart Pistol, in Shakespeare's *Henry V*, tells his captive, the French knight, that he shall die " on point of fox."

As the centuries passed swords became more and more supple and slender, while cannon became more and more huge and terrible. We have travelled a long way from the gold-and-lapis dagger of the Sumerian king, a long way from the childish-looking mangonel and the spluttering bombard; but however far we travel we shall never reach a point at which the skill and energy of the craftsmen cease to be good and beautiful things, good and beautiful in themselves, whatever ends they are made to serve.

INDEX

ALABASTER, 151
Amazons, the, 156
Apprenticeship, 167
Arabia, arts and crafts in—*see* Islamic arts and crafts
Archery, 266, 274, 276
Architecture, 128, 132, 138
Ardagh Chalice, 47
Arkwright, Richard, 117
Armourers, 267, 269, 271, 273, 275-276
Artillery, 277-280
Athens, 15, 71, 131, 185, 227
Augustus the Strong, 30

BABYLON, 124, 129, 155, 157, 249
Babylonia, 14, 124, 154
Bagpipes, 244
Bakers, 201-220
Bell, St Patrick's, 47, 51
Bells, 49-52
Bookbinding, 243
Books, 58, 242-243
Böttger, Friedrich, 30
Bottles (leather), 244-245
Bows, 266, 268, 270, 274
Brasses, monumental, 60-61
Brickwork, 124, 133, 135, 141
Britain, ancient, 18, 39, 61, 121, 123-124, 232
Bronze, 36-39
Bronze Age, 13, 37, 39, 41, 66, 93, 121, 123, 267
Buddha, 271
Builders, 122, 123-125, 127-130, 132-133, 135-136, 137-147, 152
Byzantium, 46, 63, 106-107, 109

CAPS, 157-158, 164
Carpenters, 74, 78, 79-80, 82
Carpets, 114
Carriages—*see* Chariots
Cartwright, Rev. Edmund, 118-119

Cellini, Benvenuto, 55-56
Chairs, 171, 251, 253, 255, 261
Chariots, 69, 193
Charlemagne, 48, 106
Charles I, 25, 88, 246, 257
Charles II, 29, 88, 177
Chaucer, 78, 84, 113, 211
China, arts and crafts in, 19 *et seq.*, 40, 49-50, 61, 86-87, 105, 137-138, 187, 251, 277
Christianity, 45, 50, 74
Churches, 142, 146 *et seq.*
Cobblers, 49, 228, 231, 236
Companies, City—*see* Guilds
Cooks, 201-220
Coopers, 81-82
Cotton, 117 *et seq.*
Cradles, 77, 78
Cretans, 15, 36, 70, 128-129, 157, 185
Crompton, Samuel, 119-120
Cromwell, Oliver, 54
Crowns, royal, 48
Crucifixes, types of, 76

DAMASCUS, 59, 272
Darius, 22
Doors, 51, 57, 74
Dunstan, St, 195
Dyers, 99, 110

EASTER ISLAND, images on, 152
Edward I, 249, 273
Edward III, 82, 112, 168, 236, 274
Edward IV, 168, 169
Egyptians, ancient, 13, 36, 40, 66-69, 94-96, 107, 125-128, 154, 183-185, 202-204, 222-225, 247-249, 265-267
Elizabeth, Queen, 166, 170, 171, 175, 240, 256
Embroidery, 107-108
Enamel, 61-63

281

The Book of Craftsmen

England, arts and crafts in, 18–19, 24, 47, 54, 76, 106, 109, 112, 141–142, 148, 166, 195, 236, 251, 258–262, 276
Etruscans, 17, 44, 157, 158

FERRARA, ANDREA, 280
Flanders, arts and crafts in, 60, 83, 112, 113
Fletchers, 269, 276
Flint, 121–122, 265
Forks, 52
France, arts and crafts in, 24, 27, 62, 63, 83–84, 116, 141, 147, 245, 254, 257, 258
François I, 27, 56
Fulham ware, 28–29
Furniture, 247–264

GARRICK, DAVID, 200
Germany, arts and crafts in, 18–19, 59, 62, 214, 279
Gibbons, Grinling, 88–91
Gladiators, 18, 133, 272
Gloves, 231, 236, 242, 245
Gold, 39–41, 42, 43 *et seq.*
Greeks, ancient, 15, 38, 44, 49, 61, 70, 100–104, 108, 130–133, 156–158, 185, 206, 226–228, 249, 269–271
Guilds, 74, 79, 80, 115, 133, 144, 167, 191–193, 215, 235, 276
Guns, 277–280

HARGREAVES, JAMES, 116–117
Harness (horse), 56, 222, 235
Hats, 157–158, 164–166, 174–175, 176, 178–179
Hatters, 153–180
Hebrews, 43, 50, 68, 97, 108, 129, 205, 218–219, 224, 268
Henry II, 112
Henry III, 107, 112, 236
Henry V, 274, 279
Henry VI, 166, 235, 276
Henry VII, 168
Henry VIII, 57, 88, 115, 166, 171, 276, 277
Holland, arts and crafts in, 27, 257
Homer, 37, 100, 226, 250
Houses, 83, 124–125, 133, 134–135, 138–142
Hugh, St, legend of, 232–233

ILLUMINATIONS, 194–197
India, arts and crafts in, 40, 42, 61
Ireland, arts and crafts in, 40, 47, 51
Iron, 41–43
Iron Age, 41, 66, 94
Islamic arts and crafts, 23, 85–86, 138–139, 272, 277
Italy, arts and crafts in, 26, 147, 279

JAMES II (of Scotland), 279
James IV (of Scotland), 277
Japan, arts and crafts in, 28, 61, 187, 251
Jewellery, 44–45, 46–48
Jews—*see* Hebrews
Joiners, 74, 80, 81

KAY, JOHN, 116
Khufu, King of Egypt, 13, 127
Knives, 52
Knossos, 15, 185

LACQUER, 87
Lake-dwellers, Swiss, 66, 92, 94, 204, 221, 247
Leather, workers in, 221–246
Limoges enamel, 63
Locks, 57
Lombardy, Iron crown of, 48
Looms, 94, 96, 100–103

MAHOGANY, 260–262
Manuscripts, illuminated, 194–197
Maoris, 86
Masons, 141, 142–146; masons' marks, 143
Maximilian, Emperor, 64–65, 276
Medals, 53
Merchant Taylors, 167–169
Metals, workers in, 36–65
Miserere seats, 75
Musical instruments, 72, 221
Mycenæ, 37, 130

NÜRNBERG, 59, 63–64

PAINTERS, 181–200
Pavements, tessellated, 135
Persians, 22, 61, 160, 272
Phœnicians, 69, 99, 108, 226

Index

Pipes, tobacco, 29, 62
Ploughs, 49
Pompeii, 186, 207
Porcelain, 19-22
Potters and pottery, 11-35
Pyramids, the, 13, 127

RICHARD II, 60, 212, 236
Rings, 54-55
Robbia, della, family of, 26, 65
Rome, 133
Romans, 18, 44, 48, 49, 57, 61, 105, 133-136, 158-160, 186-187, 206-208, 219, 229-231, 250-251, 271-272
Rupert, Prince, 29

SAMIAN ware, 18, 38
Sandals, 223, 226, 229
Scandinavia, arts and crafts in, 39, 42, 46-47, 100, 108, 161
Schliemann, Heinrich, 37
Sculptors, 121-123, 126-132, 133-135, 146-152
Seals, 53, 54
Sèvres china, 34
Shakespeare, 172 et seq., 217, 241, 256, 274, 279, 280
Ships, 69-71, 73, 87
Shoes, 227, 229, 237-241
Signets, 54
Silk, 105-107
Silver, 44 et seq.
Slings, 267-268
Slip-ware, 13
Smiths, 43, 49
Snuff-boxes, 62-63
Spain, arts and crafts in, 23, 26, 44, 45, 235, 257, 272, 279
Spices, 209, 217

Spinning, 92, 93, 116
Spinning Jenny, the, 116-117
Spoons, 52
Spurriers, 275-276
Steel, 58-59, 272-273
Stone Age, 12, 66, 92, 121, 123, 204, 221, 247
Stonehenge, 123-124
Sumeria, arts and crafts in, 14, 66, 124, 126, 154, 273, 280
Swords, 267, 269, 271, 272, 279

TABLES, 249, 250, 253, 256
Tailors, 153-180
Tanagra, 16-17
Tapestry, 113-114
Tara brooch, 47
Temples, 123, 132
Thrones, 249
Toby jugs, 35
Tombs, 16, 19, 60-61, 123, 150
Tools, 49, 67, 128, 142, 248, 265
Torture, instruments of, 63
Toys, 16
Trajan, Emperor, 208
Troy, 15, 37, 101
Turners, 80, 81
Tut-ankh-Amen, 41
Tyrol, ironwork in, 63-64

UR, 41, 267
Urns, cinerary, 13

VISCHER, PETER, 64-65

WEAPONS, 265-280
Weavers, 92-120
Wedgwood, Josiah, 31-34
Wood, workers in, 66-91

THE LIBRARY
ST. MARY'S COLLEGE OF MARYLAND
ST. MARY'S CITY, MARYLAND 20686

75954